Positional Analysis for Sustainable Development

Climate change, biodiversity loss, pollution of land and water, land-use changes, lack of equality and other problems at local, national and global levels represent a challenge for economics as a social science. Mainstream neoclassical economics may be able to contribute to a more sustainable society but it has also played a dominant role in a period where problems have been aggravated. A pluralist and democratic view of economics is therefore very much warranted. This book presents a multidimensional and ideologically more open view of economics: understanding economics in multidimensional terms is in accordance with the 17 sustainable development goals recognized by nations at the UN-level in 2015.

Accordingly, approaches to decision-making and accounting at the national and business levels have to be reconsidered. Neoclassical cost–benefit analysis (CBA) with focus on the monetary dimension and an assumed consensus about a specific market ideology to be applied is not compatible with democratic societies where citizens and actors in other roles normally differ with respect to ideological orientation. Environmental Impact Statements and Multi-Criteria methods are used to some extent to broaden approaches to decision-making. In this book, Positional Analysis is advocated as a multidimensional and ideologically open approach. Positional Analysis is based on a political economic conceptual framework (as part of ecological economics) that differs from neoclassical ideas of individuals, firms and markets. And since approaches to decision-making and to accounting are closely connected, a new theoretical perspective in economics similarly raises issues of how national and business accounting can be opened up to meet present demands among various actors in society. This perspective raises also numerous ethical questions at the science and policy interface that need to be properly addressed for sustainability decision-making.

Judy Brown is a Professor of Accounting at Victoria University of Wellington, New Zealand.

Peter Söderbaum is a Professor Emeritus in Ecological Economics at Mälardalen University, Västerås, Sweden.

Małgorzata Dereniowska is an associate member of Greqam, Aix-Marseille University (Aix Marseille School of Economics), CNRS and EHESS, France.

Routledge Studies in Ecological Economics

For a full list of titles in this series, please visit www.routledge.com/series/RSEE

Positional Analysis for Sustainable Development

Reconsidering Policy, Economics and Accounting

Judy Brown, Peter Söderbaum
and Małgorzata Dereniowska

Routledge
Taylor & Francis Group

LONDON AND NEW YORK

First published 2017
by Routledge

2 Park Square, Milton Park, Abingdon, Oxfordshire OX14 4RN
52 Vanderbilt Avenue, New York, NY 10017

Routledge is an imprint of the Taylor & Francis Group, an informa business

First issued in paperback 2020

British Library Cataloguing in Publication Data
A catalogue record for this book is available from the British Library

Library of Congress Cataloging in Publication Data
A catalog record for this book has been requested

ISBN: 978-1-138-63450-3 (hbk)
ISBN: 978-0-367-34116-9 (pbk)

Typeset in Bembo
by diacriTech, Chennai

Contents

List of Illustrations

Figures

Tables

Foreword

Cost–benefit analysis (CBA) has been criticized over the years but still tends to dominate as the only established approach to decision making at the societal level. Investments in infrastructure, for example roads or dams, are often depicted and assessed in this singular way. Analysis is carried out in monetary terms and refers to prices in actual or hypothetical markets, with minimal consideration of non-monetary values.

Similarly, the accounting systems that have become established at national and organizational levels are predominantly expressed in monetary terms. As in economics, there is limited discussion of the ideological underpinnings of accounting theory and practice and how the privileging of market-oriented perspectives and monetary values (e.g. shareholder wealth maximization) have impacted the culture and priorities of governments, societies and organisations. Also, the scope of ethical debate in policy analysis is limited in this context.

Both neoclassical economics and mainstream accounting reduce human beings to utility-maximizers operating in capital, labor and consumer markets, ignoring or playing down their role as citizens in a democratic society. Organizations – whether in the private or public sector context – are similarly conceived in market-like terms. Under neoliberalism, for example, accounting reforms have played a major role in embedding more corporate-like governance systems.

Sustainable development has become a legitimate vision for society since the Brundtland report (World Commission on Environment and Development 1987). It has become clear that present development trends are unsustainable in many ways. Established methods of preparing decisions and established accounting guidelines and practices do not adequately address present demands and challenges. Indeed, in many cases, they arguably reinforce unsustainable trends with ethically dubious implications as, for example, when corporations limit social and environmental accountings to those for which a 'business case' rather than a 'citizen case' can be made.

In this situation, alternative approaches to decision making and accounting practices need to be developed, and coupled with ethical analysis. For this purpose, it is unwise to focus directly and exclusively on specific alternative approaches to decision making and alternative systems of accounting. Some part of our discussion and analysis has to relate to perspectives, for example, the now dominant paradigm of neoclassical economics as well as the (related) dominant market and economic growth ideology. When it is understood that there are relevant alternative perspectives in relation to sustainable development, then the rationale for alternative decision-making methods and accounting practices, ingrained with ethical reasoning, becomes more apparent.

The role of economics as a conceptual framework and roadmap is reconsidered in the present study. Accepting a degree of complexity is important in addressing sustainability. Simplistic ideas where 'economics is about money' have to be replaced with a truly multidimensional analysis. Technocratic ideas about economists being able to identify correct ways of valuing and summarizing all impacts in monetary terms have to be downplayed in favor of more ideologically open analyses. In a democratic society there are competing political views and analysis should reflect this fact, rather than assuming one single ideological orientation. As in other areas of contentious politics, terms such as 'sustainability' and 'sustainable development' are underpinned by plural and often conflicting values and can be interpreted in many different ways, leading down quite different societal pathways.

In the present study, institutional theory in the spirit of Gunnar Myrdal and K. William Kapp will form a background in terms of perspective and positional analysis will be the alternative method for decision making and accounting presented and discussed. Positional analysis is an approach with its origins from a PhD study (Söderbaum 1973). Since then the approach has been further developed with applied studies mainly in the Scandinavian countries. There are also other methods that belong to the category of multi-criteria approaches and similar developments in other social and humanistic sciences. In this book, we have focused in particular on tendencies in business management and accounting (Chapters 5 and 6) and in philosophy and ethics (Chapters 7 and 8). In two final chapters interviews have been carried out as a way of further illuminating possibilities and remaining issues with positional analysis.

As the challenges of sustainability become ever more pressing, it is increasingly clear that groups of academics who have worked in relatively isolated circles now find that they have a lot in common. Here and in our broader writings, we have emphasized linkages between the following streams of work: some versions of heterodox economics with approaches such as positional analysis, ambitions of opening up accounting, science and technology studies and discussions of pluralism and sustainability with democratic theory, practical ethics and philosophy.

We hope this work helps encourage academics across a range of disciplines to reflect on their roles as scholars in partly different fields (in our case economics, accounting, philosophy and ethics) and the expectations upon them in relation to sustainability issues. In an era of 'post-normal' science, value-neutrality and standing outside is no longer possible. Although often presented as apolitical, neither economics nor accounting is neutral in terms of values or ideology. We have to openly discuss these issues – and engage policymakers as well as the wider citizenry – if we are to successfully address current unsustainable trends.

Judy Brown
Peter Söderbaum
Małgorzata Dereniowska

Acknowledgements

Judy Brown wishes to thank the Royal Society of New Zealand Marsden Fund for supporting this research as part of a funded project on 'Dialogic Accounting: The Challenge of Taking Multiple Perspectives Seriously', Contract No. VUW1011. Parts of Chapters 5 and 6 have been updated and reworked from the article 'Democracy, sustainability and dialogic accounting technologies: taking pluralism seriously', *Critical Perspectives on Accounting*, Vol. 20, No. 3, pp. 313–342, used by permission. Judy Brown acknowledges with thanks this permission.

In his position as Professor Emeritus, Peter Söderbaum wishes to thank the Mälardalen University, Västerås, for continued support. He also wants to acknowledge assistance by Klas Andberger with figures.

Małgorzata Dereniowska wishes to express special thanks to Jason Matzke for continuous support and feedback with this project, and for ground-shaping conversations throughout years of collaboration in general, reflected in the presented ideas; to Beata Ziemska for her indispensable assistance in the process of writing; and to Jean-Sébastien Gharbi and Yves Meinard for insightful discussions. Part of this research was supported by the A*MIDEX project (n ANR-11-IDEX-0001-02) funded by the « Investissements d'Avenir » French Government program, managed by the French National Research Agency (ANR). Małgorzata Dereniowska acknowledges this support, and extends her thanks to Michel Lubrano for generous possibilities to conduct this research within the project *Dynamics of Inequalities and Their Perceptions* (DynIPer).

The authors want to express special thanks to both Andy Humphries and Elanor Best from Routledge for their encouragement, assistance and invaluable advice and support throughout the realization of this project.

1 Democracy as a lead concept in dealing with unsustainable development

Peter Söderbaum

'Sustainable development' has become a key phrase in public and private debate since the publication of the Brundtland report in 1987. The title of the report *Our Common Future* is well turned since it points to interests shared by all human beings (and other forms of life) now and in the future. An extensive literature exists about development trends, some of which are judged to be unsustainable and require action. Such trends may refer not only to climate, ecosystems or natural resources[1] but also to the health of human beings, to social issues such as inequality and unemployment or to financial resources.

In this book, our purpose is not so much to present facts about more or less sustainable trends but rather to contribute to our understanding of the factors behind 'actually existing unsustainability' to use a phrase from the title of a book by Barry (2012). A lot can certainly be achieved by focusing directly on phenomena that are judged to be negative from a sustainability point of view. Individuals can modify their lifestyles, for example, to reduce environmental pollution or threats of climate change. Within the scope of present institutional arrangements, essential steps can be taken. However, the challenge in front of us is of such a magnitude that we also need to discuss options at a more fundamental level with respect to perspectives.

We have, for a long time, relied heavily on certain ideas about development and prosperity. Economic growth in gross domestic product (GDP) terms belongs to these ideas. Strengthening competitiveness of business corporations in a region and benefits of international trade (and of a specific kind of globalization) for all are elements of this set of beliefs. At some stage, we have to recognize that the present political–economic system, while producing some benefits to humankind, is not performing well in sustainability terms. In this situation where a considerable change in course is needed, it becomes appropriate to also consider more radical changes in perspective and institutional arrangements. This is not an easy matter, and I do not claim to know the right things to do in concrete terms. However, I am convinced that some essential options with respect to perspectives need to be discussed openly in the international community.

Democracy is a multi-facetted concept, and we return to it at many places in the present study. For the moment, emphasis is on the importance of listening to many voices at different arenas. There is a lot of inertia and path dependence in development and in the positions of actors in the development dialogue. Powerful groups may try to protect the status quo and feel threatened by the questioning of dominant perspectives. However, such attitudes should not be a barrier for new thinking, new behavior and new practices. Dialogue should not be avoided in a situation where some of us make the judgment that 'our common future' is at stake. After all, this is essentially a value or ideological issue, and we should all have some saying about what kind of future we want to live in.

A necessary dialogue about perspectives

To open the door for consideration of new institutional arrangements (in the sense of marginal or larger changes in political economic systems), we believe that fundamental perspectives of three interrelated kinds need to be discussed:

- Theories of science and relationships between science and politics.
- Paradigms in economics and management science (the latter field being closely related to economics).
- Value or ideological orientations (moral and ethical considerations included).

We argue that there are alternatives to dominant perspectives in each of the above fields. There are alternatives to positivism as a theory of science; there are alternatives to neoclassical economic theory (and all that follows from this dominant paradigm) and there are alternatives to neo-liberalism as the dominant ideological orientation with its focus on the role of markets and profit-maximizing firms. Our opinion is that such alternatives need to be explored carefully in the present situation. A degree of pluralism is needed in the sense of comparing and assessing different alternatives.

A preliminary idea of the differences between what is judged to be dominant perspectives and possible alternative perspectives is listed in Table 1.1. One issue is about the role of science in relation to the challenges of sustainable development

Table 1.1 A way of categorizing perspectives to be discussed as part of sustainability politics

	Dominant perspective	*Potential alternative perspective*
Role of science	Positivism: objectivity, standing outside, testing hypotheses	Also subjectivity: the scholar is unavoidably a political actor among other political actors
Paradigm in economics	Neoclassical theory: economic man and profit-maximizing firm assumptions	Political economics: political economic person (PEP) and political economic organization (PEO) assumptions
Ideological orientation	Neo-liberalism: focus on markets and the efficiency of business corporations	Potential ideological orientations include those that focus on specific interpretations of 'sustainable development'

and sustainability politics. It is probably still fair to attribute a dominant role to positivism. According to this view, politics should be kept at a distance and science be 'value free'. Various phenomena should be observed objectively, bias avoided and hypotheses that may explain various phenomena tested.

The right-hand column of Table 1.1 points to emerging views. A role is still attributed to some of the ideas behind positivism, but subjectivism is also considered essential. The scholar is an actor and political economic person (PEP) guided by her ideological orientation. We choose our fields of study, the problems to be approached, methods to be applied, how to present results and so on. And such choices can only be made from a particular viewpoint, or perspective, in the present language. The scholar is a responsible and accountable actor and cannot hide behind claims of only aiming at the truth in an allegedly value-neutral way. Among economists, this position was expressed at an early stage by Gunnar Myrdal:

> Valuations are always with us. Disinterested research there has never been and can never be. Prior to answers there must be questions. There can be no view except from a viewpoint. In the questions raised and the viewpoint chosen, valuations are implied.
>
> Our valuations determine our approaches to a problem, the definition of our concepts, the choice of models, the selection of observations, the presentation of our conclusions – in fact the whole pursuit of a study from beginning to end.
>
> (Myrdal 1978, pp. 778–779)

A second issue is about disciplinary paradigms in economics (Table 1.1). Here the dominance of neoclassical economic theory cannot be denied. Introductory economic textbooks have been homogenized and standardized not only regionally but also globally. Mankiw's book *Economics* (2008) is an example. At first glance, it may be considered an advantage that economists from different parts of the world speak the same language and use the same conceptual framework. However, this language is specific not only in scientific but also in ideological terms. This fact does, of course, not exclude neoclassical economic theory as a possibly relevant economics paradigm. It is the dominance, even monopoly, of neoclassical theory (with connected ideology) at university departments of economics that must be questioned. In a democratic society, one cannot limit economics to the neoclassical language and paradigm. Some degree of pluralism that better reflects the many ideological orientations relevant to citizens, politicians and political parties is called for. Will the demands for a sustainable development be well handled by exclusive reliance on neoclassical theory for example? We believe that economic science has to be opened for competition. Working along more lines than one is probably a wise idea in the present situation.

In the right-hand column of Table 1.1, a political economics view is outlined. The terminology chosen, 'political economics', points directly to the role of democracy. It questions the idea that all existing ideological orientations in a society can be reduced to one, dictated by a dominant group of economists.[2] Technocracy is here down played and democracy with a diversity of perspectives and approaches acknowledged (Söderbaum and Brown 2010). Among such perspectives, other than neoclassical theory, we certainly have our preferences (which will be indicated in the pages to follow), but we do not claim to know a single 'true' paradigm to completely replace neoclassical theory in a Kuhnian 'paradigm-shift' sense (Kuhn 1970). Reference to 'paradigm coexistence' is a more constructive position.

As part of this political economics perspective, an individual is assumed to be a PEP, that is, an actor guided by her 'ideological orientation' and the organization is similarly assumed to be a political economic organization (PEO) and actor guided by its ideological orientation or 'mission'. Ideological orientation and mission are not predetermined (as in the case of neoclassical maximization of utility and monetary profits) but something to be investigated in each case. The sustainability challenge, as an example, suggests an open attitude to ethical principles and ideological preferences.

In a democracy, many ideological orientations or socio-political viewpoints are represented rather than one but at a point in time one particular ideological orientation may dominate. For some decades, a market and economic growth ideology with connected ideas about efficiency and rationality has been dominant (Table 1.1, left-hand column). This is the ideology of neo-liberalism that was advocated among others by Margret Thatcher as Prime Minister in the United Kingdom and Ronald Reagan as President of the United States. Privatization of previously publicly managed assets and activities in the economy as a way of improving efficiency was among their recommendations. Rather than pointing to the failures of existing capitalism, they wanted more of it, arguing in 'there is no alternative' terms.

Our point is instead that there are alternative ideological viewpoints to that of neo-liberalism and that such alternatives need to be explored and articulated. Our view of human beings in the economy need not be limited to that of consumers and market-related roles, and there are organizations other than 'firms' in a neoclassical sense. And in the case of business corporations, broader and different missions than that of monetary profit maximization are relevant for those who take sustainable development seriously. Corporate social responsibility (CSR) exemplifies a relevant issue these days as does the UN sanctioned Global Reporting Initiative (GRI).

When Table 1.1 was introduced above, reference was made to different but interacting perspectives. Focusing on the left-hand column, positivism and its dominant role have certainly been a building block for neoclassical economics. The dominance of neoclassical economics, for example with Friedman and Friedman and their book *Free to Choose* (1980), in turn has certainly played an essential role for the emergence and strengthening of neo-liberal ideology. And I believe that together the three dominant perspectives (positivism, neoclassical economics and neo-liberalism) largely explain the kind of capitalist political economic system that we now experience nationally and globally. This dominance together with connected emotional and cognitive inertia among influential actors may also explain the kind of debate and dialogue about sustainability issues taking place in the media and elsewhere.

When looking for an alternative political-economic system that may perform better in relation to sustainability indicators, we can similarly think in terms of the three kinds of perspectives (right-hand column of Table 1.1). A scholar should certainly respect some traditional ideas of doing good science, but he or she should also be open about and responsible for his or her ideological orientation.[3] PEP and PEO assumptions will make our ideas of economics and the economy – and also about us as economists – more open and compatible with democratic imperatives. Finally, other ideological orientations than those framed on traditional neoclassical ideas of economics (economic growth in GDP terms, monetary profits in business) need to be considered. Our interpretations of sustainable development can be made more explicit for example.

Alternative ideas of science in relation to politics, of conceptual frameworks in economics and of ideological orientations may then together suggest smaller or larger changes in present institutional arrangements. In view of what we know today, it appears unwise not to consider also radical institutional change. At some point, one may, for example, understand that present challenges for the local, national and international community are largely non-monetary in kind. However, in our economies, the most important and influential organization, the business corporation, is defined in monetary and financial terms. Does this mean that the business corporation is legally mis-constructed in relation to present needs?

Observations from the UN dialogue on sustainability

Is it correct to argue that dialogue about fundamental perspectives is largely avoided at arenas where establishment actors meet? It may be expected that actors established as politicians, business leaders or other professionals tend to benefit from the present situation and therefore often prefer business-as-usual (BAU) ideas of development and institutional frameworks. They may accept some modification or modernization of present thinking and practices as a response to perceived problems. However, ideas of radical change are probably met with skepticism. Fortunately actors belonging to the establishment (in some sense) do not represent a completely homogenous group. And they are not the only actors in a democratic society. There are social movements suggesting that political pressures and change may come from many sources.

Let us now focus on debate about sustainable development at the UN level. To what extent does the dialogue include a consideration of fundamental perspectives as discussed above? Are issues about radical change of the political-economic system discussed or avoided? The Stockholm UN Conference in 1972 on the Human Environment is one of the earlier cooperative efforts while the previously mentioned publication of the Brundtland report (1987) in preparation for the 1992 UN Rio de Janeiro Conference belongs to the more recent events. In the year 2000, the Millennium Development Goals (MDGs) were established in a United Nations Millennium Declaration and later a Millennium Ecosystem Assessment was initiated (World Resources Institute/United Nations Environmental Programme 2005). A new UN Rio de Janeiro Conference took place in 2012, and I will focus on two documents in preparation for this conference and another UN report (2013) dealing with a proposed Post-2015 Development Agenda:

- UNEP (2011). Toward a GREEN economy. Pathways to Sustainable Development and Poverty Eradication. United Nations, New York.
- United Nations (2012). Resilient People, Resilient Planet. A Future Worth Choosing (The report of the United Nations Secretary-General's High-level panel on global sustainability). United Nations, New York.
- United Nations (2013). A New Global Partnership: Eradicate poverty and transform economies through sustainable development (The Report of the High-Level Panel of Eminent Persons on the Post-2015 Development Agenda). United Nations, New York.

The UNEP 2011 report refers repeatedly to a 'green economy' where green investments will create green jobs and replace 'brown' investments. Ecosystem services should be measured and included in 'natural capital'. Problems facing this transition tend to be perceived in terms of neoclassical economics with recommendations of full-cost pricing and monetary calculation of present value as in cost–benefit analysis (CBA). A modeling effort with focus on economic growth and where brown investments are replaced by green ones is presented. This part has been criticized by Victor and Tim (2012) who ask questions such as 'how green is green?' What kind of green (environmental) dimensions are part of the model and how? UNEP (United Nations Environmental Programme) has been heavily involved in this study and therefore bears some responsibility for the results.

Despite its promises, the green economy perspective represents a version of ecological modernization via technological fixes and market mechanisms, relying on neoclassical resource economics and focusing mostly on financial and environmental issues with limited concern for social wellbeing and equity (Brand 2012, Spangenberg 2016). It can be said that with the rise of the green economy, we are dealing with a new stage of neoclassical and neoliberal (aspirations to) hegemony.

The 2012 UN report is the outcome of work in a panel of politicians from different parts of the world. Again, the idea is to follow up from previous UN activities in preparation for the 2012 Rio de Janeiro Conference. A large number of proposals for action are listed. Concerning alternatives to mainstream neoclassical economics, reference is made to a 'new political economy of sustainable development'; 'we will bring the sustainable development paradigm from the margins to the mainstream of the global economic debate' (UN 2012, p. 13). This sounds promising, but on the same page, our politicians are back to neoclassical arguments:

> Most goods and services sold today fail to bear the full environmental and social cost of production and consumption. Based on the science, we need to reach consensus, over time, on methodologies to price them properly. Costing environmental externalities could open new opportunities for green growth and green jobs.
>
> (UN 2012, p. 13).

If the panel members argue in favor of a new approach to political economy, then they should not return to a language in terms of externalities, full cost pricing and consensus that have been around for some 30 years but instead point to a new paradigm and how it differs from the old one.

The post-2015 Agenda, our third report, refers back to previous UN activities. The aim is to build consensus for a new global partnership. Peace, absence of violence and an ambition to build open and accountable institutions are features adding to those of previous reports. Other positive elements of this agenda are a willingness to critically discuss the achievements of previous studies and UN projects, such as the Millennium Development Goals and to discuss possible weaknesses of consensus reports. There is also an attempt to identify relevant actor categories, their roles and capabilities in relation to the sustainability challenge. In the case of this report, the UNDP (United Nations Development Programme) has been the main contributing UN organization.

In the three reports, the authors are certainly conscious about the seriousness of the problems faced. Reference is made to planetary boundaries and the necessity of action. Ideas for possible reform and action are listed, that is, ideas that deserve serious attention. It is also clear that attempts have been made to listen to many voices with politicians and experts included. However, many of the actors that have been involved belong to establishment circles, suggesting that the capacity and sometimes also willingness to go beyond mainstream perspectives are limited.

In this book, we would like to encourage an ideologically open debate and action about all kinds of initiatives that can improve performance in relation to sustainability criteria. However, as already indicated, we want to warn against efforts limited to those based essentially on mainstream perspectives. At issue is if and how the three reports consider alternatives to the mainstream with respect to views of the role of science, views of economics and ideological perspectives.[4] Do they open or rather close the door for consideration of radical institutional change?

The authors of the three reports appear to be a bit divided between the need for change and the ambition to protect mainstream thinking and mainstream institutions. There is a recognition that 'the biggest risk of all may be with the status quo' (UNEP 2011, p. 39). At issue is, however, what kind of changes they are ready to consider seriously.

Also the academia is given a role in the modernization processes, for example, by developing new green technologies. The authors of the reports encourage actors in all roles to become serious about sustainability issues but otherwise seem to assume that university research and education are not part of the problems faced. Concerning economics, they rely heavily on neoclassical theory, and no references are made to publications where neoclassical theory is criticized and competing paradigms advocated. For many of us, present challenges are furthermore largely understood in ideological terms, but the word 'ideology' is avoided in the texts. Even in the case of the 2012 report with a panel of politicians, there is no serious consideration of ideological options.[5] Modification and 'modernization' of present institutional arrangements are discussed frequently, but hardly any proposal for radical institutional change can be observed.

To summarize; problems in the reports tend to be framed or formulated in terms of numbers of persons (globally or regionally) who suffer from poverty, lack of water resources, sanitation and so on and not in terms of failures of actors and institutions who bear some part of responsibility for the observations made.

In all three reports, there is a declared ambition to reach consensus. There are presumably not only reasons for such efforts but also risks. We do not as readers learn much or anything about actors (individuals and organizations) who have expressed differing opinions. New thinking, which is clearly needed, may come from them rather than from those who agree with the mainstream. In fact, the tendency to see theories of science, paradigms in economics and ideology as 'protected zones in the development dialogue' (Söderbaum 2008, pp. 37-50) can be questioned from the point of view of what we know of a well-functioning democracy. Mouffe (2005) for one argues that antagonism is not something that should necessarily be eliminated in public debate. Tensions between various groups and opinions may be regarded as the life blood of a democracy. In societies where democracy is taken seriously, we accept that individuals, groups of individuals, political parties and so on differ with respect to ideological orientation. Why is only consensus celebrated by UN organizations? Since consensus on sustainability is fairly difficult to achieve, with regard to local and global policies, we need an alternative practice that will allow us to move forward.[6]

The concepts of ideology, ideological orientation and democracy

'Ideology' is a 'contested concept' in the sense that it can be interpreted differently by different actors. In the social sciences, we have to live with a number of contested concepts (Connolly 1993), such as institution, power and ideology, suggesting that we need to clarify what we mean in each case. In the present context, 'ideology' is about 'means-ends relationships'. It is about where you are (present position), where you want to go (future positions) and how to get there (strategy). 'Ideology' is about worldviews, values and belief systems. The word 'ideology' has mainly been used at a collective level when referring to political parties, for example, the ideology of social democracy, liberal ideology, green ideology. However, ideological preferences may also be common to more than one political party or group as in the case of 'economic growth ideology'. Or large groups may (hopefully) emphasize a 'sustainability ideology' in some sense.[7]

In the present book, ideology, or rather 'ideological orientation', is used even at the level of individuals. If political parties and other organizations refer to their ideologies when turning to us as citizens in the hope of being accepted and even elected, then it can be assumed that also individuals when responding in one way or other refer to their respective ideological orientations. It is assumed that an individual as a PEP and actor is guided by her 'ideological orientation'. This can be compared with neoclassical assumptions where the individual is assumed to be a consumer related to commodity markets and maximizing utility. Our reference to ideological orientation suggests that the individual in all her roles (as citizen, professional, family member and so on) is a part of the economy and society. The ideological orientation of an individual is furthermore something to be problematized and investigated rather than taken for granted. How does individual A understand sustainable development, for example, and how does this understanding affect her decision-making and behavior? How do individual A and individual B differ with respect to ideological orientation?

The portrayal of individuals as utility maximizing consumers (and otherwise related to the market for jobs and financial capital) in neoclassical theory is quite compatible with an economic growth ideology in GDP terms. This neoclassical theory is, however, rather empty (if not dangerous) in relation to the new challenges of a sustainable development. We need a view of individuals in microeconomics that is compatible with the new demands.

As part of the present political economics view, decision-making is seen as a 'matching' process between an individual's ideological orientation (or an organization's 'mission') and expected impacts of each alternative of choice considered (Figure 1.1). The individual is searching for alternatives that are 'appropriate'[8] or 'compatible' with his or her ideological orientation. He or she may experience a good fit in relation to some alternatives or perhaps a miss fit in relation to all alternatives considered. There are many possibilities.

The ideological orientation of an individual can be expressed in qualitative, quantitative and visual terms. It is normally fragmentary (rather than complete) and uncertain (rather than certain), and the same can be said about the expected impacts connected with the choice of specific alternatives. Neoclassical ideas about optimal solutions by maximizing utility (or monetary profits) then become special cases that are realistic only in situations of (close to) complete information (or 'perfect information' as in neoclassical jargon).

As suggested in the title of this book, the political and ideological aspects of economics have to be made visible rather than remain hidden. The economy is embedded in a democratic society. Reference should be made to a political economics that is open rather than closed with respect to ideological orientations of individuals and missions of organizations. In ethical terms, the ideological orientation of an individual in a specific situation may be narrow or broad. Taking steps from trends that are unsustainable to those that are more sustainable is a matter of considering the interests of others (sometimes even those that are living in other parts of the world and future generations).

A democratic society is characterized by the existence of many ideological orientations rather than one and by critical deliberations where some reorientation of ideological views takes place. At the same time, the ideological orientation of

| Ideological orientation of individual as actor | | Expected multidimensional impact profile of each alternative of choice considered |

Figure 1.1 Decision-making as a 'matching' process.

each citizen is respected. Ideas of rationality and efficiency may come from sources outside the individual, but our individual is the final judge about rationality or 'appropriateness' in our present language.

This argument implies a move toward democracy in economic analysis. Neoclassical CBA, as an example, is built upon technocratic ideas of 'correct prices' for purposes of 'resource allocation'. Such an idea of correct prices (or methods to identify correct prices) is certainly specific in ideological terms. CBA can therefore only be used when there is a consensus in society about the values or ideological orientation built into CBA (Mishan 1980). In a society where democracy is taken seriously, each individual can (based on her ideological orientation) accept or reject the CBA ideology. A Norwegian economist, Johansen (1977), has identified the ideological orientation built into CBA as a 'net value-added' idea, that is, an economic growth ideology and I share his judgment.

The key role of social science and economics in sustainability policy formation

When dealing with presently existing unsustainable trends, we believe that conceptual frameworks in economics and management science have a specific role. Leading actors in our societies refer largely to their interpretations and views of economics in decision-making and management practices. Many years of indoctrination through education and public debate have made neoclassical economics the dominant frame of reference among establishment actors. This frame of reference has played a dominant role in a period when problems with unsustainable development have been aggravated.

Compared with neoclassical theory, we suggest a broadening of perspectives as follows:

- Strengthening of interdisciplinary openings, especially in relation to other social sciences
- Pluralist attitudes to theoretical perspectives (paradigms) in economics and other social sciences, recognizing that there may be more relevant models than one of individuals, business corporations, markets and so on.
- Broadening the view of the economy to include actors other than consumers and firms as well as ecosystems, natural resources, physical infrastructure and so on.
- Multidimensional analysis where each dimension is taken seriously and monetary (or other one-dimensional) reductionism is avoided
- Historical and evolutionary perspective. Increased focus on changes in non-monetary positions over time
- Institutional analysis with focus not only on markets but also on non-market institutions
- Moving some steps away from technocracy toward democracy by respecting differences in ideological orientation between politicians and citizens
- Focus on actors, their positions in various contexts, their responsibility and accountability in a democratic society.

Throughout this book, we address these recommendations from different perspectives and in diverse contexts, but some remarks are in order here.

The alternative perspective on economics has been presented elsewhere as 'ecological economics' (Söderbaum 2000) or 'sustainability economics' (Söderbaum 2007, 2008). Similar efforts have certainly been made by others, but the present approach can perhaps be considered as more elaborated and radical by recommending changes in the basic ideas about economics and changes in basic assumptions about individuals and organizations.

Among interdisciplinary openings, as mentioned in the above list of recommendations, the one in relation to social psychology is of particular importance. Our idea of a PEP is understood in terms of concepts such as role, relationship, motive, identity, attitude, cognition, dissonance and so on.[9] Also theories of science emphasizing subjective aspects of individuals such as narrative analysis and social constructivism can be relevant. And as has already been made clear, we are interested in the subjectivity of individuals out there in society. Personal features of the scholar matter. The scholar is a PEP and actor among other PEPs.

In the present context, pluralism implies that the neoclassical idea of one logically closed paradigm, including economy as well as economic analysis, is abandoned in favor of an open attitude to theoretical perspectives, such as social economics, ecological economics, feminist economics and institutional economics. Instead of the paradigm shift idea, we are thinking in terms of 'paradigm coexistence' (where there still may be a shift in the 'dominant paradigm'). At the level of single phenomena as part of a theoretical perspective, such as 'organization' or 'market', there may be more models than one and each model may add to the understanding offered by the others.

Consumers, firms and government are parts of the economy, but there are organizations other than firms that are influential and 'belong' to the economy. Universities, churches, Civil Society Organizations (CSOs) are examples of this. Ecological economists like me also look upon ecosystems and natural resources as essential parts of the economy rather than something outside it.

Economic analysis should be multidimensional according to the political economics perspective advocated here. Analysis should be disaggregated in the sense that expected monetary and non-monetary impacts are described separately and different non-monetary impacts in turn separated. Any decision to use prices in monetary terms as weights as part of aggregation is considered an ideological decision that one cannot leave to technocrats. The rule here is that democratic principles should apply in economic analysis.

In neoclassical analysis, history is normally considered irrelevant; only the present and the future count. Contrary to such a position, we regard the historical background as important for understanding the present situation and options for the future. As will be discussed in the chapters to follow, positional thinking, especially in non-monetary terms, is a way of bringing in different forms of inertia into the analysis (commitments, path dependence, lock-in effects and irreversibility).

Markets are no doubt important in a political-economic system, and there are many kinds of markets and models of markets. However, we are also interested in various kinds of other institutions that affect the functioning of an economy, for example, institutions where development issues are discussed and handled locally or globally. At the global level, United Nations, UNDP, UNEP, IMF, WTO and GRI (Global Reporting Initiative) exemplify institutions.

In economic analysis of the neoclassical kind, the analyst is an expert in an extreme sense ('science-speaking-truth-to-policymakers') dictating social values. Cost–benefit analysis is technocratic in the sense that a specific ideology is built into the method. In the present book, we show how economic analysis that is more compatible with democracy can be carried out.

Neoclassical theory and analysis focuses on and is limited to market-related roles of individuals, firms and national governments. As part of our present political economics, individuals and organizations are political actors in a broader sense who are responsible and accountable for their behavior and action. This means that no attempt is made to construct one single explanatory theory applicable to all individuals or all organizations. There are certainly not only similarities between actors in one category but also differences.[10]

Table 1.2 is an attempt to summarize the argument so far.

Table 1.2 A comparison between the neoclassical and the present political economics (or institutional) framework

View of	Neoclassical economics	Institutional economics
Individual	Economic man	PEP as actor guided by ideological orientation
Organization	Profit-maximizing firm	PEO as actor guided by mission
Economics	Ideologically closed idea of efficient resource allocation	Ideologically open ideas about efficiency and resource management
Decision-making	Optimization	Matching, appropriateness, pattern recognition
Approach to sustainability assessment	Cost–benefit analysis (CBA)	Positional analysis (PA), EIA and so on
Relationships between actors	Markets	Non-market and market
Market	Supply and demand of single commodities	Social (and power) relationship between single (and networks of) PEPs and PEOs
Progress in society	Growth in GDP	Ideologically open and multidimensional. Interpretations of SD among ideological options

The illusion of a value-free economics

To end this chapter, I would like to return to Gunnar Myrdal's statement that 'values are always with us' as economists and that economics is a political science in that sense. We cannot claim value neutrality. We can, however, attempt to carry out analysis that is open to more value orientations or ideological orientations than one and in that sense is more compatible with democracy.

In her book from 2014, 'Die Illusion wertfreier Ökonomie' (The illusion of a value-free economics), Tanja von Egan-Krieger focuses on three heterodox schools of thought in economics, namely feminist economics, institutional economics and ecological economics and scrutinizes what she sees as representative authors in each of these fields. She also discusses orthodox or standard economics. Her conclusions can be presented in simplified form as follows:

1   Orthodox (neoclassical) economics is not value free but specific both in scientific and value terms.
2   There is some flexibility (albeit limited) of value orientations also within neoclassical theory. A neoclassical economist can take feminist values seriously to some extent, for example.
3   Neither are the mentioned heterodox schools value free. They differ both in conceptual/scientific terms and with respect to value or ideological orientation from the mainstream.

Feminist economists claim to take the position of women in contemporary society seriously. Ecological economists ideologically emphasize present unsustainable trends and are committed to do something about these issues. Recognizing the role of values, ethics and ideology in the work by scholars and in society at large will improve the climate for dialogue. When it is understood that values and ideology cannot be avoided or eliminated in economics research and education, then we have to realize that we need to consider the role of democracy seriously in the academia.

Notes

1   Rockström et al. (2009) have attempted to present essential 'planetary boundaries' and risks as well as how far we are from constructively dealing with them.
2   Some connect the notion 'political economics' with a Marxist perspective. In the present study all schools of thought in economics, the neoclassical paradigm included, are regarded as specific in ideological terms and therefore represent cases of political economics. In relation to environmental issues 'political ecology' is similarly used in a restrictive sense (for an overview, see Robbins 2004).
3   Those of us who are active in the fields of development economics, environmental economics or ecological economics know that differences in the kind of research we are doing is not only a matter of narrow scientific criteria. Our engagements and ideological orientations often differ significantly. This aspect is particularly important when thinking in terms of pluralism, which is not just about the descriptive fact of the existence of diversity at the level of theory, but also represents the attitude of respect, tolerance,

engagement and critical conversation between scientists (Negru 2010, p. 188). Thus, the ideological orientation is an inherently normative issue that codetermines the way in which science is conducted.

4 For more elaborated comments on the report 'Resilient People ….', see Söderbaum (2012, 2013).

5 Reference is, however, at one place made to 'political perspectives': 'the choices that people make are also crucial and depend on broad considerations, such as political perspectives, habits and ethical values' (UN 2012, p. 35).

6 As mentioned before another part of the UN dialogue refers to a sanctioning of eight Millennium Development Goals (cf. follow-up study UN, 2015) which have recently been replaced with 17 'sustainable development goals'. Such a disaggregated view of development is more in line with the arguments in this book.

7 There may also be systematic differences in how 'ideology' is used in different cultural contexts. In the United States 'ideology' (as a result of the political climate, one may imagine) is sometimes used negatively. I have come across books – even on sustainable development – where the author starts by assuring his readers that he has attempted to be 'non-ideological' (Nolan 2009, p. 7). In a European context and as used in this chapter 'ideology' of some kind is necessarily present. But in the United States there are certainly also authors and other actors who use ideology in what here may be called a European way. One case in point is Nobel Laureate in physics Gell-Mann who identifies a number of necessary transitions toward sustainable development, 'ideological transition' being one (1994, pp. 359–362).

8 In his book *A Primer on Decision Making* (1994) March similarly refers to 'logic of appropriateness'. In computer language one may also refer to 'pattern recognition'. Our individual (or organization) looks for desired patterns of impacts and matches them against the expected patterns of impacts of each alternative considered.

9 It may be added that also mainstream economists increasingly recognize a need for openings in relation to social psychology. This is exemplified by a book by Kahneman *Thinking, Fast and Slow* (2011). At issue is, however, if attempts to take psychology seriously can be accommodated with neoclassical theory (Beckenbach and Kahlenborn 2016).

10 Neoclassical public choice theory can be criticized for its assumption of homogeneity in each actor category such as farmers or bureaucrats (Söderbaum 1991).

References

Barry, John, 2012. *The Politics of Actually Existing Unsustainability. Human Flourishing in a Climate-Changed, Carbon-Constrained World*. Oxford University Press, Oxford.

Beckenbach, Frank and Walter Kahlenborn, eds., 2016. *New Perspectives for Environmental Policies Through Behavioral Economics*. Springer, Heidelberg.

Brand, Ulrich, 2012. *Beautiful Green World. On the Myths of a Green Economy*. Luxemburg Argumente Nr 3, 2nd Volume. Rosa Luxemburg Stiftung, Berlin.

Connolly, William E., 1993. *The Terms of Political Discourse*. Blackwell, Oxford.

Friedman, Milton and Rose Friedman, 1980. *Free to Choose*. Penguin Books, Harmondsworth.

Gell-Mann, Murray, 1994. *The Quark and the Jaguar. Adventures in the Simple and the Complex*. Abacus, London.

Johansen, Leif, 1977. *Samfunnsøkonomisk lønnsomhet. En drøfting av begrepets bakgrunn og inhold*, Industriøkonomisk Institutt, Rapport Vol. 1. Tanum-Norli, Oslo.

Kahneman, Daniel, 2011. *Thinking, Fast and Slow*. AllanLane, London.

Kuhn, Thomas S. 1970. *The Structure of Scientific Revolutions* (second edition). University of Chicago Press, Chicago, IL.

Mankiw, N. Gregory, 2008. *Principles of Economics*. South-Western Cengage Learning, Stamford, CT.

March, James G. 1994. *A Primer on Decision Making. How Decisions Happen*. Free Press, New York.

Mishan, Ezra J. 1980. How valid are economic valuations of allocative changes? *Journal of Economic Issues*, Vol. 14, No. 1, pp. 143–171.

Mouffe, Chantal, 2005. *On the Political.* Routledge, London.

Myrdal, Gunnar, 1978. Institutional Economics, *Journal of Economic Issues*, Vol. 12, No. 4, pp. 771–783.

Negru, Iona, 2010. Plurality to pluralism in economics pedagogy: the role of critical thinking, *International Journal of Pluralism in Economics Education*, Vol. 1, No. 3, pp. 185–193.

Nolan, Peter, 2009. Crossroads. *The End of Wild Capitalism & the Future of Humanity.* Marshall Cavendish, London.

Robbins, Paul, 2004. *Political Ecology. A Critical Introduction.* Blackwell Publishing, Oxford.

Rockström, J., W. Steffen, K. Noone, Å. Persson, F.S. Chapin III, E.F. Lambin, T.M. Lenton, M. Scheffer, C. Folke, H.J. Schelinhuber, B. Nykvist, C.A. de Wit, T. Hughes, S. van der Leeuw, H. Rohde, S. Sörlin, P.K. Snyder, R. Costanza, U. Svedin, M. Falkenmark, L. Karlberg, R.W. Corell, V.J. Fabry, J. Hansen, B. Walker, D. Liverman, K. Richardson, P. Crutzen and J.A. Foley, 2009. A Safe Operating Space for Humanity, *Nature*, Vol. 461, pp. 472–475.

Söderbaum, Peter, 1991. Environmental and agricultural issues: what is the alternative to public choice theory? pp. 24–42 in Dasgupta, Partha ed. *Issues in Contemporary Economics Volume 3. Policy and Development.* International Economic Association/Macmillan, London.

Söderbaum, Peter, 2000. *Ecological Economics. A Political Economics Approach to Environment and Development.* Earthscan, London.

Söderbaum, Peter, 2007. Toward sustainability economics: principles and values, *Journal of Bioeconomics*, Vol. 9, pp. 205–225.

Söderbaum, Peter, 2008. *Understanding Sustainability Economics. Towards Pluralism in Economics.* Earthscan/Routledge, London.

Söderbaum, Peter, 2012. Democracy and sustainable development. Implications for science and economics, *Real-world Economics Review*, No. 60 (20 June 2012), pp. 107–119, http://www.paecon.net/PAEReview/issue60/Soderbaum60.pdf

Söderbaum, Peter, 2013. Ecological economics in relation to democracy, ideology and politics, *Ecological Economics*, Vol. 95 (November), pp. 221–225.

Söderbaum, Peter, and Judy Brown, 2010. Democratizing economics. Pluralism as a path towards sustainability. *Annals of the New York Academy of Sciences, Ecological Economics Reviews*, Vol. 1185, pp. 179–195.

Spangenberg, Joachim, 2016. The world we see shapes the world we create: how underlying worldviews lead to different recommendations from environmental and ecological economics – the green economy example, *Int. J. Sustainable Development*, Vol. 19, No. 2, pp. 127–146.

UNEP (United Nations Environment Programme), 2011. *Towards a Green Economy. Pathways to Sustainable Development and Poverty Eradication. A Synthesis for Policy Makers.* United Nations, New York.

United Nations, 2013. *A New Global Partnership: Eradicate Poverty and Transform Economies through Sustainable Development.* The Report of the High-Level Panel of Eminent Persons on the Post-2015 Development Agenda. United Nations, New York (un.org/publications).

United Nations, 2015. The Millennium Development Goals Report 2015. United Nations, New York.

United Nations Secretary General's High-level Panel on Global Sustainability, 2012. *Resilient People, Resilient Planet: A Future Worth Choosing.* United Nations, New York.

Victor, Peter A. and Tim Jackson, 2012. Commentary: a commentary to UNEP's Green Economy Scenarios, *Ecological Economics*, Vol. 77 (May), pp. 11–15.

World Commission on Environment and Development (The Brundtland Commission), 1987. *Our Common Future.* Oxford University Press, Oxford.

World Resources Institute and United Nations Environmental Programme (UNEP), 2005. *Ecosystems and Human Well-Being.* Synthesis Report (Millenium Ecosystem Assessment). Island Press, Washington, DC.

2 Fundamentals of sustainability economics and positional analysis

Peter Söderbaum

Positional analysis (PA) is part of a broader theoretical perspective that may be referred to as ecological economics or sustainability economics. Essential parts of this broader perspective have already been presented such as political economic person and political economic organization assumptions. In this chapter, a holistic idea of economics and an ideologically open idea of rationality are presented. Also concepts such as 'cost' and 'benefit' will be reconsidered in the light of multidimensionally and ideologically open thinking. However, first a few words about the complexity faced when approaching sustainability issues and decision-making.

Management approaches that respect complexity and are compatible with democracy

The problems that we face are complex in many ways. We can list a number of environmental problems that often are interrelated and require attention such as climate change, pollution in its various forms, biodiversity loss, depletion of natural resources, loss of agricultural land, radioactive waste, impacts on human health and so on. In some cases, problems are being mitigated; in other cases, they are getting worse. A lot of inertia is built into present development trends. We know that we cannot solve things overnight.

The complexity that we face can also be described as follows:

- Uncertainty is involved with respect to objectives (ideological orientation), alternatives to be considered and impacts.
- Objectives and impacts are multidimensional.
- Conflicts of interest are involved making ethics and ideological orientation an issue.
- The power positions of actors as decision makers or other actors concerned may differ.

Or, we can go one step further and articulate problems at the level of perspectives (worldviews) of politicians and other actors in society as in Table 1.1:

- Theories of science and the role of science in relation to politics
- Paradigms in economics

- Ideological orientations
- Institutional arrangements

When facing complex problems as indicated, one way of responding is to assume that the complexity 'does not really exist':

> We live in a world that is becoming increasingly complex. Unfortunately, our styles of thinking rarely match this complexity. We often end up persuading ourselves that everything is more simple than it actually is, dealing with complexity by presuming that it does not really exist.
>
> (Morgan 1986, p. 16)

Our preference is, however, to face some part of the mentioned complexity and to suggest and carry out economic analysis that is more compatible with (the complexity of) the problems faced. However, this means that one has to reconsider the role of the analyst carrying out the study, the role of politicians and other decision makers and the role of citizens (or other actors concerned). What is needed is a move some steps away from technocracy to democracy as listed in Table 2.1.

Neoclassical cost–benefit analysis (CBA) exemplifies an extremely technocratic approach (left-hand column of Table 2.1) in the sense that the analyst claims to know how to find out the correct values in the form of prices for different impacts. CBA is a case of 'monetary reductionism', and the analyst responds well to demands that may exist among politicians and some citizens for clear-cut recommendations and so-called optimal solutions claimed to be relevant for society as a whole. Ideological conflicts that may exist in a society are 'solved' by the analyst pointing to the recommendations made in CBA textbooks. The patterns of non-monetary (environmental, social, etc.) impacts that follow from the choice of each alternative become a non-issue since all relevant impacts have already been priced properly in monetary terms.

Table 2.1 Roles of analyst, politician and citizen in the cases of technocracy and democracy as two different cultural contexts

Role as	Technocracy	Democracy
Analyst	Optimal solution presented	Many-sided illumination of decision situation: conditional conclusions
Politician (decision maker)	Optimal solution accepted	Ideally consulted at all stages of study. Faces complexity and uses available information; extended accountability
Citizen (concerned actor)	Consulted only as dictated by analyst	Ideally active participant, consulted at all stages of study

Table 2.2 A classification of approaches to decision-making and evaluation

	Ideologically closed	*Ideologically open*
One dimensional	'a'	'b'
Multidimensional	'c'	'd'

A more open approach (right-hand column of Table 2.1) is exemplified by PA. Analysis is multidimensional, and no single dimension is prioritized or placed above the others from the very beginning. Analysis of ideological orientations, alternatives of choice and impacts is many sided in the attempt to illuminate an issue with its conflicts, irreversible non-monetary impacts, uncertainties and so on. Conclusions of this analysis are conditional in relation to each ideological orientation considered (and found relevant to the study).

Our reasoning points to a possible classification of approaches to decision-making as in Table 2.2. CBA then belongs to the 'a' category being one dimensional and ideologically closed, whereas PA belongs to the opposite corner, that is, 'd' (multidimensional and ideologically open). Again, this is seen as a movement away from technocracy toward a strengthened democracy. It is also possible to think of methods that belong to the 'b' category, for example, a method like CBA that emphasizes the monetary dimension, but where a sensitivity analysis is carried out with alternative prices for each impact identified. This would still be a case of 'monetary reductionism'. The 'c' category of closed and multidimensional analysis may then stand for an approach where specific targets have to be achieved in each dimension considered.

It should be emphasized that PA is not the only approach that belongs to the 'd' category being multidimensional (disaggregated) and open in ethical/ideological terms. Also environmental impact statement (EIS) [or environmental impact assessment (EIA)] tends to be presented in disaggregated form. Environmental laws stipulating the use of EIS exist in many countries, suggesting that this method is institutionally well established. One problem when compared with PA and CBA is, however, that EIS focuses on environmental impacts rather than all kinds of impacts. Another issue is that EIS tends to enter late in the decision process when influential actors are already committed to one specific alternative. What is achieved then is often limited to mitigation of a proposed alternative's environmental impacts.

From monetary reductionism to multidimensional and ideologically open ideas of economics

In neoclassical economics, the 'economy' is understood in terms of markets of three kinds, that is, markets for commodities, markets for financial capital and markets for labor. Each actor, individual or firm is related to markets of different kinds. Ecological economists do not deny the importance of market relationships but emphasize a broader conception of the economy. The market economy is embedded in the biosphere with natural resources and ecosystem services. The economy – and economic objectives and impacts – can no longer be reduced to markets and money. Non-monetary impacts are considered as 'economic' as monetary ones. In addition to monetary flows and positions (states), we have to seriously consider non-monetary flows and positions (states).

Natural and human resources are, according to the present view, 'economic' resources. We need not refer to prices in monetary terms. Changes in the size of an iceberg in terms of its surface or in cubic kilometers are 'economic' changes just as transformation of agricultural land to asphalt surface is an economic change. Changes in the number of persons unemployed or changes in chemical pollutants (defined in some way) in the blood of specific human beings can similarly be regarded as essential changes in economic resource positions. The 'value' of such degradation of natural resources or human resources is a matter of one's ideological orientation. According to most conceptions of sustainable development, such cases of irreversible degradation of non-monetary resources should be avoided. For those who still prefer to think exclusively in monetary terms, it can be argued that the cost is infinite, making exclusively monetary analysis more or less meaningless.

Objectives, indicators and impacts in economic analysis can then be classified in four categories as listed in Table 2.3. One distinction is made between that which is expressed in monetary and non-monetary terms and another between variables that refer to periods of time and points in time, respectively. It is argued that these distinctions are of importance not only for decision-making but also for accounting theory and practice (Brown 2009).

On the monetary side, the distinction between flows and positions (or states) is part of established and institutionalized accounting practices. A monetary flow of a business corporation is exemplified by profits while the balance sheet (assets and debts) describes monetary positions that are considered relevant. At the national level, gross domestic product (GDP) exemplifies a monetary flow variable, whereas the debts of a nation measured according to some definition exemplify a monetary position.

A new thinking is needed particularly with reference to the non-monetary side. Exploitation of minerals or pollution from a factory or a transportation system is normally measured per period, that is, as a non-monetary flow that will affect the state of the environment in specific ways and perhaps the health of individuals. Sometimes, there is a more direct relation between human activities and impacts as in the case of mining of iron ore that may lead to water pollution. In other cases,

Table 2.3 A classification of impacts in economic analysis

	Flow (referring to the period of time)	Position (referring to the point in time)
Monetary	'e'	'f'
Non-monetary	'g'	'h'

a number of human activities at many places lead to observed changes in the state of the environment.

However, positional thinking is not only about describing expected impacts in terms of states (positions) of the environment at particular points in time or the health status of individuals. Also the positions of actors participating in decision processes and market exchange in terms of their knowledge and power (in relation to other actors for example) can be described. The possibility of one actor exploiting another weaker actor can be discussed and described. The professional or other career of an individual can be described in positional terms and so on.

Similarly, the paths followed by business corporations (or other organizations) over time can be discussed in positional terms. Actually, this is where the PA project started in the late 1960s. The challenge was one of preparing for decision-making concerning alternative research and development (R&D) projects. Monetary costs for the first periods of implementing a research project can perhaps be estimated with some accuracy. However, what will happen in terms of knowledge? Will a project be successful in terms of arriving at a new technology and new products for the company? There is, of course, no easy answer to these questions. However, in addition to financial monetary impacts, a recommendation was made to think in terms of stock of knowledge as a positional variable. Changes in the stock of knowledge after one period may influence the financial outlays of moving in different directions at that future point in time. Part of the benefits may be connected with reduced monetary costs of specific further moves to acquire knowledge. The mentioned study and other early examples of positional thinking and PA are described in Appendix to this book.

One way of understanding the possible role of positional thinking is to refer to 'situatedness' as discussed in Chapter 4 of this book. The manager of R&D projects starts in some particular situation (conditioned by previous decisions). This situatedness refers to a present position with connected options for the future. Inertia is relevant in the sense that a specific move may make it more difficult, if not impossible, to arrive at specific positions in the future. Each move considered at a particular point in time will influence future options by facilitating specific future moves and making other moves more difficult or impossible. An analogy with a game of chess is relevant although a game of chess ends in a particular way while there is no predetermined end to positional thinking in relation to decision-making. A decision process starts with a situatedness in positional terms (explained in part by previous decisions) and ends with a new situatedness where further moves are normally possible.[1]

Non-monetary costs and benefits

As is made clear in the definition earlier, a multidimensional conception of economics has been chosen. Monetary costs and benefits are often involved in a decision situation but also non-monetary costs and benefits (Table 2.4). The idea (and ideological position) that everything should be expressed in monetary terms and that all kinds of impacts can be traded against each other is rejected. A disaggregated and multidimensional idea of economic analysis is preferred.

Table 2.4 Classification of objectives and impacts in economic analysis

	Costs	Benefits
Monetary	'i'	'j'
Non-monetary	'k'	'l'

Sustainable development is in itself a multidimensional concept. The monetary dimension is there, but our reasons for coining a new concept for progress are non-monetary in kind. Focus on economic growth and related monetary concepts is no longer enough. We need to focus on a number of ecological, social, health-related dimensions and so on and make them visible when managing resources or account-ing for progress – and lack of it – in society. As I see it, the monetary reductionism of neoclassical economics is not very helpful in our ambitions to get closer to a sustainable development.

In conclusion, then our ambition in the pages to follow is to respect complexity in a number of ways:

1 Rather than assuming that history does not matter we recognize that there is always a background to the present situation or position (with built in relevant aspects of inertia).
2 Rather than simplifying by assuming that value issues can be standardized as in CBA, we respect the existence of more than one ideological orientation.
3 Rather than attributing a primary role to the monetary dimension and pursue a strategy of aggregation, we describe monetary and non-monetary dimensions separately and also separately consider different non-monetary dimensions.
4 Rather than assuming that numbers alone 'count', we also consider qualita-tively or visually described impacts.
5 Rather than simplifying by assuming that uncertain impacts are certain or argue that probability analysis can easily be applied, we should point to relevant risks and uncertainties and not pretend that they can easily be considered.
6 Rather than relying on experts in a traditional sense with connected role inter-pretations for other actors, a move toward democracy is suggested.
7 Rather than accepting existing arenas and institutional arrangements (with existing power relations) for dialogue and decision-making, additional ways of strengthening democracy can be considered.

Note

1 See also how positional thinking (and situatedness) can be illustrated in terms of a specific kind of decision tree in Chapter 4.

References

Brown, Judy, 2009. Democracy, sustainability and dialogic accounting technologies: taking pluralism seriously, *Critical Perspectives on Accounting*, Vol. 20, No. 3, pp. 312–342.
Morgan, Gareth, 1986. *Images of Organization*. Sage, London.

3 Mainstream economics and alternative perspectives in a political power game

Peter Söderbaum

In mainstream economics textbooks, 'economics' is normally connected with 'allocation of scarce resources', the main idea then being that 'efficient' management of such resources can be handled in monetary terms. While scarcity is an important aspect of management, for example in relation to limited fish stocks, agricultural land and limited absorptive capacity of various pollutants, 'scarcity' is here seen as a multi-facetted and multidimensional concept with objective as well as subjective elements. Such aspects can be considered in a partly different definition of economics where democracy and the ideological orientation of individuals play a role:

> Economics is multidimensional management of (limited) resources in a democratic society

This definition implies a move away from highly technocratic ideas of economics (as in neoclassical cost–benefit analysis [CBA], for example) towards the acknowledgement of some democratic principles. In a democracy, citizens have the right to vote in support of specific politicians and political parties. Elections are taking place according to specific rules and institutional arrangements. Voting is done anonymously; results are presented openly and a majority rule is applied.

Free speech is a fundamental right in a democracy. In principle, the opinions and ideological orientation of each citizen should be respected (as long as they do not directly go against the idea of democracy itself). Individuals should also be encouraged to participate in dialogue about ideas of progress in society or direction of development. Dialogue is needed at the level of visions and ideological orientations as well as about specific problems or issues where decisions are made. Specific arenas may exist or be arranged to facilitate participation and dialogue.

In practice, there are often, if not normally, limits to public dialogue. Each individual as actor is left with his or her knowledge and cognitive capacity and relates to a context that may facilitate participation or rather make participation difficult. Participation in public dialogue can in itself be regarded as a matter of managing resources, starting from a person's power and resource position. Search costs of monetary and other kinds are involved and are related to the expected benefits (in monetary and non-monetary terms) from search. Neoclassical ideas of perfect information are rejected while Simon's (1957) and Cyert and March's (1963) concepts of 'bounded rationality' and 'satisficing behavior' are highly relevant. These authors questioned neoclassical ideas of rationality based on perfect information as not being relevant in relation to the complexities of the real world.

Respecting different ideological orientations among actors in a society is the essence of democracy. In special cases, there may be consensus about ideological orientation among citizens and actors in other roles. However, in the normal case, there are tensions and differences of opinion. Reference can also be made to conflicts of interest between stakeholders or interested parties in relation to a particular issue or decision situation. Such stakeholder interests are, however, generally perceived as limited and connected with specific activities. They differ in that respect from an actor's ideological orientation as a more comprehensive concept.

In neoclassical economic analysis, the monetary dimension is emphasized. Impacts are quantified in monetary terms to make them comparable and to 'trade' them against other impacts. Negative environmental impacts can be traded against other impacts in CBA, for example. The idea that all impacts have a price, and generally the emphasis on the monetary dimension, is specific in ideological terms.

Technocracy or democracy – the example of neoclassical CBA

While not excluding the possibility that debate and other forms of interaction between actors may lead to consensus about ideological orientation, we argue that tensions between actors advocating different ideological orientations are the normal case. Such tensions or competition between ideological orientations can be deliberately eliminated in two ways:

A   By giving priority to a technocratically decided ideological orientation as in the case of neoclassical CBA and thereby eliminating all competing world views and ideological orientations

B   By giving priority to a leading politician as dictator or a group of politicians, for example a politburo by endowing it with exclusive power and eliminating dissenting voices (which represent competing ideological orientations)

The claimed right to eliminate competing voices is common to the situations A and B. In case A, we are dealing with an extreme form of technocracy where the approach to governance and decision-making as well as to relevant ideological orientation is placed in the hands of experts. While not excluding some democratic elements, this situation can be described as highly technocratic.

Power is similarly concentrated in our second case B. Leadership is in the hands of one political dictator or other political entity, and obedience is secured in many ways, including police and military power. A society of this kind is described as a dictatorship. While power is highly centralized, minor elements of democracy may still be observed.

In case B, the concentration of power is highly visible. Also in case A, elements of political dictatorship is present but not so easily visible. In Sweden (and many other so-called developed countries), which is often understood as a democratic nation, there are tendencies to leave governance to the market. When CBA as a method is applied, all possibly relevant ideological orientations are reduced to one where impacts of alternatives are transformed to monetary terms and where economists claim the right to preach correct prices or values for each impact. Perhaps a neoclassical economist advocating CBA does not fully understand what he or she is doing. A related possibility is that he or she has internalized the ideological orientation inherent in neoclassical theory with its CBA. Neoclassical economists who understand that the CBA approach is controversial may try to hide this fact.

In her books *On the Political* (2005) and *Agonistics: Thinking the World Politically* (2013), Mouffe similarly argues that democracy should be understood in terms of antagonism between actors holding different views. These tensions are not regarded as dysfunctional in public debate but rather constructive. The idea that dialogue necessarily should aim at consensus is questioned. Mishan whose work was mentioned in Chapter 1 argues in similar terms. He himself has written a textbook on neoclassical CBA (Mishan 1971) but contends that the CBA framework can only be used if there is consensus in society about the rules of valuation in CBA (actual market prices, hypothetical market prices as when consumers are asked about their 'willingness to pay'). If no such consensus exists at a particular time, then the CBA method cannot be used (Mishan 1980). Mishan points specifically to tensions about environmental issues existing at the time of writing early in the 1980s and makes the conclusion that CBA textbooks have to be left on a shelf until some day in the future when a consensus possibly emerges. Considering the present situation year 2016 with extreme difficulties to counteract climate change, biodiversity loss, pollution of water systems, depletion of fish stocks and so on, it is probably correct to argue that consensus about the use of CBA in economic analysis is no longer a realistic expectation. Sustainability policy and action have to be built on other conceptual frameworks and methods.

Technocracy or democracy – the example of neoclassical 'full-cost pricing'

Neoclassical economists recommend the use of CBA for purposes of public decision-making. Another recommendation more connected with neoclassical environmental economics as a sub-field is 'full-cost pricing'. While it is believed that the market mechanism has a potential to solve a large number of private and public problems, it is also recognized that markets may fail. It is assumed that those directly involved in the market transaction as buyer and seller are satisfied with it (which in the real world is not necessarily the case), but that some identifiable third parties may suffer from so-called negative externalities. Such negative external impacts should be 'internalized' into the market transaction, it is argued, so that prices reflect the 'full cost'. The monetary dimension is once more at the heart of this analysis and as with CBA, neoclassical economists claim technically to be able to inform us about the corrections for externalities to be made. Reference is made to single pollutants as external impacts, and the corrections point to a different optimal solution.

K. William Kapp, institutional economist and probably the first environmental economist of all categories, argued that externalities are ubiquitous rather than appearing as single phenomena (Kapp 1950). Business corporations or firms, operating under existing institutional arrangements, systematically shift (or 'externalize') costs upon others and society at large (Kapp 1970). In this manner, monetary costs are reduced and monetary profits increased. A mining company, for example depletes natural resources and pollutes soil and water systems in a step-by-step fashion. Not only monetary costs but also irreversible costs of a non-monetary kind are involved. It is not easy – if at all possible – to find out what the 'full cost' in monetary terms is in such cases.

Having abandoned the neoclassical idea of correcting the price mechanism to arrive at full costs as identified by experts, what remains, once more, is to move away from technocracy towards democracy. The price mechanism may still be used, but prices, charges or taxes to be paid by different parties will then be based on systematic multidimensional impact studies and ethical judgments of fairness or appropriateness in relation to different actors or interested parties affected. In principle, each citizen, or actor in other roles, may have his or her own opinion about relevant policy instruments and fair prices in the case that market instruments are used. Policy is furthermore not limited to the use of market instruments. Also prohibitions can be considered. Policies and decisions are formulated and made in political assemblies where the ideological orientation of political parties and single politicians influences outcomes.

The TEEB study – Is it an example of cognitive and ideological inertia?

The UN reports commented upon in the introductory chapter suggest that CBA and 'full-cost pricing' are still taken seriously in some establishment circles. Another recent example is the so-called TEEB study, *The Economics of Ecosystems and Biodiversity. Ecological and Economic Foundations* (TEEB 2010). More than 100 economists, some of them being part of ecological economics associations, participated in this ambitious project as contributors and reviewers. The focus is on valuation of ecosystem services, and 'valuation' is equal to 'monetary valuation'. Reference is repeatedly made to early studies by Pearce with 'total economic value' in monetary terms as a key concept (Pearce and Turner 1990). The estimated value of specific ecosystem services is part of an aggregative process where all impacts are involved. Neoclassical CBA and 'full-cost' pricing are back on the scene.

The argument is underpinned by a familiar rhetoric. It is argued that 'you cannot manage what you do not measure' (TEEB 2010, p. xxv). Getting the 'metrics' right is what is needed. Later, a return to 'economic valuation' in monetary terms is recommended, the argument being that people know about money and understand a language in money terms:

> Valuations are a powerful 'feedback mechanism' for a society that has distanced itself from the biosphere upon which its very health and survival depends.

> Economic valuation, in particular communicates the value of Nature to society in the language of the world's dominant economic and political model. Mainstreaming this thinking and bringing it to the attention of policy makers, administrators, businesses and citizens is in essence the central purpose of TEEB.
>
> (TEEB 2010, p. xxvii)

A careful reading of the book reveals that at least some of the contributors understand that there are many problems involved in a project to value ecosystem services in monetary terms. Taking those arguments seriously, for example uncertainty about the nature and function of specific ecosystem services and the irreversibility of biodiversity loss could very well lead to the opposite conclusion – that monetary valuation of ecosystem services should be downplayed or abandoned in favor of other approaches to valuation (assessment) and economic analysis.

The attempt to focus on ecosystem services and to identify them and their role can only be encouraged. Similarly, the possibility to sometimes use a price mechanism to reduce biodiversity loss can be considered (as part of ethical judgments of 'fair' or 'appropriate' charges or taxes). However, the whole idea to reduce ecological services to some alleged technically determined monetary equivalent is here questioned for reasons that have already been presented. Our societies suffer from too much of monetary thinking and monetary reductionism. Sustainable development is primarily about non-monetary progress. We need non-monetary indicators and not only monetary ones. The neoclassical CBA method with its 'trade-off' reasoning is a case of 'weak' sustainability in a situation where we need 'strong' sustainability (Neumayer 2003). Or, we can refer to the distinction among a 'business as usual' (BAU) strategy, the strategy of 'ecological modernization' (Hajer 1995) and consideration of 'radical change' (e.g. Söderbaum 2000, 2008). The 'mainstreaming' strategy of TEEB can then best be described as ecological modernization in a situation where we need to consider radical change.

When Pavan Sukhdev in his preface to the TEEB study argues that we should continue to rely on 'the world's dominant economic and political model', he overlooks the possibility that this dominant model has failed in important respects and is an essential part of the problems faced. Neoclassical economic theory should not be excluded from consideration but is, as I see it, insufficient and not very constructive in relation to sustainability issues.

Biological diversity is a positive concept for many citizens and actors in other roles. Those of us who take democracy seriously similarly regard some extent of 'cultural diversity' in positive terms. In this light, the 'mainstreaming' idea of the TEEB study can be examined. Is 'ideological monoculture' in economics and development thinking the right thing to aim at?

In this book, we emphasize democracy and an open political dialogue. From this point of view, it is quite possible that the TEEB study leads to a constructive dialogue about ecosystem assessment and more generally approaches to decision-making. A number of articles have been produced by ecological economists, the present author included (Söderbaum 2013, 2015). If there is a 'mainstream', there are other streams as well. As a political economic person (PEP) among other PEPs, I hope that the TEEB study marks the end to the dominance at the UN level and elsewhere of neoclassical economic theory in relation to sustainability and environmental issues. However, the cognitive and other inertia involved should not be underestimated.

A political power game with economists and other actors involved

We have become accustomed to think of scientists as standing outside politics and not being part of it. This is the result of the dominance of positivism as a theory of science. As mentioned before, Gunnar Myrdal told us social scientists, however, that 'values are always with us', that they are necessarily present in some form. My position is that the economist (or other social scientist) is part of politics. The scholar is a PEP among other PEPs. As PEP, the scholar has to observe normal ideas of democracy in addition to other ideas of good science. To this, we will return.

The TEEB study exemplifies how politics is necessarily involved. Sukhdev as study leader is apparently glad to enter into a role where neoclassical economics and CBA with its specific ideological orientation are celebrated. In this acceptance of mainstream economics, he is supported by some well-known neoclassical environmental economists.[1] Also PEPs whose identities are more connected with 'ecological economics' participated but were not strong enough in the political power game that apparently took place.

We do not know what will finally come out of this scientific and political power game and are not yet in a 'game over' situation. The important thing for the moment is only to make it clear that politics is involved in the field of economics of ecosystems and biodiversity and that more than one view is possible. Economics is always political economics.

It should then be understood that the TEEB study is a political document where good science and good arguments do not always play the first role. As part of a massive political strategy to implement their message, specific recommendations are directed towards specific audiences:

- Actors in 'National and International Policy Making'
- Actors in 'Business and Enterprise'
- Actors in 'Local and Regional Policy and Management' (TEEB 2010, p. 5)

The United Nations Environment Programme, UNEP (which is also behind a similar Green Economy initiative mentioned in Chapter 1) has played a leading role in the TEEB project. Other policy-oriented institutions contributing to the financing of TEEB are the European Commission, the German Federal Ministry for the Environment (BMUB) and the UK Department for Environment. Additional UK institutions as well as Norway's Ministry of Foreign Affairs and the Swedish International Development Agency have supported the project. It appears that many are those who support traditional thinking in monetary market terms and economic growth ideology. The good thing is that this is done in publications that are open to deliberations and criticism.

Note

1 Public choice theory is part of neoclassical economics. I have criticized or pointed to the limits of this theory (1991) but tend to think that it reasonably well describes the category of neoclassical economists themselves. They form a 'rent-seeking' category protecting the neoclassical monopoly. Hopefully there is, or will be, some heterogeneity that at some stage opens the door for pluralism.

References

Cyert, Richard M. and James G. March, 1963. *A Behavioral Theory of the Firm*. Prentice Hall, Englewood Cliffs, NJ.

Hajer, Maartens A. 1995. *The Politics of Environmental Discourse. Ecological Modernization and the Policy Process*. Clarendon Press, London.

Kapp, K. William, 1970. Environmental disruption: general issues and methodological problems, *Social Science Information*, Vol. 9, No. 4, pp. 15–32.

Kapp, K. William, 1971 (1950). *The Social Costs of Private Enterprise*. Schocken Books, New York.

Mishan, Ezra J. 1971. *Cost-Benefit Analysis*. Allen & Unwin, London.

Mishan, Ezra J. 1980. How valid are economic valuations of allocative changes? *Journal of Economic Issues*, Vol. 14, No. 1, pp. 143–171.

Mouffe, Chantal, 2005. *On the Political*. Routledge, London.

Mouffe, Chantal, 2013. *Agonistics: Thinking the World Politically*. Verso, London.

Neumayer, Eric, 2003. *Weak versus Strong Sustainability: Exploring the Limits of Two Opposing Paradigms*. Edward Elgar Publishing, Cheltenham.

Pearce, David W. and Kerry Turner, 1990. *Economics of Natural Resources and the Environment*. Harvester Wheatsheaf, Hempsted.

Simon, Herbert, 1957. *Models of Man*. John Wiley, Hoboken, NJ.

Söderbaum, Peter, 2000. *Ecological Economics: A Political Economics Approach to Environment and Development*. Earthscan/Routledge, London.

Söderbaum, Peter, 2008. *Understanding Sustainability Economics: Towards Pluralism in Economics*. Earthscan/Routledge, London.

Söderbaum, Peter, 2013. Ecological economics in relation to democracy, ideology and politics, *Ecological Economics*, Vol. 95 (November), pp. 221–225.

Söderbaum, Peter, 2015. Varieties of ecological economics: do we need a more open and radical version of ecological economics? *Ecological Economics*, Vol. 119 (November), pp. 420–423.

TEEB, 2010. The TEEB study, United Nations Environmental Programme in Kumar, Pushpam ed. *The Economics of Ecosystems and Biodiversity. Ecological and Economic Foundations*. Earthscan, London.

4   Positional analysis as approach to decision-making, accounting and democracy

Peter Söderbaum

There are alternatives to neoclassical economic theory, and there are alternatives to cost–benefit analysis (CBA). One may ask why CBA is still recommended and used in many parts of the world in spite of criticism and the existence of alternative approaches. One factor might be that people generally, and actors in specific roles, have become accustomed to believe in science and in experts. Experts in economic analysis are expected to be able to tell us about the 'best' or 'optimal' alternative. Approaches that do not produce one single clear-cut solution are sometimes not even accepted as 'methods'.

However, clear-cut solutions have a price; problems have to be simplified in a number of ways. You have to rely on a specific paradigm and method; you have to frame the problem in specific ways by choosing variables in the equation to be optimized. Only aspects or dimensions that can be described quantitatively count and performance in one dimension has to be chosen for maximization (minimization), possibly with constraints in other dimensions. Reference to some value or ideological orientation is needed for each of these decisions. The analysis necessarily becomes built upon a single perspective while other ideological orientations among decision makers or citizens are neglected. A technocratic way to deal with this situation of conflicting ideological orientations in a society is to try to convince all actors that CBA is the only scientifically correct method. This is a strategy chosen by United Nations Environment Programme (UNEP) and other influential actors and institutions in the previously discussed *The Economics of Ecosystems and Biodiversity* (TEEB) study.

Another factor that may explain the continued popularity of CBA is its standardized character. Analysts offer an idea of how to correctly 'value' impacts of different kinds. The fact that such an idea of correct valuation represents a very specific ideology is then ignored or not understood. Cognitive and emotional inertia among actors as analysts, or professors of economics, adds to the factors that possibly explain the use of CBA. Cognitive inertia (or commitments) is a fact of life (and is also relevant for the present author). Even laziness may play a role in continuing to use the same method or repeat the 'same message as last year'.

At issue is how one can deal with the existence of inertia and other aspects of complexity while respecting democracy. If we just are interested in clear-cut solutions as quickly as possible, we do not even need CBA. Choosing one alternative rather than the other could be done by throwing dice or in the form of a lottery. However, we are not primarily interested in quick decisions but in alternatives of choice that are relevant in relation to the problems faced and in the ideological orientations of decision makers and others. We want to see to it that decision makers and other actors know what they are doing (in relation to sustainable development, for example) when choosing a particular alternative. CBA is perhaps not irrelevant in relation to sustainable development (the ideological orientation, which is our primary concern here), but it is possible to socially construct approaches that are more relevant.

Let us first discuss the kind of sustainability issues we are facing.

Nature of the sustainability problems faced

Sustainability issues are not primarily market issues with externalities that can be dealt with through full-cost pricing. Neoclassical theory in equilibrium terms is instantaneous and a bit mystical in relation to the time dimension. We argue here – what should be self-evident – that the temporal dimension plays a key role in sustainable development and that dealing with time in terms of discount rate and present value in monetary terms is a strange practice. It can only be understood in terms of an obsession with quantification and mathematical treatment in money terms.

Sustainability problems are complex in a number of ways:

- The time dimension is essential with inertia as a relevant phenomenon.
- Impacts are multi-dimensional rather than one dimensional.
- Decisions affecting sustainability performance are made not only by national governments but also by other organizations and at other levels (individual, family, local community, business corporation, European Commission, UN).
- Many actors in different roles (analyst, politician, stakeholder, citizen) are involved in decisions.
- Tensions and antagonism as well as cooperation may characterize relationships between stakeholders and between actors in different roles.
- Uncertainty is normally a relevant phenomenon, not only concerning impacts but also the ideological orientation of actors and appropriate roles for different actors.
- There is finally a tension between reliance on experts (technocracy) and participation of politicians, those affected and other citizens (democracy).

Purpose of positional analysis

The purpose of a positional analysis (PA) study is to bring some order in the study of a particular decision situation while respecting various aspects of complexity as previously mentioned. The existence of complexity suggests some humility in the approach as preferable to firm statements about correct prices and optimal solutions.

Rather than trying to 'solve' a problem in a final manner, the purpose of PA is to 'illuminate' a decision situation for politicians or other decision makers, stakeholders and other actors concerned by the issue. The actors as political economic persons (PEPs) normally differ with respect to ideological orientation suggesting that the analyst need to consider more than one ideological (value) orientation. Conclusions in the form of ranking alternatives then become conditional in relation to each ideological orientation considered. The idea is no longer one of pretending that conflicts do not exist or that the analyst knows how to solve conflicts by referring to a specific idea of welfare in society.

When illuminating a decision situation, the following aspects are normally considered as part of PA:

- Historical background
- Ideological orientations that appear relevant to decision makers and other actors (or should be considered as part of national or other policy principles)
- Alternatives of choice
- Expected impacts connected with each alternative
- Uncertainty and risks
- Inertia and irreversibility
- Conflicts of interest and tensions between ideological orientations

The approach is disaggregated where non-monetary impacts are separated from monetary ones (cf. Table 2.1). The analyst typically uses documents (newspaper articles, etc.) from public debate, interacts with stakeholders and other concerned actors, arranges meetings where stakeholders and other actors can exchange ideas and expresses their opinions. Such interactions of various kinds are documented to facilitate transparency and accountability of actors.

Why is the approach indicated more compatible with democracy than CBA? There is an ambition to make actors and their arguments visible. This transparency plays a role for responsibility and accountability. All actors, the analyst included, are regarded as PEPs, each with his or her ideological orientation. The possibility that an information base for decision makers is manipulated by powerful actors and/or the analyst is counteracted by an imperative of 'many sidedness' in analysis. Analysis should be many sided, for example with respect to ideological orientations and alternatives of choice considered.

A scheme of analysis

PA can be described in the form of a scheme of analysis. Later some elements in the scheme will be further elaborated:

- Reference is made to PEP and Political Economic Organization (PEO) assumptions, for example the idea of decision-making as a matching process between ideological orientation and expected impacts of each alternative considered (cf. Figure 1.1).

- Historical background of the study: Are there previous studies and documents related to the same issue? Are there commitments already made that may limit the options available?
- Dialogue among analyst, stakeholders and concerned actors about how problems are perceived and how to deal with the problems in a process of interactive learning.
- Identification and articulation of relevant ideological orientations among decision makers and other actors concerned. Ideological orientations that should be considered according to national policy or European Union commitments should be included even if they play a peripheral role in the ideological orientations of the actual decision makers.
- Identification of relevant first-stage alternatives (cf. below about multiple-stage decision-making). Listening to the actors is here a good idea. It is also possible to search for alternatives starting with the ideological orientations that have been identified. Are there alternatives that have a good chance of matching a specific ideological orientation?
- Equal treatment of alternatives considered.[1] The fact that one influential stakeholder advocates a specific alternative should not lead to this alternative being given priority position in the evaluation
- A multi-dimensional and ideologically open idea of economics, rationality and efficiency
- Systems thinking as a way of identifying impacts and their extension in space. What kind of systems will be affected differently depending on which one of the alternatives that is chosen? What is the spatial extension of these affected systems? How does the specific decision situation relate to broader policy issues, for example at the national level?
- Systematic focus on how non-monetary and monetary impacts over time differ between alternatives.
- Positional thinking as a way to consider inertia (e.g. path dependence, irreversibility) and more generally impact on future options by choosing one alternative rather than another.
- Analysis of commonalities and conflicts of interest in relation to various affected activities (of individuals and organizations).
- Conditional conclusions of analysis in relation to previously identified ideological orientations to be presented for decision makers and other actors.
- Feedback from all actors, ideally at all stages of the analysis and decision process with the purpose of improving the information base.
- A non-monetary and monetary framework for the monitoring of impacts and ex post evaluation (follow-up studies).

This list is certainly ambitious, but simplified versions of PA have been used and can be considered. The way of thinking recommended in the scheme of analysis can also have a value in itself in relation to sustainability issues even in situations where no written analytical study is made.

The time dimension – a multiple-stage process

The time dimension refers to relationships between the past, the present and the future. It is, for example about equality between the present generation of people and future generations. Are we systematically degrading the life-support systems of future generations? To get an idea of how the future is affected, we need to distinguish between monetary and non-monetary dimensions (cf. Table 2.3). Direct monetary impacts of an investment in oil drilling, iron ore mining or highway transportation will tell us only part of the story. Moreover, there will be many kinds of non-monetary impacts. Less oil or iron ore or land for non-transportation purposes will be available in the future. Soil, water and air may be polluted at the time of extraction of natural resources and later when oil or iron is transformed and used for different purposes, for example in-house construction or transportation. Such pollution may be accumulated over time at various places, human bodies included.

When building a new road, agricultural land and land covered by forests may be bought from real estate owners at some monetary price. These monetary costs and financial outlays are certainly relevant, but the fact of often irreversible transformation of land is an additional and different cost of a non-monetary kind. The idea that such non-monetary costs (and benefits for that matter) can and should be transformed to some monetary equivalent is heroic, to say the least. The best we can do is to describe and discuss such impacts as part of a multi-dimensional profile over time for each investment project considered with the uncertainties involved. Systematic analysis is possible also in cases of uncertain impacts.

Cost and benefit, be they monetary or non-monetary, have also to be related to the value or ideological orientation of the observer. The fact that agricultural land and forest cover is reduced is important for some of us but not for all. That which is a non-monetary benefit for one person may be a non-monetary cost for another. A new road will facilitate transportation for some but produce noise and pollution for those living nearby. Ecosystems will be affected, and the road may be a barrier for animals. Traditional analysis in CBA terms tends to downplay, if not eliminate, many non-monetary costs. The way forward here is to take different ideological orientations seriously in our attempt to inform decision makers and other actors.

Inertia is present in monetary as well as non-monetary dimensions. Monetary impacts are often emphasized, as we have seen, in neoclassical economic theory, whereas inertia on the non-monetary side does not fit well into the neoclassical conceptual framework. Inertia relates the past to the present and limits or opens the door for possible futures. The necessary existence of inertia suggests that decision-making be regarded as a multiple-stage process in multi-dimensional terms. An initial position can be identified, and choosing a specific option rather than another leads to a new position or state at a later point in time that in turn facilitates or hinders specific decisions and moves at that stage (Figure 4.1). A decision today where one alternative is chosen is only regarded as a first decision in a series of decisions and moves that follow. The logic is the same as in a game of chess. Each move by one of the chess players will condition the possible moves in the future.

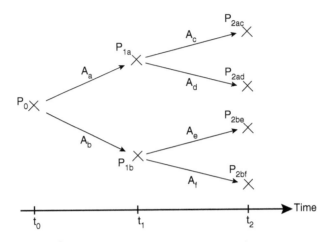

Figure 4.1 Decision tree in positional terms.

In Figure 4.1, P_0 stands for the starting position of an object of description at time t_0. A_a and A_b are two alternatives considered at t_0. A_a is expected to lead to position P_{1a} at point in time t_1, while choosing A_b at t_0 will result in a position P_{1b} at t_1. P_{1b} differs qualitatively and quantitatively from P_{1a}. Assuming that A_a was chosen at t_0 then the options at t_1 will differ from the options at t_1 for the case that A_b had been chosen at t_0.

This may sound both abstract and trivial. It is trivial in the sense of being close to our everyday experiences. If I have time to read one of two books during a particular period, my position in terms of knowledge and other experiences at the end of the period will differ depending on which one of the books I choose to read. Similarly, staying at home working in Uppsala for one particular day will probably lead to a different position at the end of the day from the option of commuting to my office in Västerås. We will later turn to issues more relevant for sustainable development where states or positions related to the environment and natural resources are involved.

It may be observed that the present kind of decision trees differs from that used in game theory (Neumann and Morgenstern 1944). In game theory, the different branches generally end with a pay-off (in monetary terms, one can imagine) while our end positions are qualitative as well as quantitative and also represent initial positions for further moves. In neoclassical game theory, performance is measured in monetary terms where impacts can be traded against each other while in the present analysis, non-monetary impacts and positional changes are also considered potentially relevant.

All kinds of dimensions can be relevant for description of inertia in its different forms (Söderbaum 1973). The physical dimension is, of course, of crucial importance. Some ecological economists see Georgescu-Roegen's (1971) analysis of inertia and irreversibility in energy and entropy terms as fundament of their discipline, but it is here argued that inertia is a multi-faceted phenomenon that should also be considered in physical terms other than energy and in other non-monetary terms than those that are physical.

Land-use changes can certainly be interpreted not only in energy terms but also in other physical as well as biological-chemical terms. In Figure 4.2, a specific case of land-use change is illustrated where thinking in multiple stages is relevant. For a certain plot of agricultural land, the options at t_0 are assumed to be 'continued use as agricultural land', a transfer to 'agro-forestry' or to 'asphalt' surface (connected with road construction). In the case of agroforestry, there is a possibility later to return to agricultural land, if desired at that time (see Figure 4.2). There is no arrow back from the position 'asphalt', suggesting that this is an irreversible change. Politicians or other decision makers may in specific cases accept such irreversible impacts. As a minimum, such consequences should be illuminated so that the decision makers know what they are doing and can consider their responsibilities.

A distinction can be made between the following forms of inertia in non-monetary terms:

- Path dependence
- Lock-in effects
- Commitment
- Irreversibility

Inertia is not only relevant for the study of the impacts of specific alternatives but is also relevant for the study of institutions. North (1990) has pointed to the role of 'path dependence' in understanding institutional change processes or the absence of institutional change. Institutions are modified or change a little bit all the time and even radical institutional change is a possibility. Some institutions are strengthened over time; others lose legitimacy among actors and become less important. What happens to institutions is a matter of their role in the worldviews

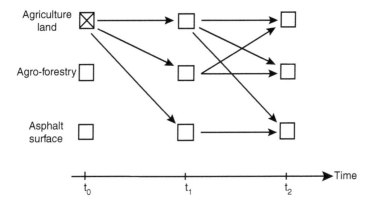

Figure 4.2 Decision tree applied to land-use planning. Options at different points in time can be illustrated or 'illuminated' for decision makers or other concerned actors.

and ideological orientations of different actors. An institution such as a standardized environmental management system, ISO 14001, that is regarded in positive terms by an increasing number of actors will play a more important role.

'Lock-in effect' as an aspect of inertia (and an extreme version of path dependence) may refer to situations where an actor perceives certain undesired impacts of a change in positional terms. In a game of chess, one of the players may realize that he or she has made a mistake and that his or her options for success in the game are radically reduced. Also in the previous case of land-use changes, some may perceive the transformation of land-use to asphalt as a serious lock-in effect. The asphalt surface is not easily changed.

Reference to 'commitments' as aspects of inertia can be subdivided. The decision process itself can be understood in terms of a series of commitments of different kinds that influence the direction of the process. Distinction can, for example be made between the following commitments:

- Cognitive commitment
- Social commitment
- Legal commitment
- Physical commitment

In a city, a politician as actor may at a point in time to other actors present his ideas of a new bridge across a river. If other actors support the idea, social commitments are perhaps added to previously existing cognitive and emotional commitments. When contracts are signed with suppliers and construction companies, it is no longer easy to get away from the project. We may speak of 'successive commitments' that lead in a specific direction. When work has started with excavators and thereby 'physical commitments' are added, there is no longer any way out. Adding one commitment after another can, of course, be a way of manipulating the decision process. Such manipulation by reducing the options available should be counteracted in a democratic society until some stage when a satisfactory information basis for decision-making is available.

Systematic comparison of expected impacts

Impact studies as part of PA should be multi-dimensional and disaggregated. In a written document, the analyst can describe each expected impact qualitatively and/or quantitatively while observing issues of inertia and uncertainty. This is done in the spirit of PA where the analyst openly points to simplifications made and where conclusions are conditional rather than unanimous.

At some stage, attempts can be made to summarize impacts, for example by ranking alternatives in relation to each impact. A matrix can be used as in Table 4.1. In this hypothetical case, no alternative ranks number 1 in relation to all impacts. Alternative A_2 appears promising, but this depends on the importance of dimension 'a' in relation to other dimensions as judged by each decision maker or other actor. Again the actor's ideological orientation becomes crucial. And decision makers and other actors normally differ more or less with respect to ideological orientation.

Table 4.1 Alternatives can be tentatively ranked in relation to each impact dimension considered

Expected impact	Alternative A_0	Alternative A_1	Alternative A_2
a	1	2	3
b	2	3	1
c	3	2	1
d	3	2	1

Making a study according to PA where many sidedness is observed and where one listens to many voices does not follow a path that is predetermined in detail. A scheme of analysis can be used but also the creativity of the analyst and others involved plays a role. It may even be argued that elements of art enter the scene.

Tensions between ideological orientations and interests

Neoclassical economists refer to specific ideas of a 'welfare economics' to legitimize their CBA. This technocratic approach to evaluation of alternatives is here rejected. Progress in society is a matter of the ideological orientation of individuals as actors. Conflicting ideological orientations are normally relevant in relation to a specific decision situation. Any conclusions will therefore be conditional in relation to each ideological orientation articulated and considered.

Having established that there is more than one ideological orientation in a democratic society – how do we deal with this fact in more practical terms as part of preparing an information basis for decision-making? Listening to the politicians as decision makers and other concerned actors is a first advice. The analyst or some other actor can also arrange meetings on specific arenas so that actors can learn from each other while respecting remaining differences of opinion.

The role of the analyst in this part is then to articulate three or four different ideological orientations that appear relevant to decision makers and other actors. If these ideological orientations do not include specific values that are the result of national or international (European Union, UN) commitments, for example a specific interpretation of sustainable development, then the analyst may include this ideological orientation to make decision makers aware of these obligations.

As previously mentioned, the number of ideological orientations considered may be three or four. A specific actor as decision maker may not see his or her own ideological orientation as being equal to (matched by) any of the ideological orientations considered. He or she is hopefully still helped by the many-sided analysis carried out.

Another possibility as part of PA is to focus on the interests of those affected. This is rather a stakeholder analysis of conflicts of interest and more limited in scope than the analysis in terms of ideological orientations. Based on a limited set of alternatives considered, the analyst can try to identify those *activities* by individuals and organizations that will be affected differently depending on which one of the alternatives considered that is chosen. In the case of construction of a new road, for example such activities may include living in houses in an area close to the proposed new road, commercial activities by organizations at specific places, specific transportation activities and perhaps all kinds of activities of the global population for the case that the new road is expected to contribute to increased CO_2 emissions compared with the previous situation.

When focus is limited to one activity at a time, such as commercial activity in one area, then it is possible to make reasonably realistic *assumptions about goal direction* connected with the activity. For the commercial activity mentioned, increased sales may be assumed; for houses close to a new road (or in some other area) reduced noise and reduced exposure to pollution can be assumed to be a relevant goal direction. On the basis of such assumptions, it becomes possible to rank the alternatives considered from the point of view of each activity identified and considered.

Activities with assumed interests (goal directions) can then be related to alternatives of choice in a matrix (Table 4.2). This will be useful as an overview of the conflicts of interest involved in a decision situation. Also commonalities of interest are visualized. Table 4.2 represents a decision situation with three alternatives A_0, A_1 and A_2 considered and four activities k, l, m and n identified where A_0 stands for no new investment in a road (or energy system), and A_1 and A_2 represent different locations of a new road.

In the case illustrated in Table 4.2, it is clear that no alternative is the best in relation to all activities. Alternative A_1 appears promising, but the 'best' alternative when bringing everything together (impacts, conflicts of interest, etc.) is up to each decision maker or actor with his or her ideological orientation.

It should be observed that the present kind of analysis builds on *assumptions* of goal direction for each identified activity. However, in practice, individuals (organizations) involved in one activity may not share the same goals. A person living close to a road may appreciate a lot of traffic rather than prefer less noise and so on. Two alternatives may get the same ranking from the point of view of one activity; uncertainty may be involved that can be indicated with a question mark and so on. Some individuals (organizations) will be part of more than one affected activity identified, suggesting that conflicts of interest of this kind may even be

Table 4.2 Ranking of alternatives in relation to activities with assumed goal direction (interest)

Activity with goal direction	Alternative A_0	Alternative A_1	Alternative A_2
k	1	2	3
l	3	1	2
m	2	1	3
n	3	2	1

internal to individuals. In such cases what matters for the individual is his or her ideological orientation and we are back to the previously presented broader analysis.

The analysis of activities and interests is presented in more detail at other places (Söderbaum 2000, pp. 102–103, 2008, pp. 1472–1473). What matters here is that tensions between different ideological orientations and between specific interests are taken seriously, visualized and indeed regarded as constructive in the search for carefully prepared decisions. The ambition to reach consensus on the basis of technocratic approaches with connected ideology (such as in the case of CBA) is abandoned. In my understanding, a CBA study does not recognize any conflicts or tensions in society.

Experiences of applied PA studies

In relation to the different elements of the scheme of analysis previously presented, practical experiences from PA studies can be discussed.

Assessment of various options at the societal level is often done in an anonymous and allegedly objective way. With democracy as a leading principle, actors in different roles such as analyst, politician (or other decision maker), stakeholders, that is, those affected, and concerned citizens are instead made visible and responsible for their arguments and actions. It is my experience that naming these actors is not a problem. They accept and even prefer to be visible in this sense and participate in a problem-solving process. Each actor can learn by interaction with other actors, and mutual respect is facilitated when it is understood that actors, decision makers included, differ with respect to ideological orientation. The idea of only one optimal solution for society as a whole is abandoned in favor of conditional conclusions.

A PA study begins at a certain point in time. The scheme of analysis stressed suggests that the historical background of a decision situation is normally relevant to describe and document. The analyst may point to previous studies of similar issues elsewhere, newspaper articles that deal with the present issue and so on. Often a relatively short text is enough as background and reminder of the fact that analysis does not start from nowhere. Commitments may be made by local governments or private actors, for example.

The analyst is in a key position to approach decision makers, stakeholders and other actors with questions about how they perceive the problem(s) and the ideas these actors may have about alternatives and ways of dealing with problems. Again some of the key arguments put forward should be documented in the written study.

While CBA starts with one ideological orientation and idea (close to neoliberalism) of markets and correct prices for purposes of public evaluation, PA is an attempt to bring in and handle also other ideas of progress in society. New ideas of progress such as some version of sustainable development where markets play a less dominant role will never get a chance if we stick to CBA and economic growth in GDP terms as the only approach.

Articulation of different ideological orientations represented among decision makers or other concerned actors, while listening to and cooperating with these actors, is a key aspect of PA. The aim of this is not to come up with alternative ideas of quantitative optimization but should represent an opening also to other (qualitative, visual, etc.) ways of visioning the future. When considering options for new transportation lines (roads or railways), benefits in terms of time savings may stand against protection of nature and ecosystems, for example where there is no single scientifically and ideologically correct 'trade-off' between impacts of the two kinds.

The ideological orientations considered in a PA study need not be limited to those articulated by the actual decision makers in a local context. Official objectives articulated at the national, European Union or UN levels are also potentially relevant. One recent example is the 17 sustainable development goals (SDGs) acknowledged at the UN level (United Nations 2015). It need not be added that these objectives strengthen the relevance of disaggregated approaches such as PA.

It should be repeated that it is not possible to exactly match and map the ideological orientation of each single decision maker or other actor. In practice, the analyst has to limit herself to three or four ideological orientations. The principle here is many sidedness. The analyst has to be open-minded and should not exclude what some actors may consider extreme or 'controversial' ideological orientations, for example those that take climate change seriously.

Issues of irreversibility are at the heart of PA. There are often non-monetary (and monetary) costs in terms of excluding future options. Ways of analyzing road construction on agricultural land or in areas of sensitive ecosystems have already been discussed. Again the principle of many sidedness (designed to strengthen performance in terms of democracy) is essential in identifying alternatives. This will counteract the possibly tactical tendencies of some actors to limit thinking in terms of alternatives to essentially varieties of one thing.

Neoclassical economists (and many others) are used for analysis that ends with clear-cut solutions. For them rational behavior for each of the consumer, the firm or at the level of society has ideally one single meaning. PA is far from these ideas. There are 'many rationalities' rather than one, each connected with an ideological orientation. Alternatives may differ in kind and impacts are multi-dimensional and fragmentary. The technocratic idea of assuming complete information about impacts is abandoned. While still making some simplifying assumptions, a degree of complexity is acknowledged.

There is a role for objectivity and established ways of describing and measuring things in PA. However, the subjectivity of the analyst is also an issue. Does he or she use his or her power position to manipulate things in specific directions in favor of specific (influential?) actors? Such possible manipulations may refer to the ideological orientations considered, alternatives considered or dimensions for considering various monetary and non-monetary impacts. Again many sidedness in analysis and a living democracy is the way of counteracting manipulation. Journalists, citizens and other actors can be helpful in calling attention to possibly manipulative behavior. At the same time, it should be made clear that there are many ideas rather than one about a 'balanced' analysis and that democracy in any sociocultural context can always be improved or strengthened.

All this suggests that the role of the PA analyst differs significantly from the role of the CBA analyst. There is still some element of technocracy in PA but in a different sense. The analyst needs to learn about economics and its different schools of thought, to improve his or her interdisciplinary competence and also his or her understanding of democracy. He or she also needs to know about methodological options such as CBA and PA and how they relate to broader issues of technocracy and democracy. Since democracy is constitutionally acknowledged in our societies, the choice between CBA and PA should be easy, but there may, of course, be other methods not known by the present author that take democracy seriously.

Will the use of PA guarantee that sustainability issues are taken seriously in analysis? The recommendation is certainly to articulate sustainable development as one among the ideological orientations considered. However, other, for example traditional ideas of progress will be articulated and considered as well. A transformation of society from present unsustainable trends has to involve and engage as many individuals and organizations as possible. Dialogue is needed and necessary as preparation for step-wise changes in more sustainable directions. Sustainability issues are not exclusively technical. They are as much, or primarily, a matter of social movements and protests to call attention to specific risks and other issues. And no actors, analysts included, can completely deny their subjectivity and ideological orientations. There is no meaningful, purely technical analysis.

Principles of performance measurement and accounting

For those actors who take sustainable development seriously, it becomes clear that a focus on monetary variables and indicators such as GDP at the national level and monetary profits in business is not enough. Emphasis on non-monetary indicators and accounting practices is needed. In Tables 2.3 and 2.4, a classification of impacts in economic analysis was presented where it was argued that non-monetary impacts are as 'economic' as monetary ones. Non-monetary impacts were divided into flows and positions (states) where the former refers to periods of time and the latter to points in time.

Concerning sustainability indicators and new accounting practices (in addition to, or sometimes to replace, monetary accounting), the following recommendations are made:

- Focus on non-monetary indicators, flows as well as positions.
- Specific focus on non-monetary positions over time: Are environmental, natural resource and health states improving over time or are they degrading?
- Avoidance of attempts to frame sustainable development in one-dimensional terms as indexes or in other ways.
- Acceptance of multi-dimensionality, fragmentation and uncertainty.
- Continued dialogue about how to improve indicator systems at various levels (organization, local community, national community, European Union).
- Standardization of new accounting practices is a possibility but should not be a barrier to experiments based on new thinking.

New indicator systems and accounting practices will not come about by themselves. Research in this area is extremely important as exemplified in Chapters 5 and 6 by Judy Brown in this volume. A continued dialogue about the mainstream paradigm in economics and pluralism in the discipline is needed. Similarly, neo-liberalism as a mainstream market ideology needs to be challenged. Hopefully, this will gradually lead to changes in institutional arrangements, including legitimate accounting systems.

Conclusion – why PA?

In the first four chapters of this volume, neoclassical theory and traditional CBA has been challenged. Some readers may ask if this comparison with CBA is really necessary. A new perspective and method should be able to stand on its own feet.

Just as CBA and PA each claim to be methods of comparing and assessing alternatives in decision situations at the public level, there may be a similar need to compare the methods that claim to be useful. Comparing one method with another should therefore rather be encouraged. It may be argued, however, that the assessment of CBA as a method and PA as a method has not been fair since PA has systematically been advocated. This may be so, but it should then be remembered that CBA is still the method recommended by mainstream economists and that there are few signs among CBA advocates that they recognize the many weaknesses of their approach. The TEEB study (2010) previously discussed rather suggests that CBA advocates try to demonstrate their strength even in relation to sustainability issues.

I will here point to only five criteria of comparison that appear to be of special importance:

1 CBA lacks a conceptual framework that can make inertia in non-monetary terms and non-monetary impacts visible. PA deals systematically with these issues.
2 CBA is an extremely technocratic approach in the sense of dictatorship by experts. Not only methodological issues but also value issues – the ideology to be applied – are 'solved' by the experts. Any existing conflicts or tensions among decision makers or other actors are neglected or regarded as being external to analysis. PA is on the contrary an attempt to deal systematically with such tensions and differences in terms of ideological orientations.
3 There is a larger issue involved of comparing neoclassical theory with its microeconomics with a political economics close to institutional theory in the Myrdal–Kapp tradition. Here again, it is argued that a new conceptual framework is needed for sustainability purposes.
4 Uncertainty and other aspects of complexity are characterizing sustainability issues (Funtowicz and Ravetz 1991). Attempts to deal with such issues in terms of a simple mathematical language with optimal solutions and so on are not very helpful. Approaches that better match the complexities of the 'real world' are needed. While a mathematical language has a role, the primary role should be played by other languages.

5 When comparing paradigms in economics or methods to prepare decision-making, one possibility is to ask whether a certain method is useful not only at the public level of national and local governance but also for everyday decision-making by individuals. It seems to me that the conceptual framework with PEP and PEO assumptions, ideologically open ideas of efficiency and rationality, positional thinking and so on, is as useful at the level of individuals while CBA is less useful. However, when making such judgments, we are back to our ideological orientations. Some have 'internalized' monetary thinking to such an extent that they would prefer what has here been called 'monetary reductionism'.

Studies of various issues can be carried out using PA as a method. However, the first important step is to influence the thinking of politicians and other actors. Those who are skeptical and dislike elements of neoclassical economics and CBA may need other approaches to make their thoughts more legitimate. Moving away from the technocratic approach of CBA with single solutions toward an approach of a more democratic kind, where issues are illuminated rather than solved in a final manner, may be a big step for many.

This debate about the pros and cons of different theoretical perspectives and methods will hopefully continue. It is my experience, however, that some actors, for example those with vested interests in CBA, tend to avoid dialogue as much as possible. We then return to the monopoly position of neoclassical economists at most university departments of economics. Only when it is understood that each scholar or other professional is a PEP acting in a democratic society will there be openings for dialogue.

There are, of course, exceptions to this tendency to avoid dialogue. Initiatives by outsiders such as ecologists are possible. A case in point is one symposium at Roskilde University Center where three persons were invited to present their differing views. Hanley presented the CBA method, Costanza a more pragmatic view (in the sense that 'the ends justify the means') and the present author PA as an alternative (Hanley and Black 2006; Costanza 2006; Söderbaum 2006).

Just as investment projects in new airports, roads or energy systems need to be 'illuminated', the same holds for theoretical perspectives and methods in economics. However, it should always be remembered that democracy with open dialogue as one of its features does not necessarily exist in the scientific community. Corporate social responsibility (CSR) has become an issue. University social responsibility remains a similar challenge in front of us.

Note

1   It may be noted that this recommendation is also made in CBA studies.

References

Costanza, Robert, 2006. Thinking broadly about costs and benefits in ecological management, *Integrated Environmental Assessment and Management*, Vol 2, No. 2, pp. 166–173.
Funtowicz, Silvio and Jerome Ravetz, 1991. A new scientific methodology for global environmental issues, pp. 137–152 in Costanza, Robert ed., *Ecological Economics: The Science and Management of Sustainability*. Columbia University Press, New York.

Georgescu-Roegen, Nicholas, 1971. *The Entropy Law and the Economic Process*. Harvard University Press, Cambridge, MA.

Hanley, Nick and Andrew R. Black, 2006. Cost-Benefit Analysis and the Water Framework in Scotland, *Integrated Environmental Assessment and Management*, Vol. 2, No. 2, pp. 156–165.

Neumann, John von and Oskar Morgenstern, 1944. *Theory of Games and Economic Behavior*. Princeton University Press, Princeton, NJ.

North, Douglass C., 1990. *Institutions, Institutional Change and Economic Performance*. Cambridge University Press, Cambridge.

Söderbaum, Peter, 1973. *Positionsanalys vid beslutsfattande och planering. Ekonomisk analys på tvärvetenskaplig grund [Positional Analysis for Decision-Making and Planning, Economic Analysis based on an Interdisciplinary Frame of Reference]*. Esselte Studium, Stockholm.

Söderbaum, Peter, 2000. *Ecological Economics. A Political Economics Approach to Environment and Development*. Earthscan, London.

Söderbaum, Peter, 2006. Democracy and sustainable development – what is the alternative to cost-benefit analysis? *Integrated Environmental Assessment and Management*, Vol. 2, No. 2 (April), pp. 182–190.

Söderbaum, Peter, 2008. 10th anniversary focus: from mainstream 'environmental economics' to 'sustainability economics'. On the need for new thinking, *Journal of Environmental Monitoring*, Vol. 10, No. 12, pp. 1467–1475.

United Nations, General Assembly, 2015. Transforming our world: the 2030 Agenda for Sustainable Development. Resolution adopted by the General Assembly on 25 September 2015. United Nations, New York.

5 On the need for broadening out and opening up accounting

Judy Brown

There is wide-ranging recognition of the need for new accountings that help to deepen democracy by facilitating participatory forms of governance. This is particularly evident in the sustainable development and social and environmental accounting literatures,[1] with increasing calls for more pluralistic forms of accounting in both public and private sector contexts. However, as in other disciplinary fields, much work remains in developing new forms of appraisal that help to open up, rather than close down, discussion and debate over sustainability issues (Brown and Dillard 2014; Stirling 2008). A particular challenge in areas such as accounting and economics is the way power intrudes so as to deny heterogeneity and privilege dominant groups and perspectives. In this chapter, I discuss the need for broadening out and opening up accounting and outline a critical pluralist approach to the development of dialogic accountings that respect difference and take ideological conflicts seriously. In the following chapter, I illustrate how Peter Söderbaum's work on pluralist economics and positional analysis can contribute to the conceptual and operational development of dialogic accounting.

In recent years, there has been growing appreciation of accounting's significance beyond a means of 'merely representing' reality. Accountants do not only convey information; their representations and reports play an active role in (re)constructing social relations (Cooper and Morgan 2013; Brown and Dillard 2015a, 2015b). Accounting is one of the sociopolitical practices through which people's subjectivities are shaped and a means by which power is exercised. Through its influence on economic and social exchanges and the mediation of conflicts, it impacts significantly on people's lives. Cooper and Morgan (2013, p. 419), for example highlight 'how accounting subtly impacts the culture and focus of governments, societies and corporations', for example in 'the ways accounting encourages financialization and fails to account for externalities and the environment'. Importantly, and contrary to the views of many accounting practitioners and researchers, all accountings are political and value laden. To believe that accounting self-evidently 'represents reality is to assume that there is a well-defined and widely accepted definition of reality, or perhaps more accurately, that there is agreement about both what aspects of reality are to be represented and also that such representations can be depicted in only one way' (Cooper and Morgan 2013, p. 422). A major concern is that mainstream accounting theory and practice focuses on business and finance capital perspectives – in particular, neoliberal understandings – at the expense of broader citizen and public interests.

Appreciation of the power of accounting in shaping social realities has been accompanied by an interest in reconfiguring calculative technologies. There is widespread recognition both in and outside of the accounting discipline of the need for new accountings that facilitate citizens' voice and accountability. Much of this relates to dissatisfaction with technocratic decision-making tools rooted in positivism and neoclassical economics, as exemplified by debates surrounding the use of cost–benefit analysis and similar techniques (e.g. see Bebbington et al. 2007a; Leach et al. 2010). Philosophically, as Söderbaum's work emphasizes, appeals for new methods are embedded in the democratic rather than capitalist traditions of Western societies. This is particularly evident in the sustainable development and social and environmental accounting literatures, with calls for approaches that recognize the plurality inherent in liberal democracies and that promote more critically reflective discussion and debate (O'Dwyer 2005; Brown and Dillard 2014). For this group, providing a range of perspectives on sustainability issues is far more democratic than providing a single, value-laden view that – intentionally or otherwise – privileges business and finance capital over other sectors of society.

Over the years, various social accounting tools have been proposed as a means of promoting democratic interaction (e.g. social and environmental accounts, social audits and integrated reports). Most recently, these have included attempts to promote dialogic accounting technologies and participatory forms of engagement. However, the results in practice have often been disappointing; and, in particular, very underdeveloped in terms of the ability to engage divergent ideological perspectives and open up space for those seeking to challenge neoclassical economic thinking, policies and practices (especially as manifested in neoliberal capitalism). In part because of the failure to appreciate the deeply political character of economics and accounting, the field has been inadequately theorized to address difference and diversity despite its claimed pluralist underpinnings.

In the rest of this chapter, I briefly review the accounting literature and related literature in other disciplines to elaborate on the need for dialogic tools that promote democratic debate and decision-making. I then look more closely at what is involved in reworking 'calculation and democracy' (Power 1992, p. 492) and the move from monologism to plurality that underpins it. Key principles for a critical pluralist framework are outlined that aim to respect difference, take ideological conflicts seriously and highlight power dynamics. These principles form the basis for discussion of Söderbaum's work on positional analysis in Chapter 6 as one possible means of operationalizing dialogic accounting.

Accounting – from monologism to dialogism

More than two decades ago, Power (1992) observed that there was much work to be done in assessing the acceptable limits of calculative technologies and warned of the risks they presented for democracy. Economic reason, he cautioned, through its ability to portray itself as 'merely technical' and thus divorced from sociopolitical interests had the capacity 'to *eclipse* other forms of knowledge and other forms of social life' (p. 477, emphasis in original). Rather than abandon accounting, Power encouraged accounting theorists to reconceptualize 'the relationship between forms of calculation and democracy' (p. 492), to build on traditions of quantitative thinking that recognized the potential of developing new forms of accounting capable of incorporating democratic norms. In this regard, he suggested that environmental accounting provided an important 'space of possibility' (p. 494).

Proponents of dialogic accounting have sought to take up this challenge, arguing that a shift from monologic to dialogic accounting principles that take ideological differences seriously is a key requirement for democratizing accounting technologies. Both mainstream accounting and much of social and environmental accounting are currently dominated by a monologic approach although those working in the latter area increasingly recognize the need for more pluralistic perspectives to inform debate regarding sustainability issues and engage divergent views (see Deegan 2016 for a recent review) notwithstanding the significant challenges of displacing current monologic practices.

Monologic accounting

Mainstream accounting is highly monologic in approach. Notwithstanding the ambiguity and subjectivity of accounting, its official narrative is deeply rooted in the assumptions of positivism and capitalism (Chua 1986; Cooper and Sherer 1984). Although presented as '*a* true and fair view', financial reports implicitly assert the status of an all-encompassing truth – a 'view from nowhere' (Nagel 1986). In refusing to recognize or glossing over the social situatedness of knowledge, this supposed impartiality operates coercively. The pre-given or axiomatic values and assumptions on which accounting is based are centered on the needs and perspectives of business and finance capital. These purportedly objective standards are assumed to benefit everyone regardless of their ideological standpoints. As such, they delimit the parameters of debate and deny voice to alternative perspectives. Powerful elites entrench their meanings and preferences and (wittingly or unwittingly) universalize their own partial positions. Monologic accounting also reflects a finality orientation, reinforcing a view that facts and numbers 'speak for themselves'.

Mainstream accounting depoliticizes accounting through a denial of the political. Where politics is acknowledged, monologic accounting is portrayed as providing a neutral framework within which different stakeholders can pursue their interests. Accounting is thus claimed to serve pluralism. Solomons (1991), for example, argues that accountants should merely report 'the facts', neutral information that users can then use in their social and economic exchanges (although he admits that accountants have shown little interest in the information needs of constituencies such as labor and consumers). There is a denial – or attempt to claim a consensus for – the value judgements underpinning accounting technologies. Where competing interests or perspectives are recognized, the dominance of capital markets and their information needs is taken for granted.[2] Alternatively, accounting is treated as a commodity, with promoters of economic rationalism seeking to leave the 'optimal' level of production to market forces (Watts and Zimmerman 1979). In the sustainability area, as in other contexts, such approaches are more likely to undermine rather than enhance democratic participation. However, the ideological ties to neoclassical economics and aggregative models of democracy that conceive of politics in market-like terms – as opposed to deliberative or agonistic understandings of democracy – are evident (see Brown and Dillard 2015a, 2015b for discussion).[3]

In arguing that accounting is monologic, there is no intention to deny the flexibility of accounting. As discussed below, accounting audiences can and do reinterpret the reports they receive. The boundaries of what is 'in' and 'outside' of accounting are also permeable, albeit that some groups have far more influence than others to define and police these boundaries. Indeed, it is recognition of accounting's potentialities that motivates the attempt to pursue more democratic approaches.

Dialogic accounting

Proponents of dialogic accounting argue for the legitimacy (and inevitability) of 'the political' in accounting.[4] They reject the notion of a 'view from nowhere' and, in particular, the idea that finance capital's point of view (even assuming that can be talked about in singular terms) is a valid standard for the claimed objectivity of accounting. They seek to foster accountings that are more receptive to the conflictual elements of a plural society; ones that are attuned to a diversity of ideological orientations. Furthermore, they emphasize the importance of avoiding a 'naive pluralism' that ignores power asymmetries in society.

It is now well recognized – inside and outside accounting – that social actors do not have unmediated access to the world 'out there'. Accountants are unavoidably involved in interpretation. Moreover, any single perspective involves the nonreporting of others, and thus, monologic accounting inevitably takes sides where there are conflicting viewpoints. It helps to naturalize particular social pathways by creating and reinforcing taken for granted meanings. The linking of actions to axiomatic values such as shareholder wealth maximization allows decision makers to distance their actions from their political and moral contexts (Dillard and Ruchala 2005) and to mark certain topics or viewpoints as off-limits. Wider social and ecological issues are relegated to externality status at best. Instrumental reason thereby helps convert political acts and standpoints into technical issues. As O'Leary (1985, p. 100) puts it, to remain silent about the fundamental contestability of such practices 'is to licence a violence upon people' through the imposition of truth claims that impact significantly on their lives and welfares.

Dialogic accounting – in recognizing heterogeneity and refusing to privilege capital markets – allows for a more pluralist expression of public interests aimed at countering instrumental rationality. It rejects the idea of a universal narrative that will account for everyone's perspectives. Rather democratic institutions need to be exposed to a diversity of ideological viewpoints, and here it is arguably helpful to think of multiple publics rather than rely on a singular public interest. Accounting thus becomes viewed as a vehicle with the potential to foster democratic dialogue and contestation (Brown and Dillard 2015a, 2015b) rather than a set of techniques to maximize shareholder wealth and impose neoclassical-neoliberal thinking, policies and practices on others.

For many, the social accounting project is rooted in the norms of democracy and pluralism. Various methods have been advanced as a means of promoting democratic dialogue and accountability. Recently, the focus has been on efforts to create new environmental and social visibilities through such mechanisms as triple bottom line reporting, full-cost accounting and integrated reporting. There has also been a concern to promote stakeholder engagement in report preparation and more participatory forms of social organization. This work stands in marked contrast to managerialist/eco-modernist approaches to social and environmental accounting, which remain embedded in a positivist, neoclassical economic agenda.

From a dialogic perspective, there is a need to develop models based on multidimensional, participative approaches that are cognizant of power asymmetries in society. Thomson and Bebbington (2005), for example advocate a social and environmental accounting that takes stakeholder engagement seriously; one that recognizes conflicts among stakeholders, engages multiple viewpoints and explicitly addresses power dynamics. Social accounting needs to create spaces for individuals and groups to deal critically and imaginatively with problems and support them in participating actively in the (re)constructions of their world(s) (Thomson and Bebbington 2005, p. 524). Bebbington et al. (2007b) conceptualize organizational and social change as a dialogic process and suggest ways accounting researchers may actively engage in facilitating that process.

Boyce (2000) addresses the issue of accounting as a social technology – 'a form of social power' (p. 27) that may serve an enabling or constraining function. He suggests that accounting has the potential to play a major role in developing accountability in a participatory democracy. It could promote transparent decision-making by creating environmental and social visibilities and exposing the standpoints of interested parties. He cautions against models aimed at bringing decisive closure. Given the essentially contested nature of sustainability, new accountings should not be aimed at producing incontrovertible accounts. Societal worth should be judged not in terms of the expert production of 'the right answer' but in the facilitation and broadening of debate:

> any form of social and environmental accounting (and much financial accounting) will produce outputs which are contestable and open to debate. The utility of such accounting is not in its representation of 'infallible truth' but in its creation of a range of environmental and social visibilities and exposure of values and priorities that become inputs to wider democratic processes of discourse and decision making.
>
> (Boyce 2000, p. 53)

Accountants need to develop accounting systems that 'prevent premature closure' and 'which infuse debate and dialogue, facilitating genuine and informed citizen participation in decision-making processes' (Boyce 2000, p. 55). In doing so, they might also help make power relations more transparent.

Calls for more dialogic approaches are not confined to accounting.[5] Increasing numbers of academics and practitioners in other social sciences are embracing more pluralistic understandings of their disciplines. In fields such as organization studies, law, public policy, politics, economics, development studies and education, there is growing resistance to the domination of positivism and economic rationalism and advocacy of more hermeneutic and critical understandings. Calls for democratization are also apparent in the traditional 'hard' areas of science, as evidenced by the emergence of areas such as post-normal science. In contrast to Kuhn's (1970) conception of normal science as the solving of well-defined disciplinary puzzles, post-normal science is based on assumptions of ideological diversity and 'a plurality of legitimate perspectives' (Funtowicz and Ravetz 1993, p. 739). It seeks to seriously address the uncertainties in real-world organizational and public policy contexts and recognizes the importance of values in a world where, to varying extents, people chose their futures.

Framework for a critical dialogic approach in accounting

As discussed above, any attempt to democratize accounting technologies requires a move from monologic to dialogic accounting principles. This section outlines a set of eight principles as the basis for a critical dialogic framework aimed at helping to develop more democratically responsive accountings: the need to recognize a diversity of ideological orientations, the importance of avoiding monetary reductionism, being open about the inherent contestability of calculations, enabling access for non-experts, ensuring effective participatory processes, being attentive to power relations, recognizing the transformative potential of dialogic accounting and resisting new forms of monologism. Each of these themes is examined in turn below. In the following chapter, I show how Söderbaum's work on positional analysis can help in operationalizing this framework.

Recognize multiple ideological orientations

Dialogic accounting recognizes that people with different values, perspectives and assumptions will seek to account differently – for different things and in different ways (Morgan 1988). It aims to facilitate the expression of divergent perspectives and to encourage individuals and groups to engage in democratic interaction across a range of organizational and societal contexts. This requires the establishment of a broad citizen-oriented base, including recognition of those not powerful enough to command a 'seat at the table' as opposed to the current situation where (reinforced by neoclassical economics) non-shareholder constituencies are often excluded on the basis that an organization has no direct accountability relationship with them.

It also emphasizes the need to enable actors to express themselves in accordance with their own sociopolitical perspectives. Neoliberals, social democrats and radical democrats, for example may all seek to approach issues (e.g. interpretations of values such as equality and liberty) in different ways. Relationships – between human beings, between humans and other species – will be judged as 'fair' or 'unfair' in relation to a particular ideological orientation (Vinnari and Dillard 2016). For dialogic literary theorists, an illuminating novel is one that represents 'all the social and ideological voices of its era … all the era's languages that have any claim to being significant' (Bakhtin 1981, p. 411). An illuminating dialogic accounting analysis should arguably do the same.

An emphasis on democratic contestation does not necessarily mean embracing total pluralism. Difference – under a critical dialogic framework – is valued only insofar as it challenges domination and inequality by surfacing marginalized perspectives and bringing ignored or obscured issues to the fore. At the same time, engaging with more authoritarian positions may assist understanding what in those discourses resonates with particular constituencies. This is arguably important where, as in accounting, a primary aim is to expose and challenge dominant (monologic) institutionalized ideologies.

Avoid monetary reductionism

Advocates of full-cost accounting have emphasized the value of developing a common monetary metric 'to "*get the prices right*"' (Bebbington et al. 2001, p. 8, emphasis in original). With the critics of instrumental rationality, proponents of dialogic accounting argue that impacts should not be reduced into a single 'bottom-line' in search of an optimal solution meaningful for all interested parties. Rather the aim is to illuminate the contested terrain of 'technical' information along the lines of post-normal science – more transparency around complex sociopolitical choices (Bebbington et al. 2007a). This recognizes that 'number assignment' always involves 'very strong value and reality assumptions' (Churchman 1971, p. 31), which signals the importance of considering a plurality of perspectives.

Monetization can dehumanize and devalue non-monetary values, contributing to the 'commodification of everything' (McGarity and Shapiro 1996). For some, such efforts reduce the values actors hold as citizens to consumer preferences and thereby privilege the neoclassical economic view of humans as self-interested utility maximizers (Sinden 2004a, 2004b; Sagoff 1998). All activities become socially constructed as economic and regarded as tradeable against each other in a market-like fashion. As such, narrow economic rationalism may exacerbate rather than prevent social and environmental exploitation (Hines 1991; Lehman 1996). Dialogic accounting seeks to provide a range of quantitative and qualitative data so individuals and groups can see diverse effects for themselves and make their own judgements about monetization, incommensurability and the extent to which 'trade-offs' are acceptable.

Be open about the subjective and contestable nature of calculations

The 'allure of numbers and scientific calculation' evident in technocratic approaches – in particular, the false promise of determinacy and misleading impression of objectivity – provides a serious threat to democratic decision-making (Sinden 2004b, p. 194). Social actors, from a dialogic perspective, should be invited to participate in open, transparent discussion. This requires intellectual honesty in terms of both the 'hard-factual' and 'inherently contestable' aspects of different accountings (O'Leary 1985). The theory-laden nature of accounting means that it produces few, if any, 'brute facts'; although clearly, depending on the specific contexts and sets of actors involved, some facts may be easier to agree inter-subjectively than others. Dialogic accounting aims to surface the inherent contestability of accounting, recognizing that subjectivity and uncertainty are important parts of democratic exchange, elements that help 'to promote and engage the process itself' (Wilkins 2003, p. 402).

Dialogics is based on a social constructionist epistemology. While recognizing that there may be things 'out there', it emphasizes that they do not come indelibly labelled as accounting events or as costs or benefits. As humans, we choose what to include in our calculations, whose perspective to take and apply subjective value weightings. Moreover, this process always occurs in a social and political context. Preferences are endogenous, arising in sociopolitical exchanges, and involve debate over ends as well as means. If actors are serious about democratic participation, they need to be more open about the values and assumptions on which their account-ings are based, so that others can challenge and reconstruct them. Rights of opposi-tion or dissent are important so that individuals and groups may object to policies and practices they perceive as harmful to themselves or others.

While there is a need to recognize that there is no neutral measurement point, it is also important to be wary of opportunistic interpretation. The aim of dialogic accounting is to foster the legitimate pursuit of divergent interests, concerns and perspectives in a pluralist society, not to encourage 'blatant propaganda' (O'Leary 1985, p. 100).

Enable accessibility for non-experts

For transparency and social accountability initiatives to have impact, citizens must have confidence in the information they are provided with as well as the capacity to process, analyze and use information (Gaventa and McGee 2013). Citizens' abilities to make use of information can be supported through, inter alia, an active media, collective action and the use of information intermediaries who can translate tech-nical data into more accessible formats (Fung et al. 2007). One way of helping to provide confidence that a range of pertinent views has been canvassed is through the development of extended peer community quality assurance processes such as those proposed in post-normal science (Frame and Brown 2008) where scientists are expected to communicate epistemic, ideological and ethical uncertainties to interested parties. The aim here is to provide information in multi-layered ways – in formats that are accessible to non-specialists as well as more technical forms that enable independent testing by heterodox experts.

In monologic approaches, technical information is often used – explicitly or implicitly – to exclude people from political processes. Those seeking to document and challenge the harmful effects of neoclassical economics and neoliberalism may require support to help them access pertinent knowledge to problematize conven-tional analyses, for example through labor and civil society education initiatives.

Here there are arguably many opportunities for heterodox economists, social and environmental accountants and social movements to work together to contest the damaging impacts of neoclassical-neoliberal thinking (Brown and Dillard 2013). As Stanford (2015, p. 233) emphasizes, this requires relationship building and mutual respect as 'it is naive, verging on arrogant' for heterodox experts 'to simply assume that their analyses and policy proposals should automatically be taken up by social and political activists'.

There is also a need to facilitate the development of critically reflective prac- titioners able to engage across a range of disciplinary and ideological perspectives. To this end, experts themselves (particularly mainstream experts) need to develop greater self-awareness of the values and assumptions underpinning their models and to be more open about the disagreements they have with each other. As Söderbaum (2008) argues, intellectual pluralism not only safeguards against excessively partial analysis in public policy contexts but also fosters creativity. Analysts should be held accountable if they have not illuminated issues in a multi-perspectival way although responsibility for decisions still rests primarily with decision makers (Söderbaum and Brown 2010).

Ensure effective participatory processes

Democratic participation in decision-making processes is important not only to assist people to reflect on their preferences but also to enable them 'to describe and take account of costs and benefits in their own ways' (Anderson 1988, p. 65) and thereby foster democratic debate.

Achieving effective participation in practice presents significant challenges. Lessons learned in participatory contexts in and beyond accounting suggest a need to involve a diverse range of interested parties early in decision-making processes and to develop procedural rules aimed at surfacing and examining different ideological perspectives. Dialogic entitlements – for example legislative rights to information and participation – are also important to expand the range of viewpoints addressed in organizational and civil society settings (but offer significant challenges of their own; see Davenport and Brown 2002 for discussion in the field of labor relations). In this sense, dialogic accounting relies on broader structural change and requires close attention to power dynamics in participatory settings. Following Gaventa's (2006, pp. 25–30) 'power cube' framework, this calls for consideration of three dimensions:

> *Spaces for participation*: spaces for discussion and engagement may be provided/ closed spaces that are tightly controlled by dominant elites; invited spaces where, as a result of external pressures or attempts to increase legitimacy, pol- icymakers or corporates encourage stakeholders to share their opinions on issues of mutual interest; or claimed/created spaces where less powerful groups develop their own agendas and networks to pursue common concerns.
> *Places and levels for participation*: these may be local, national or global arenas, with, for example local actions to build power 'from below' enabled or con- strained by broader national or transnational conditions, for example legal frameworks and/or codes of conduct relating to corporate responsibility.

Forms of power: these may be visible forms of power, for example formal laws, rules, structures and procedures; hidden forms of power whereby powerful actors and institutions control decision-making processes, excluding or marginalizing the views of less powerful individuals or groups (e.g. through agenda-setting, controlling the selection of experts, resource dependencies); or invisible forms of power (e.g. internalized norms and values) that operate by shaping how individuals or groups conceive of their place in society, their awareness of alternatives and/or possibilities for action, helping explain why people often fail to question existing power relations.

Understanding the relations between these dimensions in contextually sensitive ways assists not only in understanding how different actors or viewpoints can be marginalized but also in identifying strategies that help to deepen democracy. I return to this issue below when looking at accounting specific issues relating to power relations.

Dialogic tools in participatory settings are valued more as a basis for generating critical reflection, discussion and debate than for their potential to provide a final determinative calculation. They help to demonstrate why democratic participation in complex, uncertain and politically contentious areas is so challenging and highlight the importance of taking a decentered, conflict-sensitive approach to governance (Griggs et al. 2014). Pluralistic approaches to accounting and economics, by opening up rather than closing down discussion and debate, are important in helping challenge conventional assumptions and securing new forms of democratic practice.

Be attentive to power relations

Numbers, because of their aura of objectivity, wield considerable power and authority. They provide a way of obscuring value judgements and intensify power imbalances by rendering decision-making processes vulnerable to manipulation (Sinden 2004b, p. 228). Managerial and other power elites have the ability to filter information they disseminate and to take opportunistic advantage of the numerous layers of subjectivity and uncertainty in statistical and financial analyses. This is exacerbated by a general lack of public appreciation of the value-laden and contestable nature of accounting information (O'Leary 1985).

Attention to the power dynamics inherent in any accounting situation is vital to ensure that counter-hegemonic viewpoints are addressed in participatory processes and that the concerns and priorities of marginalized groups are not defined out of technical models (Brown and Dillard 2014, 2015a, 2015b). Collective action is important given the difficulties individuals *qua* individuals experience in questioning decisions or providing resistance in isolation. Oppositional analysis can be used to deconstruct the analyses of others as a way of highlighting contradictions and introducing new perspectives. Activist groups have contested the way cost–benefit analysis values land, forests, fisheries and livelihoods, its reliance on unaccountable experts and its neglect of equity issues. They have countered contingent valuation methodologies by refusing to measure non-traded goods (e.g. species preservations) in monetary terms or by placing infinite values on them (Sinden 2004a, 2004b). In some cases, they have employed a concurrent reliance on and distrust of technical and scientific discourse (Tillery 2003). The value of oppositional analysis or counter-accounting has also been recognized within the accounting literature (e.g. the work of Counter Information Services in the 1970s and, more recently, by authors such as Apostol 2015, Cooper et al. 2005, Gallhofer et al. 2006 and Thomson et al. 2015).

However, counter-accountings on their own have limitations from a dialogic perspective. Some combination of insider and outsider forms of engagement argu-ably provides the most effective form of engaging for social change. This entails some social actors seeking to effect incremental or transformative change from the 'inside' (e.g. working with business and policymakers to reform or transform insti-tutions from within) and others working more combatively from 'outside' main-stream institutions (e.g. with activist groups) (Brown and Dillard 2013; Brown et al. 2015). Specific actors might also favor dualistic strategies on the basis that the pur-suit of enduring social change requires 'multiple tramping of the same soil' (Cooper 2001, p. 129).

Recognize the transformative potential of dialogic accounting

Accounting intervenes in subtle and complex ways in both representing and con-structing social reality, with significant implications for individuals, organizations and societies. As Cooper and Morgan (2013, p. 422) emphasize, 'technologies are inevitably imbued with the assumptions and values of the technology builder'. Thus, far from being 'boring bookkeeping', accounting and accountability systems have the capacity to reinforce dominant views as well as open up new possibilities.

Dialogic accounting aims to encourage social actors to become more critically reflective (at individual, meso and macro levels) and to facilitate democratic engage-ment across groups with divergent ideological perspectives. It promotes the idea of agonistic debate and dialectic learning in pluralistic environments rather than pro-ceeding according to a pre-conceived formula. It seeks to facilitate multi-perspectival analysis, involving consideration of a range of diverse situated viewpoints, a process 'whereby people's unexamined preferences can be scrutinized and … revised, aban-doned, or retained with a deeper meaning than existed initially' (Galsto 1994, p. 361). Accountings are designed to both broaden out in terms of the topics canvassed and open up in terms of the contested nature of sustainability issues. As Mouffe (2000, p. 70, emphasis original) argues, 'the creation of democratic forms of individuality is a question of *identification* with democratic values', which take place through a diverse range of practices and discourses. There is no one correct understanding of account-ing, economics or sustainability that all rational people should accept. From an ago-nistic perspective, the coexistence of different understandings will lead to struggles between adversaries, but 'far from being a danger for democracy', this is 'its very con-dition of existence' (Mouffe 2000, p. 74). The aim is to assist in bringing the limiting beliefs and assumptions of all actors into consciousness in a way that allows them to engage in democratic struggle and potentially transform their limit situations.

Dialogics facilitates reflection on and (re)construction of perspectives as actors are exposed to critiques and new ideas, without aiming to erase diversity. Showing the grip of dominant discourses on our thinking and practices, for example helps illustrate the pathways that have been closed down. Exposure to divergent ways of seeing things not only helps foster democratic identification but also brings the possibility of 'aspect change' (Norval 2007, Ch. 3) that helps open up new individual, organizational and societal realities. Monologic dialogue, by contrast, only contemplates a 'banking' concept of communication in which authoritative speakers 'deposit' their beliefs, values and assumptions into the heads of others (Thomson and Bebbington 2004, 2005) although it should not be assumed those at the receiving end of dominant discourses necessarily accept them unquestioningly. As Scott's (1992) seminal work on 'hidden transcripts' shows, people may appear to acquiesce to dominant understandings in front of those with power over them but express quite different views in their own spaces. Dominant groups can also engage in 'backstage' talk that reinforces their power.[6]

Resist new forms of monologism

Dialogics is not about replacing one form of monologism with another. It is sensitive to critiques levelled at the tendency of some critical commentators to engage in knowledge imposition and guide people to pre-identified 'right answers'. Attempts to rescue people from their 'false consciousness' – no matter how progressive the intentions – can amount to another form of authoritarianism. They risk repeating the monologic assumptions and anti-democratic approaches that dialogic accounting seeks to challenge. We need to avoid suggestions that people are only 'enlightened' when they 'agree with us'.

There are no guarantees that conflicts of values or interests will be resolved. Indeed, the dialogics proposed here seeks to help surface conflict and preserve democratic contestation. It aims to provide a tool that enables people to voice and reflect on their own perspectives, recognizing the possibilities for both consensual outcomes (albeit often of a 'conflictual' type) and rational disagreement.

The objective is not necessarily to reach agreement but rather a richer appreciation of complex issues and to allow divergent perspectives to be confronted. Social change is seen to be dependent on sociopolitical interaction, contestation and learning – discussing and debating one's own and other peoples' interests, concerns and values. Dialogic tools are best viewed as reflexive rather than technical innovations, and civil conservations should not be too managed or predictable. Likewise, ongoing disagreements – for example between those on the 'left' and 'right' of the political spectrum – should not be regarded as a sign of failure. To the contrary, the drive for a 'final' resolution of conflict puts democracy at risk, by implying the elimination of the political (Mouffe 2005, 2013).

The following chapter considers how the framework outlined above might be put into practice in a sustainability context, drawing on Söderbaum's work on positional analysis.

Notes

1   The literature in this area is extensive, dating back to at least the 1980s. See, for example, Boyce (2000), Brown and Dillard (2015a, 2015b), Brown et al. (2015), Cooper and Morgan (2013), Deegan (2016), Gray (2002), Morgan (1988), O'Dwyer (2005) and O'Leary (1985).

2   Some professional accounting bodies admit a bias in favor of investors but assert that in meeting their information needs, other users will be catered for. For example, the International Accounting Standards Board (IASB 2010, p. 11) in its conceptual frame-work advises that 'Other parties, such as regulators and members of the public other than investors, lenders and other creditors, may also find general purpose financial reports use-ful. However, those reports are not primarily directed to these other groups'. The IASB (2010, p. 5) favors 'focusing on financial statements that are prepared for the purpose of providing information that is useful in making economic decisions' and 'believes that financial statements prepared for this purpose meet the common needs of most users'.

3   See Brown (2009, especially pp. 318–323) for discussion of aggregative, deliberative and agonistic conceptions of democracy and their implications for accounting. In that paper and more recent work, I have worked with colleagues to elaborate an agonistic approach to dialogics on the grounds that it more fully expresses the plural nature of contempo-rary democracies; enables accounting to engage with more (conflicting and consensual) perspectives on economic, social, environmental and cultural matters; recognizes the value-laden and political nature of all perspectives; is more sensitive to complex power dynamics in social relations and offers promising avenues for pursuing progressive social change.

4   There are many ways of understanding 'the political'. The agonistic approach I have developed with colleagues follows the work of Mouffe (2000, 2005, 2013) in seeking to acknowledge the dimension of antagonism inherent in all human societies. 'The political' refers to this antagonistic dimension 'that can take many forms and can emerge in diverse social relations', while 'politics' denotes 'the ensemble of practices, discourses and institutions that seeks to establish a certain order and to organize human coexist-ence in conditions that are always potentially conflicting, since they are affected by the dimension of "the political"' (Mouffe 2013, pp. 2–3). Rather than trying to design insti-tutions and accountings 'that, through supposedly "impartial" procedures, would recon-cile all conflicting interests and values', the aim is 'to envisage the creation of a vibrant "agonistic" public sphere of contestation where different hegemonic political projects can be confronted', where, as in positional analysis, participants with divergent ideological orientations can 'decide between clearly differentiated alternatives' (Mouffe 2005, p. 3).

5   Indeed a strong case can be made that accounting is just catching up in this regard.

6   Mainstream accounting academics and practitioners are often more open about the con-testability of accounting in private than when they take the public stage (see, e.g. Chua 1986, p. 618, discussing how accounting becomes a 'sacred' language, with 'profane talk' handled in private so 'that rationality and the appearance of order are maintained'). This is a further example of the way mainstream accounting denies its inherently political character.

References

Anderson, Elizabeth, 1988. Values, risks, and market norms, *Philosophy and Public Affairs*, Vol. 17, No. 1, pp. 54–65.

Apostol, Oana Mihaela, 2015. A project for Romania? The role of the civil society's counter-accounts in facilitating democratic change in society, *Accounting, Auditing & Accountability Journal*, Vol. 28 No. 2, pp. 210–241.

Bakhtin, Mikhail M., 1981. *The Dialogical Imagination*. Emerson, Caryl and Michael Holquist (trans.). University of Texas Press, Austin, TX.

Bebbington, Jan, Judy Brown and Bob Frame, 2007a. Accounting technologies and sustainability assessment models, *Ecological Economics*, Vol. 61, No. 2/3, pp. 224–236.

Bebbington, Jan, Judy Brown, Bob Frame and Ian Thomson, 2007b. Theorizing engagement: the potential of a critical dialogic approach, *Accounting, Auditing & Accountability Journal*, Vol. 20, No. 3, pp. 356–381.

Bebbington, Jan, Rob Gray, Chris Hibbitt and Elizabeth Kirk, 2001. *FCA: An Agenda for Action*. ACCA Research Report No. 73, ACCA, London.

Boyce, Gordon, 2000. Public discourse and decision making: exploring possibilities for financial, social and environmental accounting, *Accounting, Auditing & Accountability Journal*, Vol. 13, No. 1, pp. 27–64.

Brown, Judy, 2009. Democracy, sustainability and dialogic accounting technologies: taking pluralism seriously, *Critical Perspectives on Accounting*, Vol. 20, No. 3, pp. 313–342.

Brown, Judy and Jesse Dillard, 2013. Agonizing over engagement: SEA and the 'death of environmentalism' debates, *Critical Perspectives on Accounting*, Vol. 24, No. 1, pp. 1–18.

Brown, Judy and Jesse Dillard, 2014. Integrated reporting: on the need for broadening out and opening up, *Accounting, Auditing & Accountability Journal*, Vol. 27, No. 7, pp. 1120–1156.

Brown, Judy and Jesse Dillard, 2015a. Dialogic accountings for stakeholders: on opening up and closing down participatory governance, *Journal of Management Studies*, Vol. 52, No. 7, pp. 961–985.

Brown, Judy and Jesse Dillard, 2015b. Opening accounting to critical scrutiny: towards dialogic accounting for policy analysis and democracy, *Journal of Comparative Policy Analysis: Research and Practice*, Vol. 17, No. 3, pp. 247–268.

Brown, Judy, Jesse Dillard and Trevor Hopper, 2015. Accounting, accountants and accountability regimes in pluralistic societies: taking multiple perspectives seriously, *Accounting, Auditing & Accountability Journal*, Vol. 28, No. 5, 626–650.

Chua, Wai Fong, 1986. Radical developments in accounting thought, *The Accounting Review*, Vol. 61 No. 4, pp. 601–632.

Churchman, C. West, 1971. On the facility, felicity, and morality of measuring social change, *The Accounting Review*, Vol. 46, No. 1, pp. 30–35.

Cooper, Christine, Phil Taylor, Newman Smith and Lesley Catchpowle, 2005. A discussion of the political potential of social accounting, *Critical Perspectives on Accounting*, Vol. 16, No. 7, pp. 951–974.

Cooper, David J. and Wayne Morgan, 2013. Meeting the evolving corporate reporting needs of government and society: arguments for a deliberative approach to accounting rule making, *Accounting and Business Research*, Vol. 43, No. 4, pp. 418–441.

Cooper, David J. and Michael J. Sherer, 1984. The value of corporate accounting reports: arguments for a political economy of accounting, *Accounting, Organizations and Society*, Vol. 9, Nos. 3–4, pp. 207–232.

Cooper, Davina, 2001. Against the current: social pathways and the pursuit of enduring change, *Feminist Legal Studies*, Vol. 9, No. 2, pp. 119–148.

Deegan, Craig, 2016. Twenty five years of social and environmental accounting research within *Critical Perspectives of Accounting*: hits, misses and ways forward, *Critical Perspectives on Accounting*, in press. Available online at http://dx.doi.org/10.1016/j.cpa.2016.06.005 (accessed 6 December 2016).

Dillard, Jesse F. and Linda Ruchala, 2005. The rules are no game: from instrumental rationality to administrative evil, *Accounting, Auditing & Accountability Journal*, Vol. 18, No. 5, pp. 608–630.

Frame, Bob and Judy Brown, 2008. Developing post-normal technologies for sustainability, *Ecological Economics*, Vol. 65, No. 2, pp. 225–241.

Fung, Archon, Mary Graham and David Weil, 2007. *Full Disclosure: The Perils and Promise of Transparency*. Cambridge University Press, Cambridge.

Funtowicz, Silvio and Jerome Ravetz, 1993. Science for the post-normal age, *Futures*, Vol. 25, No. 7, pp. 739–755.

Gallhofer, Sonja, Jim Haslam, Elizabeth Monk and Clare Roberts, 2006. The emancipatory potential of online reporting: the case of counter accounting, *Accounting, Auditing & Accountability Journal*, Vol. 19, No. 5, pp. 681–718.

Galsto, Miriam, 1994. Taking Aristotle seriously: republican-oriented legal theory and the moral foundation of deliberative democracy, *California Law Review*, Vol. 82, No. 2, pp. 331–399.

Gaventa, John, 2006. Finding the spaces for change: a power analysis, *IDS Bulletin*, Vol. 37, No. 6, pp. 23–33.

Gaventa, John and Rosemary McGee, 2013. The impact of transparency and accountability initiatives, *Development Policy Review*, Vol. 31, No. s1, pp. s3–s28.

Gray, Rob, 2002. The social accounting project and *Accounting Organizations and Society*: privileging engagement, imaginings, new accountings and pragmatism over critique? *Accounting, Organizations and Society*, Vol. 27, No. 7, pp. 687–708.

Griggs, Steven, Aletta J. Norval and Hendrik Wagenaar, 2014. *Practices of Freedom: Decentred Governance, Conflict and Democratic Participation*, Cambridge University Press, New York.

Hines, Ruth, 1991. On valuing nature. *Accounting, Auditing & Accountability Journal*, Vol. 4, No. 3, pp. 27–29.

International Accounting Standards Board, 2010. *Conceptual Framework for Financial Reporting 2010*, IASB, London.

Kuhn, Thomas S. 1970. *The Structure of Scientific Revolutions* (second edition), University of Chicago Press, Chicago, IL.

Leach, Melissa, Ian Scoones and Andy Stirling, 2010. *Dynamic Sustainabilities: Technology, Environment, Social Justice*, Earthscan, London.

Lehman, Glen, 1996. Environmental accounting: pollution permits or selling the environment, *Critical Perspectives on Accounting*, Vol. 7, No. 6, pp. 667–676.

McGarity, Thomas O. and Sidney A. Shapiro, 1996. OSHA's critics and regulatory reform, *Wake Forest Law Review*, Vol. 31, pp. 587–646.

Morgan, Gareth, 1988. Accounting as reality construction: towards a new epistemology for accounting practice, *Accounting, Organizations and Society*, Vol. 13, No. 5, pp. 477–485.

Mouffe, Chantal, 2000. *The Democratic Paradox*, Verso, London.

Mouffe, Chantal, 2005. *On the Political*, Routledge, London.

Mouffe, Chantal, 2013. *Agonistics: Thinking the World Politically*, Verso, London.

Nagel, Thomas, 1986. *The View from Nowhere*, Oxford University Press, New York.

Norval, Aletta, 2007. *Aversive Democracy*, Cambridge University Press, Cambridge.

O'Dwyer, Brendan, 2005. Stakeholder democracy: challenges and contributions from social accounting, *Business Ethics*, Vol. 14, No. 1, pp. 28–41.

O'Leary, Ted, 1985. Observations on corporate financial reporting in the name of politics, *Accounting, Organizations and Society*, Vol. 10, No. 1, pp. 87–102.

Power, Michael, 1992. After calculation? Reflections on *Critique of Economic Reason* by André Gorz, *Accounting, Organizations and Society*, Vol. 17, No. 5, pp. 477–499.

Sagoff, Mark, 1998. Aggregation and deliberation in valuing environmental public goods: a look beyond contingent pricing, *Ecological Economics*, Vol. 24, Nos. 2/3, pp. 213–230.

Scott, James C. 1992. *Domination and the Arts of Resistance: Hidden Transcripts*, Yale University Press, New Haven, CT.

Sinden, Amy, 2004a. The economics of endangered species: why less is more in the economic analysis of critical habitat designations, *Harvard Environmental Law Review*, Vol. 28, pp. 129–214.

Sinden, Amy, 2004b. Cass Sunstein's cost-benefit lite: economics for liberals, *Columbia Journal of Environmental Law*, Vol. 29, No. 2, pp. 191–241.

Söderbaum, Peter, 2008. *Understanding Sustainability Economics: Towards Pluralism in Economics*. Earthscan/Routledge, London.

Söderbaum, Peter and Judy Brown, 2010. Democratizing economics: pluralism as a path towards sustainability, *Annals of the New York Academy of Sciences*, Vol. 1185, pp. 179–195.

Solomons, David, 1991. Accounting and social change: a neutralist view, *Accounting, Organizations and Society*, Vol. 16, No. 3, pp. 287–295.

Stanford, Jim, 2015. Towards an activist pedagogy in heterodox economics: the case of trade union economics education, *Journal of Australian Political Economy*, Vol. 75, pp. 233–256.

Stirling, Andy, 2008. "Opening up" and "closing down" power, participation, and pluralism in the social appraisal of technology, *Science, Technology & Human Values*, Vol. 33, No. 2, pp. 262–294.

Thomson, Ian and Jan Bebbington, 2004. It doesn't matter what you teach? *Critical Perspectives on Accounting*, Vol. 15, No. 4/5, pp. 609–628.

Thomson, Ian and Jan Bebbington, 2005. Social and environmental reporting in the UK: a pedagogic evaluation, *Critical Perspectives on Accounting*, Vol. 16, No. 5, pp. 507–533.

Thomson, Ian, Shona Russell and Colin Dey, 2015. Activism, arenas and accounts in conflicts over tobacco control, *Accounting, Auditing & Accountability Journal*, Vol. 28, No. 5, pp. 809–845.

Tillery, Denise, 2003. Radioactive waste and technical doubts: genre and environmental opposition to nuclear waste sites, *Technical Communication Quarterly*, Vol. 12, No. 4, pp. 405–421.

Vinnari, Eija and Jesse Dillard, 2016. (ANT)agonistics: pluralistic politicization of, and by, accounting and its technologies, *Critical Perspectives on Accounting* Vol. 39, pp. 25–44.

Watts, Ross L. and Jerold L. Zimmerman, 1979. The demand for and supply of accounting theories: the market for excuses, *The Accounting Review*, Vol. 54, No. 2, pp. 273–305.

Wilkins, Hugh. 2003. The need for subjectivity in EIA: discourse as a tool for sustainable development, *Environmental Impact Assessment Review*, Vol. 23, No. 4, pp. 401–414.

6 Positional analysis in relation to other pluralistic accounting practices

Judy Brown

This chapter focuses on Peter Söderbaum's work on positional analysis and how it could be applied to existing sustainability assessment tools (SATs) to foster democratic engagement in participatory settings. The chapter discusses how dialogic accounting could be operationalized through positional analysis to promote critical reflection and ideologically open discussion on sustainability issues. In this sense, positional analysis can be seen as part of a larger body of work aimed at broadening out and opening up forms of appraisal and decision-making. The chapter also addresses the challenges of implementing pluralist accountings and positional analysis in monologic business and policy environments.

Operationalizing dialogic accounting through positional analysis

Positional analysis provides a way of responding to Morgan's (1988) challenge to adopt an openly interpretive approach to accounting and to develop forms of practice that emphasize how accounting representations 'should be regarded and used as elements of a *conversation* or *dialogue*, rather than as foundational claims asserting a particular kind of objectivity or "truth"' (p. 484, emphasis in original). In common with others who have pointed to the importance of multiplicity in accounting, the aim is to help develop spaces of possibility for 'thinking, and speaking that allows for openness, plurality, diversity and difference' (Tong quoted by Gallhofer 1992, p. 41; see also Gallhofer et al. 2015). This calls for broad-based accountings that can be used as platforms for action as actors with different perspectives reflect on unsustainable development trends and possible alternatives.

Sensitivity to issues of values, plurality and situated knowledges is arguably particularly critical in the sustainability arena. There is increasing acceptance that the complexity of the area – both in terms of scientific uncertainty and socio-political controversy – requires a multidimensional and ideologically open approach. As O'Connor (1999, pp. 674–675) observes,

> where decision stakes are high and there are scientifically non-resolvable uncertainties, value-plurality and social controversies over decision criteria tend to emerge as glaring social facts … many different points of view can be

expressed, none of which is wholly convincing (to everybody, all the time …), none of which deals entirely adequately with all aspects of the situation, but none of which can be wholly rejected (by everybody) as having nothing at all relevant to say about the situation and what should be done and why.

There are growing calls for more participative approaches to decision modelling and analysis; particularly within fields such as science and technology studies, urban planning and development studies. In discussing science as a post-normal practice, O'Connor (1999) highlights the need for a 'complexity epistemology' that works with several irreducible analytical perspectives in a 'permanent conversation'. Stirling (2008) calls for greater attention – in both analytic and participatory appraisals – of the need for approaches that open up rather than close down governance commitments in the science and technology field. A particular concern is that more traditional narrow, closing down forms of appraisal such as cost–benefit analysis privilege particular dimensions of sustainability issues, while ignoring or obscuring equally, if not more, important non-monetary dimensions. Moreover, too often this selective visibility operates in a way that favours prevailing values and dominant elites. There are clear parallels here between proposals for dialogic accounting, positional analysis and what the science and technology literature refers to as 'empowering designs' for sustainability, namely:

> … diverse, deliberately configured processes for consciously engaging with the challenges of sustainability – involving a 'broadening out' of the inputs to appraisal and an opening up of the outputs to decision-making and policy. In particular, empowering designs for appraisal aim at eliciting and highlighting marginalized narratives and thus exposing and exploring hidden pathways. In this way, 'inclusion' goes beyond simply the bringing of frequently excluded groups to the table – but extends to detailed and symmetrical treatment of alternative pathways for social, technological and environmental change. Crucially, these empowering designs for appraisal also aim at facilitating processes of negotiation between protagonists of different narratives and thus promote explicit deliberation over the detailed implications of contending possible pathways.
>
> (Leach et al. 2010, p. 99)

Progress towards broadening out/opening up forms of analysis relies on researchers, practitioners, policymakers and civil society actors who are willing and able to engage with multiple perspectives. However, existing contexts of exclusion, unequal power relations and vested interests make this very difficult to achieve in practice (e.g. in an accounting context, see Brown and Dillard 2014, 2015a, b).

For the purposes of framing the following discussion, Table 6.1 summarizes the major features distinguishing traditional (e.g. cost–benefit analysis) and dialogic approaches to accounting (e.g. positional analysis). It should be emphasized that accounting tools are not inherently monologic or dialogic. It would, for example, be possible to develop cost–benefit analysis in more dialogic directions, but this

Table 6.1 Comparing traditional and dialogic approaches to accounting

	Traditional accounting	Dialogic accounting
View of accounting	Prioritizes the perspectives, goals and values of business and finance capital (e.g. shareholder wealth maximization, economic growth). Broader financial, social and ecological impacts of organizational decision-making accounted for where a 'business case' can be made. Accounting technologies also play a key role in introducing market-like metrics in neoliberal governance regimes in both public sector and developing country contexts.	Seeks to democratize accounting by developing pluralistic accounting systems responsive to the decision-making and accountability needs of a range of actors for use in organizational and civil society contexts. Recognizes a diverse range of goals and values including, inter alia, efficiency, economic growth, sustainable livelihoods, labour rights, fair trade, cultural identity and social justice.
Relationship of accounting to broader public interests	Accounting theory and practice portrayed as technical, neutral and apolitical. Technical standardization around business, investor and capital markets perspectives – underpinned by neo-classical economics and neoliberal logics – is asserted to also serve broader public interests.	Accounting theory and practice are inherently political and value-laden. Aims to deal openly with plurality, contestability, uncertainty and the value-laden nature of accounting appraisals. Focus on the need for broadening out/opening up forms of accounting that take divergent socio-political perspectives seriously and thereby support democratic participation and decentred governance practices.
Treatment of uncertainty and controversy	Focus on stability of extant systems through managerialist strategies; for example, sustainability challenges framed as risk management issues (e.g. protecting profits against external 'shocks', mitigating negative reputational effects) to be addressed through technical methods and stakeholder management initiatives.	Contested framings, policy controversies, social justice and power key foci: questions about accounting and reporting of what, for whom, in what ways, and who gains or loses? Different forms of incomplete knowledge – risk, uncertainty, contestability and ignorance – recognized.

(continued)

Table 6.1 Comparing traditional and dialogic approaches to accounting (*continued*)

	Traditional accounting	Dialogic accounting
Styles of sustainability assessment	Narrowly framed expert-based quantitative methods (e.g. cost-benefit analysis, probabilistic risk assessments) that close down around business framings. Costs and benefits assessed in financial terms, longer term highly discounted, models underpinned by instrumental economic logic. Distributional questions beyond impacts for shareholders and capital markets rarely addressed.	Need for cross-disciplinary expertise and new appraisal approaches. Focus on assessment methods that broaden out in terms of inputs, open up issues for critical reflection and wide-ranging debate (e.g. positional analysis, Q methodology, counter-accounts, external social audits). Substantive exploration of divergent socio-political framings of issues.
Approach to governance and social change	Top-down approach to governance. Mainstream accounting/business case framings sedimented through accounting education, professional socialization and institutional structures (e.g. business domination in accounting rule making). Minimal or instrumental approach to stakeholder engagement.	Decentred understanding of governance. Far-reaching innovation and change seen as unlikely from working solely through prevailing institutions. Consensus-oriented approaches susceptible to domination by incumbent elites. Need for concerted engagement in several arenas, with formal policymaking processes sitting alongside citizen engagement and mobilization.
Implications for engaging actors with divergent ideological orientations	Does not admit divergent socio-political perspectives. Closes down appraisal processes by focusing on the information/accountability needs of business and finance capital. Public interest issues, when considered at all, framed in terms of neoliberal values and capital markets.	Looks for empowering designs that go beyond finance capital-oriented understandings of accounting and accountability. Targeted efforts to work with groups whose information and accountability needs are currently ignored, marginalized and/or not well understood. Broad-based alliance building linking those interested in developing pluralist approaches to accounting.

would deeply challenge its roots in neoclassical economics. There is similarly a risk that positional analysis could be applied in an overly narrow way, for example, depending on how applications are facilitated and who is invited to participate.

However, given the pluralistic philosophy that underpins positional analysis – and its explicit objection to monetary reductionism – appropriate implementation requires facilitation by heterodox experts and a diverse range of participants. Thus, it offers a much more pertinent approach to operationalizing dialogic accounting than conventional narrowing in/closing down approaches such as cost–benefit analysis (see also Leach et al. 2010, p. 106).

Positional analysis

As discussed in previous chapters, Peter Söderbaum has written widely on ecological economics, democracy and sustainability. He is a strong critic of the monologism of neoclassical economics, as reflected, for example, in the highly aggregated, ideologically closed approach of cost–benefit analysis. He approaches sustainability as a contested concept and seeks forms of analysis that acknowledge and engage the ideological diversity evident in democratic societies (Söderbaum 2008, 2015). His work is firmly rooted in pluralist traditions and coheres well with the critical dialogic accounting approach outlined in Chapter 5.

Söderbaum argues that democratization requires a move to ideologically open models and a view of individuals as political economic persons rather than rational economic men. He proposes a positional approach to analysis, focused on illuminating a situation in a way that is as many sided as possible rather than providing a solution assumed to be optimal for all actors. The aim is to elucidate decision-making situations with all of their 'conflicts, uncertainties, and other complexities' (Söderbaum 1987, p. 152) and to facilitate dialogue and debate. There is an assumed consensus about the imperatives of democracy as framing principles (i.e. more than one ideological orientation, more than one alternative, the need to open up spaces for dialogue and debate). However no *a priori* agreement is assumed about the way problems should be represented, the correct principles of valuation, what counts as a cost or benefit and, thus, what amounts to an 'optimal' solution. Individuals and groups with different ideological orientations will have different views about what sustainability involves and thus what elements to account for, why and how. Their willingness to quantify impacts in monetary terms or the materiality they attach to particular aspects will also differ. Business groups might seek to privilege financial over social, environmental and cultural dimensions of sustainability; others the reverse. The focus in positional analysis 'is to look for a many-sided set of alternatives considered that correspond reasonably well to a many-sided set of ideological orientations that appear relevant to interested parties and actors in relation to the decision situation' (Söderbaum 2015, p. 422). Here it is also important to appreciate the ways in which wider socio-political and institutional contexts (e.g. legal frameworks, social norms, knowledge of alternatives) operate as important influences in mediating options and preferences. As Söderbaum (2013) highlights in relation to policy documents and expert reports on sustainability, too much emphasis on consensus thinking, adapting to existing dominant models, and over-used rhetoric about not being able to 'manage what you do not measure' severely limits the possibilities for moving beyond mainstream thinking.[1]

In short, positional analysis calls for a 'political turn' in economics and accounting with both individuals and organizations 'understood as political actors in a democratic society' (Söderbaum 2014, p. 2756). Democratizing economics and accounting, as well as revitalizing democracy more generally, are viewed as important steps in moving towards a more sustainable society. Continuing to rely on the dominant political economic system and mainstream thinking that, for many commentators, played a major role in producing current unsustainable trends is not simply questionable but dangerous to society (Söderbaum 2013, p. 222). To open up space for a politics for sustainable development – and demonstrate that there are alternatives to neoclassical economics and neoliberalism – awareness of plurality and the inherently political character of economics and accounting are crucial. Approaching sustainability as a contested concept – with recognition of both dominant and alternative narratives – means that ideas about science, economics and accounting as being somehow:

> separable from values, ideology and politics should be abandoned. It is not possible to deal with political issues in an exclusively scientific manner. In relation to politics for sustainable development there are options with respect to theoretical framework, method, way of presenting results etc. and each choice is necessarily made from some vantage point. Reference can be made to scientifically established method but again; there may be more than one established method and the reasons why some methods are avoided may be political rather than scientific.
>
> (Söderbaum 2011, p. 1019)

A key feature of positional analysis is its systematic treatment of both monetary and non-monetary dimensions of sustainability. Warning against monetary reductionism, Söderbaum has highlighted from his earliest engagements for ecological economics that changes in resource positions such as intellectual capital, health and safety, or the environment can be expressed in many ways (see the Appendix to this book for the early history of positional analysis). Positional analysis also seeks to deal openly with scientific uncertainty, for example, by reporting estimates in terms of ranges rather than single numbers. Non-monetary management and accountability systems may be designed and changes observed through a positions (points in time) and flows (periods of time) approach. These can be presented in quantitative forms along with narratives or visual images, for example, photographs of an environmental site after completion of a project. This recognizes that numbers (and especially narrow monetary-oriented views of sustainability) are not everyone's first – or preferred – language (Chua 1996).

Indeed those who see sustainability values and impacts as primarily qualitative in character regard attempts to reduce everything to monetary aspects – such as 'sustained economic growth' in GDP terms or 'sustained monetary profits' in business contexts as more likely to reinforce, rather than encourage critical reflection on, neoclassical economic-neoliberal orthodoxy (Söderbaum 2008, p. 2). Again a plurality of ideological perspectives makes this a contested position, with different groups having their own ideas about the most effective forms of communication and social change processes. In marked contrast to those who seek to address sustainability through a 'total economic value' approach based on monetary valuation, Söderbaum (2015, p. 422) highlights the weaknesses of trying to address contemporary crises by continuing to rely on the mainstream economic theory that has played such 'a significant role in the road-maps used by influential actors in a period when many negative trends have been established'. New thinking, rather than intensified application of the dominant paradigm, is required to move beyond unsustainable 'business (almost) as usual' practices (see also Gray 2006, pp. 803–809 in contrasting managerialist, triple bottom line and ecologically/eco-justice informed approaches to sustainability reporting).

Rationality in positional analysis is defined hermeneutically involving compatibility with an actor's ideological orientation rather than in instrumental terms, whereby particular values and ends (e.g. economic growth, shareholder wealth maximization) are regarded as axiomatic. There may be a good fit between the ideological orientation of an actor and a particular alternative or a mismatch. An individual or group that places a high value on deontological rights (e.g. animal rights, rights to self-determination) might strongly object to utilitarian approaches. Definitions (e.g. of critical natural capital) and levels of substitutability across capital categories will be debated among advocates of weak and strong forms of sustainability. Those concerned with eco-justice (e.g. intra- and intergenerational equity) will seek to interrogate the distributional impacts of projects – how costs and benefits are distributed among different groups. Where there is agreement to monetize, there is still the issue of how to monetize, for example, the acceptability of market valuation methodologies and/or the choice of an appropriate discount rate. Discounting of environmental liabilities, for example, may be resisted on the basis that it discriminates against future generations. Contingent valuation methods based on willingness to pay may give rise to concerns about ability to pay or the appropriate group to be surveyed. The social value of particular products or services (e.g. highways, airport expansion, defence) is also highly controversial.

Positional analysis aims to illuminate issues through dialogue and multi-perspectival analysis rather than provide definitive answers. Reaching decisions is not a matter of maximizing an objective function 'given from outside' (Söderbaum 2006, p. 187) such as economic efficiency. Rather it is about articulating competing ideological orientations that facilitate a search for relevant alternatives. Technical analyses – utilizing different disciplinary and theoretical lenses – support and are supported by participatory processes. This involves dialogue between interested parties and multi-paradigmatic experts about problems, perceptions and ideas in an interactive learning process. Appropriate ways of organizing this process depend on the type of issue and local context. As in science and technology studies, technical and value aspects of analysis are recognized as inextricably intertwined.

Contingency in relation to ideological orientations may be related to differences in scenarios of the future and/or value priorities. Two groups might contest the evidence surrounding the 'impacts of climate change on endangered species, or they might differ in the values they assign to the perpetuation of rare species, or both' (Dietz et al. 2005, p. 346). Or they might differ in terms of the features of risk they consider relevant, for example, whether risk is assumed voluntarily, technological alternatives, distribution of risks and benefits or catastrophic potential.[2] Different actors may seek different levels of disaggregation of the distributional impacts of various aspects of sustainability (e.g. economic well-being, health and safety risks, environmental issues) across different social groups, geographical locations, generations or on non-human species. Multicultural societies give rise to 'deep conflicts' that 'include differences over the legitimate grounds for adjudicating disputes' (Baber 2004, p. 333). A specific decision maker will look for alternatives that best match their ideological orientation, including their attitudes to risks and uncertainties. Through dialogue, decision makers and affected stakeholders may move closer to or further away from each other (Söderbaum 2006, p. 188). The aim, as in dialogic accounting, is to encourage democratic engagement that enables us to acknowledge, confront and learn from diverse ideological perspectives.

Söderbaum (2004, p. 50) warns that conscious and unconscious attempts may be made to subvert positional analysis by focusing on only a few very similar alternatives. This is exacerbated by the fact that some interests are institutionally better organized and more influential than others. He suggests that such difficulties can be counteracted by directly engaging a wide range of stakeholders and other concerned actors from the initial stages of decision modelling or by the analyst identifying the different ideological perspectives related to an issue and highlighting under-represented viewpoints. This is supported by findings in other areas that suggest, for example, that citizens who are engaged early on in formulating policies are more likely to play an active role in monitoring them, thereby increasing social accountability (Carlitz 2013; Gaventa and McGee 2013). Particular care needs to be taken to ensure that positions supporting both dominant and alternative narratives are represented (Leach et al. 2010). Dryzek and Neimeyer's (2008) concept of 'discursive representation' is valuable here as it highlights that groups that are at one level diverse (e.g. corporate boards with a mix of women, men, ethnic minorities) can still share a common ideological orientation.

Positional analysis and social and environment accounting

Positional analysis might be applied to experimental social and environmental accounting technologies as a way of developing them along more critically dialogic lines. For illustrative purposes, this section focuses on its potential application in the area of sustainability assessment. To date, ideas and tools for sustainability assessment in accounting have often been based on models that attempt to translate social and environmental impacts into monetary terms with the aim of producing a single 'full-cost' account (Bebbington et al. 2007). As such, they are vulnerable to the critiques of monologic approaches such as cost–benefit analysis, with its emphasis on monetization and reliance on neoclassical economic valuation methodologies.

As noted earlier, positional analysis and dialogic accounting are not the only approaches that recommend more ideologically open analyses. Science and technology studies scholars, in particular, also emphasize the need for new methods that broaden out and open up issues to democratic contestation. This is exemplified by Stirling's (2008) work in relation to participatory technology assessment and Leach et al.'s (2010) calls for a new 'pathways approach' to address sustainability challenges. Their pathways approach highlights the importance of understanding social dynamics, complexity, divergent perspectives and the inherently value-laden nature of sustainability assessments. By taking pluralism seriously, it helps to demonstrate how particular pathways dominate policy thinking – even when they are not successful in producing desired outcomes – and to identify alternative possible pathways. Science and technology studies offer many valuable insights in terms of both the reasons for and ways of introducing more pluralistic approaches into accounting, in the interests of developing more empowering designs for sustainability.[3] In this respect, there is much potential for academics and practitioners interested in pluralistic appraisal methods to work together to develop alternatives.

Positional analysis would assist to move SATs in more critical dialogic directions. Groups with different ideological orientations (in conjunction with multi-paradigmatic experts that understand how technical and value issues are inextricably intertwined) would be encouraged to construct their own SATs. Separate SATs rather than integration into a unitary account leave actors with the ability to exchange SATs as a way of explaining and justifying their perspectives and differences and allow them to interrogate each other's accounts. Crucially, it enables alternative views to be expressed in more than token ways. For example, prior research suggests that unions favour a stronger conception of sustainability than managerial groups (Springett and Foster 2005) and have a particular interest in exploring the social impacts of organizational activity (e.g. work environment, human rights, democratic participation). Tensions between environmental and social aspects of sustainability have also led to complex relations of cooperation and conflict between labour and environmental groups (Obach 2004) with implications for the construction of SATs. Similarly, indigenous groups might seek to give more visibility to aspects of cultural heritage – for example, protecting culturally significant sites, common property, rights to participate in the management of natural resources (Rockloff and Lockie 2006). Context-sensitive representations and decision rules might be developed, based on different value perspectives (e.g. divergent understandings of accountability) and/or different epistemologies (e.g. indigenous knowledge). This might help to challenge tokenistic or co-optive forms of participation where stakeholders are assimilated into dominant 'business case' approaches to sustainability.

In fostering ideologically open SATs, caution needs to be taken about assuming identities that *unify* particular stakeholder groups, for example, 'the employee point of view'. Any claim to speak for 'all employees' will inevitably privilege the voices of some and marginalize others. The aim is to let others into the conversation without imposing new forms of monologism. There are commonalities and differences within as well as across groups (e.g. ethical versus neoclassical investors: liberal, radical, socialist and eco-feminists). Core values also vary across organizations (e.g. socially responsible and profit-maximizing firms). Rather than over-essentialize individual or group perspectives, agonistic exchanges could be structured around documented typologies of competing ideological discourses such as those provided by Brown and Fraser (2006). An open approach is also important from the perspective of identifying potential political coalitions that might plausibly collaborate to pursue specific social change initiatives (Brown and Dillard 2013a; Brown et al. 2015).

Table 6.2 illustrates how the eight principles outlined in Chapter 5, together with positional analysis, might be applied to SATs.

Table 6.2 Applying critical dialogic principles and positional analysis to sustainability assessment tools

Critical dialogic principle	Examples of application of positional analysis to SATs
Recognize multiple ideological orientations	Engagement with a diverse range of stakeholders and ideological perspectives – actors treated as 'political economic people' rather than 'rational economic men' Different SATs constructed, consistent with particular ideological orientations (rather than looking for a 'unified' SAT)
Avoid monetary reductionism	Utilize monetized SATs to illustrate the limits of calculative technologies and question whether monetization is appropriate for particular items Expand the possibilities for non-financial indicators of performance and presentation of SATs as part of a larger set of dialogic methods (e.g. encompassing visual material, narrative accounts)
Be open about the subjective and contestable nature of calculations	Recognize the subjective and contestable nature of what is included, how items are included and the decision rules as to what constitutes a move towards sustainability Recognize divergences of viewpoints within and between groups of experts
Enable accessibility for non-experts	Role for 'organic' experts who work with marginalized groups to develop SATs that cohere with their own values and assumptions (i.e. experts who share the ideological orientation of those they work with) as well as 'border-crossing' experts who facilitate multi-perspectival dialogue and debate Extended peer quality assurance processes – 'non-experts' able to challenge expert analysis – experts learn from 'non-experts' Recognize the complex nature of relationships between knowledge, expertise and power (e.g. accountants are often oblivious to the values and assumptions underpinning their technical methods)
Ensure effective participatory processes	Pay particular attention to the context of application (e.g. whether settings enable people to express non-hegemonic views and engage in robust debate) Engage for democratically supportive environments (e.g. ones that provide legal rights to information and participation)

Critical dialogic principle	Examples of application of positional analysis to SATs
Be attentive to power relations	Use SATs to challenge power elites (e.g. to expose the frames dominating specific decision outcomes and their distributional impacts)
	Recognize a need for capacity building (e.g. developing skills and the means to articulate currently marginalized voices in accounting terms)
	Do not rely on 'invited' or 'provided/closed' spaces of engagement controlled by dominant elites, but also develop claimed/created spaces where less powerful groups develop their own agendas and networks to pursue common concerns
Recognize the transformative potential of dialogic accounting	Use SATs as a tool for agonistic exchange – discussion, debate, reflection
	Look for conflicts and convergences across different sets of social actors as a basis for collective action

Benefits of a positional approach

Positional approaches have several benefits from the perspective of dialogic accounting. By explicitly addressing sustainability as a contested concept, positional analysis and SATs help to encourage greater transparency around the value judgements, assumptions and uncertainties involved in any accounting. They allow different social actors to formulate their own accountings (broadly defined) and thus provide a fuller expression of the plural nature of contemporary democracies. By encouraging actors to make their values and assumptions explicit, differences in perspective are brought to the fore rather than obscured. Separate accounts rather than synthesis into a unified account allow individuals and groups with strongly felt value commitments to express themselves more authentically. Positional analysis also permits those with mixed positions to illustrate their tensions. Actors may, for example, be able to give clearer expression to conflicts they experience between their working lives and personal beliefs. Individuals and groups become more dialogically accountable to each other and the opportunities for knowledge imposition more limited. Rather than accept a powerful pre-set framing that closes down debate, multiple publics can exchange accounts as a way of justifying and advocating different courses of action and problematizing each other's situated positions.

A plurality of situated knowledges can thus help to diffuse power. Inclusion of the perspectives of marginalized groups promotes reflexivity, because they are more likely to surface the unstated values and assumptions of dominant groups. This helps to problematize narrowing in/closing down forms of analysis by showing how inevitably partial perspectives are presented as apolitical, objective and neutral. It also highlights that the institutional adoption of any particular standpoint (e.g. the privileging of the interests of finance capital in accounting) is an exercise of power that excludes other possibilities. This opens space for imagining alternatives and allows actors to pursue both co-operative and oppositional forms of engagement. Critical dialogics recognize that it is possible to forge links between demands that are not always obviously connected. In pursuing local action or developing progressive transnational coalitions, disparate individuals and groups may build loose (and sometimes improbable) alliances or 'novel partnerships' (Cohen 2006, p. 75). For example, in their case study of a campaign against the construction of a second runway at Manchester airport in the United Kingdom, Griggs and Howarth (2013) show how direct action environmentalists and local residents – 'the Vegans and the Volvos' – developed a new temporary political identity. Similarly, various actors interested in developing pluralistic forms of accounting and economics, while having their own positions, share a common aversion to monologic mainstream approaches.

By stimulating critical self-reflection and imagination, positional analysis can play an important role in the (re)construction of preferences and social change. Exposure to new frameworks may challenge actors' self-understandings and confidence in the naturalness of their opinions and thereby unsettle the taken for granted. People learn to read situations in different ways. Ideas about corporate accountability, for example, may shift as perspectives interact and problematize each other. Increasing numbers of stakeholders may extend their interpretations of performance beyond the capital markets and profits for shareholders. Or they may retain the same views but in a new way. Thicker, more complex understandings help to promote democratic subjectivity and cultivate an agonistic ethos of engagement. By highlighting the limits of overly consensus-oriented approaches (Brown and Dillard 2013b), positional analysis is much better equipped to deal with deep conflicts over both ends and means.

In short, dialogic accounting proposes that truth and fairness require access to competing perspectives. Sustainability can be represented and understood in many different ways depending on our geographical locations, interests, values and worldviews. There is no complete, unified accounting that captures the definitive truth in complex and politically contentious areas such as sustainability. This does not mean, as many critics seem to fear, accepting an unbridled 'anything goes' relativism or 'hopeless nihilism'. As Sheila Dow highlights in a recent roundtable dialogue on pluralism (Reardon 2015, p. 287), 'there is no contradiction between pluralism and fierce argument; the need to argue for one's own approach inevitably reflects an acceptance of alternatives as legitimate objects of critique'. From an agonistic perspective, pluralism is about individuals and collectives confronting their ideological differences and protecting against participation being used as a means of co-optation and control.

Positional analysis is particularly helpful here as it enables new types of questions to be asked. How do interpretations of sustainability differ? What values and assumptions underlie different interpretations? Are particular perspectives privileged? What impacts flow – directly or indirectly – from currently dominant neoliberal and neoclassical economic understandings? Whose perspectives are ignored or glossed over? Do people recognize or acknowledge their situatedness? Who believes particular ideas and why? What accounts for the grip of dominant narratives? Are people aware of alternatives? In recognizing situatedness, contingency and antagonism as integral aspects of human being, there is an emphasis on taking responsibility for one's viewpoints and the social realities they help to create. Relatedly, while those favouring non-mainstream positions – both in and outside academia – will have their own preferred alternatives, they may be able to form alliances and take collective action that helps to challenge neoclassical-neoliberal orthodoxy (Brown and Dillard 2013a; Stanford 2015). In these ways, a positional approach can help to deepen and revitalize democracy. As Frank Stilwell emphasizes, pluralism in economics is fundamentally concerned with 'the exploration of diverse 'ways of seeing' economic issues in a manner that challenges the 'conventional wisdom' of orthodox economics' (Reardon 2015, p. 279). Individual challenges are unlikely to make much of an impact unless associated with broader collective action on the part of both academics and civil society groups.

The challenges of implementing dialogic accounting and positional analysis

This chapter has focused on exploring how dialogic accounting might be advanced through Peter Söderbaum's work on positional analysis. In summary, as an ideologically open model, positional analysis can help to

- Expose the values and assumptions of traditional accounting models and create new visibilities
- Help social actors recognize the situated nature of all knowledge claims
- Promote hermeneutically rational decision-making (e.g. both within a particular ideological orientation and across different ideological perspectives)
- Facilitate stakeholder dialogue and accountability (e.g. helping actors to articulate how particular positions resonate with or fail to speak to their needs or concerns)
- Encourage individuals and groups to critically reflect on prevailing organizational and social practices
- Highlight power relations by exposing the frames dominating specific decisions
- Guard against various forms of monologism and preserve space for ongoing contestation

The strength of any position in theory is, of course, no guarantee of success in practice. Realizing the possibilities of dialogic accounting and positional analysis will not be easy. There are a number of barriers to be overcome, including implementation issues and related socio-political barriers.

There will be difficulties in obtaining data to provide multi-perspectival accounts. Modelling in a sustainability context is knowledge intensive (e.g. identifying impacts, establishing relevant boundaries). The conscious or unconscious bias of existing expert and organizational information systems means much relevant data will not be available in a systematic form (Blackburn et al. 2014). In the labour context, for example, attempts to develop dialogic approaches are often thwarted by managerial responses that information is 'not collected' (Davenport and Brown 2002, pp. 204–207). There is also much to learn about the ways that experts as facilitators can most effectively present information (e.g. of decision alternatives, modelling subjectivity and uncertainty) so as to promote dialogic interaction and learning. Positional analysis may require significant investments of time and resources, especially in the early stages. As with the establishment of any other area, it might be expected that the issues related more straightforwardly to technical operationalization would dissipate over time; the socio-political barriers are likely to prove far more problematic.

The diffusion of new accounting models typically relies heavily on the advocacy of powerful actors and epistemic communities. Social accounting initiatives have often met with resistance from both managers and the accounting profession, especially where they move beyond 'win–win' eco-efficiency agendas. This is consistent with findings in other disciplines of managerial fears that dialogic approaches may generate challenges for power elites and lead to heightened stakeholder demands (Livesey 2001). Decision makers also often object to participatory approaches on the basis that they are time consuming and costly and have strongly resisted dialogic entitlements in the form of legislated information and participatory rights (Brown and Dillard 2014; Owen et al. 2001).

Moving outside the organization – for example, by engaging social movements – may help to stimulate broader interest in dialogic accounting and positional analysis. However, new accountings are not enough on their own; providing new accounts does not necessarily allow users to effectively respond. Some citizens, even if they are interested in alternative approaches, will find it difficult to secure effective voice in sustainability decision-making. Voluntarist stakeholder engagement initiatives rely on managements and policymakers being prepared to experiment with new approaches and being open to discussion of divergent socio-political perspectives. Knowledge and power differentials mean there is significant potential for capture by dominant elites in the absence of broader institutional change. As Gaventa (2006, p. 23) highlights 'the use of terms such as "partnership" and "shared ownership" by large, powerful actors like the World Bank and the International Monetary Fund (IMF) invite engagement on a "level playing field" but obscures inequalities of resources and power'.

Resistance to dialogic accounting and positional analysis is also likely to come from those seeking to determine right answers on behalf of others. Positional analysis requires actors to be open about their situatedness and engage in political dialogue. Some may be reluctant to admit that they have ideological orientations. They may feel uncomfortable with the uncertainty associated with the absence of pre-specified foundations. Such approaches may seem too complex and challenging to facilitate. Notwithstanding the inroads being made by interpretive approaches in some policy settings, officials trained in technocratic paradigms are still likely to privilege supposedly 'neutral' analysis. If engagement is not sufficiently plural, participatory processes are likely to be dominated by a relatively narrow range of interests (Archel et al. 2011; Brown and Dillard 2015a, b). Here the threat goes beyond managerialism; differences within different communities also need to be respected.

Hagendijk and Egmond (2004, pp. 8–9) point to the potential for multi-perspectival approaches to lead to their own forms of pseudo-participation. While stakeholders may outwardly welcome dialogue, they may not listen to other voices but merely talk at each other from well-entrenched positions. However, even here agonistic exchange is possible. As Torfing (2005, p. 19) observes, actors are rarely trapped within a particular discourse so as to be unaffected by others they encounter. Social reality is 'constantly disarticulated and rearticulated' through both cooperative and conflictual encounters.

Concerns have also been expressed that pluralistic approaches will lead to uncritical relativism and paralysis. This ignores that actors rarely accept that 'all claims are equally valid' (Torfing 2005, p. 19). More typically, they are participants in discourses that provide 'values, standards, and criteria for judging something to be true or false, right or wrong, good or bad' (Torfing 2005, p. 19). Social situatedness and indeterminacy do not signify an 'absence of meaning' but rather choice among meanings (Burton 1997, p. 575). A critical dialogic approach also recognizes the need for action and thus the need for 'talk' to come to an end at certain points. However, it does not seek to depoliticize this act of judgement; the responsibility to otherness exists in tension with the responsibility to act (Feldman 1999). Agonistic dialogic ethics requires people to take responsibility for their beliefs and actions – including any decision not to choose or act – and to be prepared to have them interrogated by others. It also does not seek to depoliticize this in the 'universal reason' of some forms of deliberative democracy or the 'local reason' of communitarianism; the judgements remain political and, as such, open to future political contestation (Brown et al. 2015).

The scope for democratic intervention in contemporary neoliberal societies is currently very restricted in many governance areas. Dialogic accounting and positional analysis need to be part of a far more decentred approach to politics (Griggs et al. 2014) that considers both formal institutional settings and spaces. As O'Leary (1985, p. 98) observes, taking pluralism seriously:

> requires at least the establishing of a legitimacy and a set of institutions and arenas in which people gain at least a right of opposition and bargaining, and preferably of democratic decision making, through all areas of social life, including the corporation. It requires a recognition of politics at the level of people's routine, daily social activities.

There is a need for dialogic entitlements (e.g. information and participation rights) and institutions where views can be debated in a robust fashion. Issues of accountability and access to competing sources of information are key, requiring consideration of not just top-down but also citizen-led transparency and accountability initiatives (Gaventa and McGee 2013). Development of dialogic accounting tools also needs to be dovetailed with related work aimed at a major rethink of areas such as education, economics, corporate governance, information technology and public policy. This requires significant inter- and transdisciplinary alliances, as well as civil society pressures for change.

Concluding comments

The need for dialogic and participatory accountings has been recognized for over 30 years in the accounting discipline and has a lengthy pedigree in many other disciplines. The shortcomings of monologic, technical approaches have become particularly evident with the rise of interest in sustainability accounting. At the same time, it is also recognized that 'accounting and democracy' is grossly under-theorized and that much work remains in terms of operationalizing dialogic accounting.

This chapter has focused on showing how Peter Söderbaum's work on positional analysis – based as it is on assumptions of a plurality of legitimate perspectives – can enable social actors to engage in wide-ranging discussion and debate about the kinds of organizations and societies they want to help (re)create in a manner that respects their diverse perspectives. Such an approach, by encouraging critically reflective dialogue, arguably has considerable transformative potential in areas such as sustainable development. At the same time, new accounting technologies face challenging barriers in terms of their operationalization. The application of dialogic accounting and positional analysis in actual settings still needs to be examined more thoroughly.[4] In line with the spirit of heterodox economics, we hope this book will help stimulate empirical projects in a variety of contexts and other endeavours aimed at tackling the democratic deficits that characterize contemporary accounting.

Notes

1   Under positional analysis, by contrast, quantitative measures merely become part of the information base for decision-making, based on the view that "you cannot manage if you rely exclusively on quantities, and even worse on one-dimensional monetary measures" (Söderbaum 2013, p. 222). Relatedly, you cannot have democratic participation without ideologically open approaches to assessment and evaluation.

2   See, for example, Anderson (1988, p. 60) contrasting the self-understanding of workers of their risk decisions with the view presupposed by cost-benefit analysis.

3   See, for example, Brown and Dillard (2014) for discussion in the context of recent proposals for integrated reporting and Brown and Dillard (2015a) in relation to opening up and closing down forms of participatory governance.

4   See the special issue of the *Accounting, Auditing and Accountability Journal* on "Accounting in Pluralistic Societies" Vol. 28 No. 5 (2015) for examples of pertinent work.

References

Anderson, Elizabeth, 1988. Values, risks, and market norms, *Philosophy and Public Affairs*, Vol. 17, No. 1, pp. 54–65.

Archel, Pablo, Javier Husillos and Crawford Spence, 2011. The institutionalisation of unaccountability: loading the dice of corporate social responsibility discourse, *Accounting, Organizations and Society*, Vol. 36, No. 6, pp. 327–343.

Baber, Walter F., 2004. Ecology and democratic governance: toward a deliberative model of environmental politics, *Social Science Journal*, Vol. 41, No. 3, pp. 331–346.

Bebbington, Jan, Judy Brown and Bob Frame, 2007. Accounting technologies and sustainability assessment models, *Ecological Economics*, Vol. 61, No. 2/3, pp. 224–236.

Blackburn, Nivea, Judy Brown, Jesse Dillard and Val Hooper, 2014. A dialogical framing of AIS-SEA design', *International Journal of Accounting Information Systems*, Vol. 15, No. 2, pp. 83–101.

Brown, Judy and Jesse Dillard, 2013a. Agonizing over engagement: SEA and the 'death of environmentalism' debates, *Critical Perspectives on Accounting*, Vol. 24, No. 1, pp. 1–18.

Brown, Judy and Jesse Dillard, 2013b. Critical accounting and communicative action: on the limits of consensual deliberation, *Critical Perspectives on Accounting*, Vol. 24, No. 3, pp. 176–190.

Brown, Judy and Jesse Dillard, 2014. Integrated reporting: on the need for broadening out and opening up, *Accounting, Auditing & Accountability Journal*, Vol. 27, No. 7, pp. 1120–1156.

Brown, Judy and Jesse Dillard, 2015a. Dialogic accountings for stakeholders: on opening up and closing down participatory governance, *Journal of Management Studies*, Vol. 52, No. 7, pp. 961–985.

Brown, Judy and Jesse Dillard, 2015b. Opening accounting to critical scrutiny: towards dialogic accounting for policy analysis and democracy, *Journal of Comparative Policy Analysis: Research and Practice*, Vol. 17, No. 3, pp. 247–268.

Brown, Judy, Jesse Dillard and Trevor Hopper, 2015. Accounting, accountants and accountability regimes in pluralistic societies: taking multiple perspectives seriously, *Accounting, Auditing & Accountability Journal*, Vol. 28, No. 5, 626–650.

Brown, Judy and Michael Fraser, 2006. Approaches and perspectives in social and environmental accounting: an overview of the conceptual landscape, *Business Strategy and the Environment*, Vol. 15, No. 2, pp. 103–117.

Burton, Mark, 1997. Determinacy, indeterminacy and rhetoric in a pluralist world, *Melbourne University Law Review*, Vol. 21, pp. 544–583.

Carlitz, Ruth, 2013. Improving transparency and accountability in the budget process: an assessment of recent initiatives, *Development Policy Review*, Vol. 31, No. S1, pp. s49–s67.

Chua, Wai Fong, 1996. Teaching and learning only the language of numbers-monolingualism in a multilingual world, *Critical Perspectives on Accounting*, Vol. 7, No. 1, pp. 129–156.

Cohen, Maurie J., 2006. The death of environmentalism: introduction to the symposium. *Organization and Environment*, Vol. 19, No. 1, pp. 74–81.

Davenport, Geoff and Judy Brown, 2002. *Good Faith in Collective Bargaining*. LexisNexis Butterworths, Wellington.

Dietz, Thomas, Amy Fitzgerald and Rachael Shwom, 2005. Environmental values, *Annual Review of Environment and Resources*, Vol. 30, pp. 335–372.

Dryzek, John and Simon Niemeyer, 2008. Discursive representation, *American Political Science Review* Vol. 102, No. 4, pp. 481–493.

Feldman, Leonard C., 1999. Political judgment with a difference: agonistic democracy and the limits of 'enlarged mentality', *Polity*, Vol. 32, No. 1, pp. 1–24.

Gallhofer, Sonja, 1992. M[othering] view on: 'The non and nom of accounting for (M)other nature'. *Accounting, Auditing and Accountability Journal*, Vol. 5, No. 3, pp. 40–51.

Gallhofer, Sonja, Jim Haslam and Akira Yonekura. 2015. Accounting as differentiated universal for emancipatory praxis: accounting delineation and mobilisation for emancipation(s) recognising democracy and difference, *Accounting, Auditing & Accountability Journal*, Vol. 28, No. 5, pp. 846–874.

Gaventa, John, 2006. Finding the spaces for change: a power analysis, *IDS bulletin*, Vol. 37, No. 6, pp. 23–33.

Gaventa, John and Rosemary McGee, 2013. The impact of transparency and accountability initiatives, *Development Policy Review*, Vol. 31, No. S1, pp. s3–s28.

Gray, Rob, 2006. Social, environmental and sustainability reporting and organisational value creation? Whose value? Whose creation? *Accounting, Auditing and Accountability Journal*, Vol. 19, No. 6, pp. 793–819.

Griggs, Steven and David Howarth, 2013. *The Politics of Airport Expansion in the United Kingdom: Hegemony, Policy and the Rhetoric of 'Sustainable Aviation'*, Manchester: Manchester University Press.

Griggs, Steven, Aletta J. Norval and Hendrik Wagenaar, 2014. *Practices of Freedom: Decentred Governance, Conflict and Democratic Participation*, Cambridge University Press, New York.

Hagendijk, Rob and Myrthe Egmond, 2004. The GM food debate in the Netherlands, 1999–2002. Science Technology and Governance in Europe (STAGE), Discussion Paper 14, August.

Leach, Melissa, Ian Scoones and Andy Stirling, 2010. *Dynamic Sustainabilities: Technology, Environment, Social Justice.* Earthscan, London.

Livesey, Sharon M., 2001. Eco-identity as discursive struggle: Royal Dutch/Shell, Brent Spar, and Nigeria, *The Journal of Business Communication*, Vol. 38, No. 1, pp. 58–91.

Morgan, Gareth, 1988. Accounting as reality construction: towards a new epistemology for accounting practice, *Accounting, Organizations and Society*, Vol. 13, No. 5, pp. 477–485.

Obach, Brian K., 2004. *Labor and the Environmental Movement: The Quest for Common Ground.* MIT Press, Cambridge.

O'Connor, Martin, 1999. Dialogue and debate in a post-normal practice of science: a reflexion, *Futures*, Vol. 31, No. 7, pp. 671–687.

O'Leary, Ted, 1985. Observations on corporate financial reporting in the name of politics, *Accounting, Organizations and Society*, Vol. 10, No. 1, pp. 87–102.

Owen, David L., Tracey Swift and Karen Hunt, 2001. Questioning the role of stakeholder engagement in social and ethical accounting, auditing and reporting, *Accounting Forum*, Vol. 25, No. 3, pp. 264–282.

Reardon, Jack, 2015. Roundtable dialogue on pluralism, *International Journal of Pluralism and Economics Education*, Vol. 6, No. 3, pp. 272–308.

Rockloff, Susan F. and Stewart Lockie, 2006. Democratization of coastal zone decision making for Indigenous Australians: insights from stakeholder analysis, *Coastal Management*, Vol. 34, pp. 251–266.

Söderbaum, Peter, 1987. Environmental management: a non-traditional approach, *Journal of Economic Issues*, Vol. 21, No. 1, pp. 139–165.

Söderbaum, Peter, 2004. Decision processes and decision-making in relation to sustainable development and democracy – where do we stand? *Journal of Interdisciplinary Economics*, Vol. 14, pp. 41–60.

Söderbaum, Peter, 2006. Democracy and sustainable development. What is the alternative to cost-benefit analysis? *Integrated Environmental Assessment and Management*, Vol. 2, No 2, pp. 182–190.

Söderbaum, Peter, 2008. *Understanding Sustainability Economics: Towards Pluralism in Economics*, Earthscan, London.

Söderbaum, Peter, 2011. Sustainability economics as a contested concept, *Ecological Economics*, Vol. 70, pp. 1019–1020.

Söderbaum, Peter, 2013. Ecological economics in relation to democracy, ideology and politics, *Ecological Economics*, Vol. 95, pp. 221–225.

Söderbaum, Peter, 2014. The role of economics and democracy in institutional change for sustainability, *Sustainability*, Vol. 6, pp. 2755–2765.

Söderbaum, Peter, 2015. Varieties of ecological economics: do we need a more open and radical version of ecological economics?, *Ecological Economics*, Vol. 119, pp. 420–423.

Springett, Delyse and Barry Foster, 2005. Whom is sustainable development for? Deliberative democracy and the role of unions, *Sustainable Development*, Vol. 13, No. 5, pp. 271–281.

Stanford, Jim, 2015. Towards an activist pedagogy in heterodox economics: the case of trade union economics education, *Journal of Australian Political Economy*, Vol. 75, pp. 233–256.

Stirling, Andy, 2008. 'Opening up' and 'closing down': power, participation, and pluralism in the social appraisal of technology, *Science, Technology, & Human Values*, Vol. 33, pp. 262–294.

Torfing, Jacob, 2005. Discourse theory: achievements, arguments, and challenges. In: Howarth, David and Torfing Jacob (Eds.). *Discourse Theory in European Politics: Identity, Policy and Governance.* Palgrave, Basingstoke.

7 Sustainability, ethics and democracy

A pluralistic approach to the navigation of disagreements

Małgorzata Dereniowska

Introductory remarks

Positional analysis as developed by Söderbaum offers an alternative approach to decision-making and planning. Both as a tool of analysis and an approach to problem solving at the interface among science, society and policy, positional analysis is designed to deal with complexity that involves uncertainty, indeterminacy and risk in sustainability research and practices. Based on an ethically open conception of economics, it aims to avoid reductionism at each step of economic and policy[1] analysis that could lead to an irresponsibly quick and potentially harmful loss of ethically relevant information, concerns or values that a policy-making process should account for. Positional analysis is not only well crafted for case-driven and problem-based approaches but also it fosters a broader institutional change process toward sustainability.

Since 1987, the term 'sustainable development' (or simply, sustainability)[2] has been widely acknowledged as a normative concept of global policy importance (WCED 1987), concerned with the relationship among nature, society and economy and grounded in principles of intra- and intergenerational environmental justice. In particular, it has aimed to address the mutual causality between economic development and environmental degradation. Prior to this, neither environmental problems nor their interconnections with social and economic spheres were of primary concern in public and political debates. Although it was intended to provide a framework for the social and economic transformations needed to meet the challenges of ongoing environmental change, the concept of sustainability is inherently a contested concept. It can mean many different things for political actors, and it includes important political and ethical components that must be properly accounted for in policy analysis and decision-making practices.

Furthermore, sustainability, which is frequently presented as a universal process of change at the institutional and cultural levels (Brown 2002; Edwards 2008), raises the questions of social and political legitimacy. Since the notion of sustainability is concerned with a wide range of issues that fit broadly under such diverse headings as the ecological, economic and social, it includes inherent tensions reflected in the commitment to often conflicting priorities such as economic development and social or environmental justice. This poses difficulties for policy development and implementation. Behind each priority lies various social values, an awareness of which has led to a growing need to address values and related assumptions behind facts and alternative policy options. Moreover, to be successfully realized, policy priorities must be legitimated by society, which requires ethically open, democratic processes.

Both in terms of the theory and practice of sustainable development, the complex question becomes how positive global change for more sustainable development can be initiated and encouraged. Discussing sustainability transition suggests a requirement of moral transformation, an issue that is subject to much debate. The rise of environmental ethics as a distinct field of theoretical and applied studies has been founded on the recognition that dealing with ecological crises requires a shift in value systems and normative orientations, attitudes and behaviors – in other words, in lifestyles and thinking on individual and collective levels. Yet global problems (e.g. climate change) that call for international, universal solutions and actions,[3] run against the fact of culturally based difference. Therefore, formulating sustainability objectives and solutions is not only about smart and progressive outcomes but also about the process and strategies of collectively arriving at them. The mediating task here pertains to strategies that go beyond polarization that impedes progress without negating antagonisms as being merely expressions of errors or without assuming away differences.

Attentiveness to the processes and procedures that lead to sustainable outcomes exposes the complexity of the multifaceted issues for small- and large-scale decision-making. This complexity is evident, among other things, in the uncertainty and risk inherent in scientific policy advice and the lack of consensus on various matters of facts (e.g. how much sea-level rise will occur as a result of climate change). Policy formation regarding sustainability objectives, such as addressing climate change, usually rests on predictive understandings of science. Scientific advice is often conceived as an objectively correct blueprint for policy making and a source for how climate change or other environmental phenomena should be socially understood. Scientific consensus regarding the scope and severity of climate change is anticipated by decision makers to help them avoid political and moral risk. In the meantime, actions to reduce climate change effects are often postponed by commissioning further scientific research. However, despite overwhelming consensus on some key points of humanly induced climate change, little agreement exists in the scientific community regarding particular future scenarios and the effects of climate change (Gardiner 2010a). This is due to an awareness of the unpredictability of highly complex natural systems, which in turn leads to the development of new accounts of uncertainty and risk (Van der Sluijs 2006). Thus, one of the questions that arise is how to develop policy despite uncertainty and while taking seriously the existence of different and often competing scientific advice. Such a task requires taking ethical arguments as seriously as scientific ones.

Actions directed toward climate change or other sustainability problems are, ultimately, morally laden actions. However, as in policy-advice science, the moral realm is characterized by inherent pluralism. This restates the question of how to make progress on matters of policy in the face of factual and moral uncertainty in situations in which there is no single, unambiguous set of moral principles or rules to follow. In light of competing moral frameworks (e.g. consequentialism and deontology) and axiologies (e.g. anthropocentric and non-anthropocentric or instrumental and non-instrumental values) for grounding human responsibility toward others, posterity, and to the environment, the practical question of moral pluralism arises: how can we embrace descriptive and moral pluralism without unwanted eclecticism and ethical relativism? The problem between lacking of standards (which, on one possible interpretation, translates into indifference toward outcomes) and needing some kind of distinguishing rules at the cost of possible or unforeseen unfairness has been a major point of contention in democratic thought and moral philosophy. Furthermore, how we can draw constructive potential out of differences as to provide a foundation for democratic action for sustainability?

This chapter tentatively maps some of the issues that positional analysis raises at the intersection of sustainable development, ethics and democracy. Specifically, I explore the potential for cooperative democratic action in a process-oriented view of sustainability decision-making and policy formation that inevitably includes making moral judgements on questions of values. The reminder of the chapter is organized as follows. Part one discusses some of the challenges on the road to sustainability transition in light of various aspects of factual and moral complexity, pointing to the need for participatory democratic processes. It is argued that taking seriously ethical arguments and articulating normative assumptions of sustainability stakes is essential for enacting suitable policy and capacity building for cooperative collective change. In the second part, I will briefly sketch the main tenets and tensions within the concept of sustainable development, tracing them to different normative perspectives. In the last part, after outlining some of the links between sustainability and democracy implied by positional analysis, questions of democratic legitimacy and a more nuanced account of moral pluralism are raised. Throughout the chapter, I provide some conceptual clarifications of various notions and positions related to ethics of sustainability and moral pluralism. The motivation for this inquiry is that positional analysis as an alternative economic method of analysis based on an ethically open conception of economics offers effective tools for explicitly addressing the often missed ethical points in public discourse and decision-making.

Sustainability transition and moral complexity

Due to the development of new forms of capitalism and its globalization, on the one hand (Kośmicki 2010), and persistent consequences of value pluralism, on the other hand (Kane 1996), our contemporary time can be called an 'axial period'. The term 'axial period' was introduced by philosopher Karl Jaspers (1953) to mark periods in human history where some old and outdated ideas were challenged on a grand scale and new ones born (although not in disconnect with history and tradition). Every period and generation has its own problems to deal with, although many of our current issues, such as the global ecological crisis, are unique in quality, scope, severity and risk. As Robert Kane puts it, 'even those who wish to retrieve the wisdom of the past acknowledge that the extent of modern challenges … is unprecedented' (Kane 1996, p. 7). The reference to axial period is relevant to think about the challenges of sustainable development in the sense that far-reaching transformation of human society and economy is implied, and it is our choice where this transformation will take us collectively. This intuition underlies the sustainability debate in the reference to 'our common future' in the famous Brundtland Report (WCED 1987).

One of the challenges of current crises is the necessity and urgency to make difficult decisions without clear guidance and unambiguous protocols. These situations are also sometimes called 'wicked problems' – a notion that was introduced to differentiate the complex problems of social policy from the classical problems of standard scientific approaches, so-called tame problems (Rittel and Webber 1973). The latter are easily delineated, described and fully decomposable by the standard methods of science.[4] While they pose no applied difficulties due to a solid knowledge base, 'wicked' problems are not susceptible to traditional, 'normal' science methods and problem-solving approaches at the levels of problem definition, evaluation, analysis and policy advice. They require different epistemological commitments to problem solving – ones that emphasize participatory methods and interdisciplinary collaborations between various actors at all stages. 'Wicked' problems occur specifically in situations where the stakes are high, decisions urgent, facts uncertain and values disputed. These are the defining characteristics of postnormal situations (Funtowicz and Ravetz 1993). Today many of the environmentalsocial issues have such characteristics (Mugerauer and Manzo 2008), and sustainable development has been widely acknowledged as essentially a 'wicked' problem that calls for new approaches to doing science and policy formation (Pryshlakivsky and Searcy 2013; Waddock 2013; Batie 2008). From an ethical perspective, the attunement to the challenge of wicked problems includes the necessity to accommodate differences and to make choices that preclude some other possibilities, sometimes equally important, legitimate and rationally irreducible in their justifications. The ethical challenge can be framed as how to perform in situations of dilemma and conflict when a decision is necessary and our knowledge limited. In such situations, characterized by ignorance, we cannot clearly foresee the consequences of our actions, are unable to determine one single, most reasonable answer and are dealing with risk.

The most popular definition of sustainability comes from the Brundtland report, which defines it as 'development that meets the needs of the present without compromising the ability of future generations to meet their needs' (World Commission on Environment and Development (WCED) 1987). Depending on whether we are focused on outcomes or processes, different aspects come to the fore. Debates have naturally arisen regarding how to accomplish sustainable outcomes. Should policy makers and experts set the sustainable objectives and programs for a society? Or rather, should we jointly deliberate on these matters? These questions underlie the controversies that arise at the crossroads among regulatory policies, substantive (environmental and otherwise) rights and public participation in decisionmaking (see e.g. Williams and Matheny 1998). One of the points of contention is whether sustainability policy should be defined in terms of a universal guideline to be applied to cases in a top-down fashion or in a decentralized approach left to arise from self-organized local collectivities attuned to local place in a bottom-up approach. An illustration of the former is Agenda 21, whose policy implementation occasionally led to stagnation due to the poor institutional governance setup ill adjusted to the demands of sustainability transition (these include factors such as poor communication among various levels and units, lack of coordination and integration, and existing jurisdictional boundaries; see Thorseth 2015). The latter, decentralized approach has been advanced, for example, within bioregionalist circles, of which Cato's (2013) bioregional economy provides a prominent, comprehensive vision. Here, political power is devolved to the level of self-governing, self-reliant bioregions, with no cross-regional comparative standards for sustainability practices. What this illustrates is that sustainability displays profoundly ethical questions about who develops and enforces, and in what way, the normative orientation, and about the scope of participatory processes on the road to much needed transition.

Although the debate over sustainable development (with the problem of climate change as the sharpest example) is usually framed as a debate about scientific facts, it is also fundamentally an ethical issue. What is at stake is not only the limits of scientific uncertainty but also, in Stephen Gardiner's words, 'how we decide what to do under such circumstances' (2010a, p. 9). Since the challenges that climate change poses cannot be addressed only by accumulating more factual knowledge and technical fixes, an engagement with questions about the meaning we make of the world and the values we identify as important needs to become a component of policy analysis (Jamieson 2010). Complexity in terms of ethical debate is, however, deficient in this regard (Gillroy and Bowersox 2002).

The ethical complexity of sustainability includes the problem of collective, as opposed to merely individual, choices and attitudes – and, by implication, responsibility. Woods's (2015) criticism concerning the argument for framing climate justice in terms of harm illustrates this point. That climate change induced by human actions leads to highly disaggregated benefits and harms throughout the globe is agreed upon by theorists. The dominant position on grounding our obligations relies on the notion of harm and responsibility as a basis for our obligations. However, received notions of harm may have limited capacity to justify the responsibilities due to its individualistic underpinnings. Woods points out that it is not a set of discrete actions that are constitutive of the unprecedented moral challenge. While disaggregation of impacts makes it difficult to clearly identify and delineate harmful actions, this is not the main issue at stake. It is the multiple patterns of actions that are more than an aggregate of individual outcomes that make up the collective characteristic of the moral challenge of climate change (Woods 2015). Broadening perspectives on moral evaluation from individuals to collectives has far-reaching consequences. Woods explains this problem further by discussing the requirements of climate justice:

> What climate justice demands is that we recognize that our conceptions of the good life are importantly wrong or ill-founded, insofar as they license a collective way of life that is beyond the planet's ecological means … On the basis of

that judgment, agents of climate justice must make multiple, coordinated, more or less small, more or less costly reassessments and adjustments to the practice of living together as ecologically embedded beings (2015, p. 101).

Both analytically and practically the idea that moral agents, by being members of a collectivity, need to participate in the assessment and allocation of responsibilities for deeds that were not intended as harm, and when the risk of potential harm is uncertain, is quite demanding. Part of the analytic challenge comes from the very characteristics of environmental goods (e.g. fresh air, oceans, lakes). Even if environmental goods are both social and shared (thereby having to do with the general question of social justice), they are often also non-excludable and unavoidable (it is difficult not to consume them). That common-pool resources (to which some environmental goods belong) are prone to be overused causes the concern that present individual interests will override any commitment to enlarged responsibility and the benefits of cooperation toward joint goals.[5] Furthermore, the intertemporal dimension complicates already complex spatial and institutional attributes of climate change that together constitute, as Gardiner (2010b) argues, a setting that encourages moral corruption, indifference and the incapacity to undertake collective action. He highlights the fact that the elements constitutive of the climate change problem as a policy issue render it impossible to address the problem's symptoms without questioning the underlying ethical considerations along with epistemological questions of climate science, policy making and the general functioning of society (Gardiner 2010b).

Part of the ethical challenges of sustainable development arises from the fact that in many respects, individualism has been a feature of the internalized concepts of ethics as a solitary enterprise. In Deane Curtin's words, 'what we lack is a public, cooperative sense of ethics that is not just a dreaded set of rules [to be applied to situations], but an evolutionary direction through which one can become fully human' (2005, p. 197). The quest for a 'cooperative sense of ethics', and cooperative action in general, may provide a fruitful perspective for sustainability, shedding light on various aspects of sustainability action across differences.

Thorseth (2015) diagnoses that one of the major obstacles, or even threats, to realizing sustainability is the problem of coordinated action. She concentrates on 'the problem of the public as it comes to the fore in the sustainability context': the lack of coordination. Thorseth sees the lack of coordination of action as a Deweyan communicative problem of the lack of procedures and methods for informing the public. According to Thorseth, the remedial power of multiperspectival, reflective judgement exercised in a deliberative democratic setting can provide a good basis for more integrated and more efficient communication across various axiological and ideological positions (2015). The requirement of better, more integrated and efficient communication across differences is one of the entry points for thinking about the possibility of a broader collective transformation toward sustainability.

In every society, there are common understandings of various phenomena, which are reflected in the language and rules of behavior. Shared ways of interpreting phenomena and behaving similarly in response by a group of actors are characteristics of institutions (Söderbaum 2007). This includes structured social orders, rules of social discourse, ethical frameworks and reciprocal relationships of individual, social and organizational patterns of thought and behavior. The institutional dynamics, when unexamined, can reinforce old schemes in understanding new concepts and, consequently, in actions. Thus, when thinking about sustainability, it is important to extend the framework beyond its widely acknowledged three pillars (the ecological, social and economic) to include the more comprehensive dimensions of our ontological, epistemological and value commitments (Söderbaum 2007; Dereniowska et al. 2015). Collective norms are meant to put some constraints on individual behavior, but individual behavior can also contribute to changes in collective norms. This interdependence suggests at least a partial explanation for how collective norms can evolve. As institutions are constantly changing, some kinds of institutional transformation occur as a by-product of this process – the extent, direction and form of which is yet undetermined. In a similar vein, Söderbaum suggests that despite the uneasiness felt with changes in behavior, 'small changes in visions and actions occur all the time and why shouldn't the positive changes toward sustainability dominate? Such changes will lead to institutional change processes that in turn will facilitate further change in vision and action' (2008, p. 22).

In society, both power games and dialogue occur (Söderbaum 2008). The prevalence and unavoidability of the former notwithstanding, it is not a purely idealistic blunder to consider dialogue as a means of problem solving. If we collectively reaffirm that sustainability concerns are legitimate and important concerns, it is through the promotion of human capacity to deal with conflict that advancements can be made in the direction of sustainability transition. The task is, then, to identify factors that might encourage dialogical modes of communication and conflict resolution among competing positions, grounded in different, sometimes divergent values. Martha Nussbaum traces the problem of value clashes among individuals, cultures and social groups and within an individual, to two inescapable tendencies of the human condition, which is reflected in the classical *one-many* ethical paradox: 'If the real clash of civilizations is ... a clash within the individual soul, as greed and narcissism contend against respect and love, all modern societies are rapidly losing the battle, as they feed the forces that lead to violence and dehumanization and fail to feed the forces that lead to cultures of equality and respect' (Nussbaum 2010, p. 143). How can 'the forces that lead to cultures of equality and respect' be encouraged? The dynamics and changeability of the real-world pose adaptive challenges that can be taken up by cooperation and interconnectivity among groups of interests and societies (Nussbaum 2010, p. 79). Any kind of normative project for world betterment requires solutions that directly engage practical skills, abilities and competences, such as critical, reflexive and enlarged thinking, or cultivation of global citizenship and care (Berlin 2000; Nussbaum 2010), to name a few. To rephrase Nussbaum's question in the context of the need for institutional change processes, one can note that an institutional challenge has multiple dimensions; clearly, new institutions and mechanisms that would allow, through legitimizing procedures, a proper balancing of various intra- and intergenerational interests are in dire need. One of the common stakes in both adjusting existing institutions, or developing and enacting new arrangements, pertains to fostering fruitful and effective dialogue and strategies for dealing with differences and conflict within and across them. It seeks constructive expressions of difference through processes that enhance these capacities. Making visible ideologies and normative frameworks is one of the entry points to this end. When different paradigms and positions are made visible and become subjects of public dialogue based on democratic, pluralistic discourse within all institutional spheres, then social learning and expanding shared understanding are more likely to occur.

Normative narratives of sustainable development: The case for a pluralistic approach

Sustainability is a concept of global policy importance with a wide variety of meanings, conceptualizations and interpretations. It carries potential to induce change in individual attitudes and behaviors and the environmental practices of institutions (Dereniowska et al. 2015), but its theoretical basis as an economic and philosophical concept of justice is far from clear. The importance of normative analysis is that depending on the specific conceptualization of sustainability and its philosophical grounding, different conceptions of justice will follow along with metrics and indicators that will be used for public policy formation. Usually, the choice of indicators is seen as one that relies solely on scientific expertise, and the use of numeric indicators, efficient and easily usable is considered a practical advantage. Yet differing conceptualizations of sustainability reveal distinct underlying philosophical assumptions that reflect disagreements over policy goals and priorities. These views range from narrow, instrumental, economic views to holistic, moral ideals (Kothari 1994). Asking the question of democratic legitimacy necessitates making clear assumptions that underlie each specific policy alternative. Another reason for this is that valid factual policy information still can be ignored for ideological reasons or it can be judged differently by competing belief systems – thus its factual usability can be properly ascertained upon examining it against normative assumptions and perspectives (Fischer 2009). In what follows, I will briefly sketch the main tenets of the normative narratives entangled in the sustainability discourse. In doing so, I will draw on the pluralistic approach presented by Dereniowska et al. (2015). Although the differences and details of various positions cannot be contained by this outline, an understanding of the values underpinning different conceptions of sustainable development is a vital part of the argument for a pluralistic approach to moral and practical reasoning (as elements of decision-making) and for an emphasis on democracy.

Two of the major contrasting approaches to sustainable development – needs satisfaction and freedom-oriented capability approach – illustrate how different philosophical assumptions, such as differing representations of the economic agent result in alternative policy narratives. The basic needs approach comes from the Brundtland report (WCED 1987). Sustainable development from this perspective aims to sustain a decent level of basic needs satisfaction and to balance present and future generations' interests. In the freedom-oriented sustainability approach proposed by Amartya Sen, sustainable development is defined as 'development that prompts the capabilities of present people without compromising capabilities of future generations' (2013, p. 11). The contrast between the freedom-oriented and needs-oriented views is 'not in terms of precision and ambiguity, but in terms of the underlying evaluative conception' (Sen 2013). The capability approach extends sustainability considerations in the light of justice in the sense that it opens up questions of human freedom, not just human needs.[6] According to Sen, this difference amounts to not treating human beings merely as the locus of needs but seeing human beings primarily as people whose freedom really matters and as active agents of change. Herein lies the paradox of the sustainability concept: on the one hand, human agency is at the center of sustainability transformation, but on the other hand, people are very often seen as patients that require being cared for.[7] Looking at the role of people as agents, not just as patients, is vital, according to Sen, to the success of development as process. Söderbaum, from a different perspective, has long argued that the role of an individual as an active driver of change cannot be underestimated for sustainable development (Söderbaum 2007, 2014).

The three pillars of sustainability, as it is often described, are economic, social and ecological development, a formulation that has supposedly expanded the informational basis of the traditional economic-growth approach. This issue is one of the main points of contention regarding sustainable economic development: Is sustainable development 'only' an enlargement of the informational basis of the traditional economic-growth approach, or is it the economic system embedded in the physical system that sets limits to the provision of both environmental and economic goods and services? Depending on the perspective taken, a different take and weight may be given to questions such as which forms of capital to preserve (and how much), what is to be sustained and what is doing the sustaining (see e.g. Neumayer 1998; Bartelmus 2012; O'Neill et al. 2008, Chapter 12).

Economic sustainability is understood as non-declining (or inter-generationally fair) economic welfare, or in terms of the maintenance of natural and manufactured capital stock of the economy (Pezzey 1992), which raises issues about the possibility and the extent of trade-offs between them. The issue of sustainable levels of capital substitution leads to a crucial distinction between two kinds of sustainability: weak and strong (Neumayer 1998 2013; Bartelmus 2012; Ekins et al. 2003) that constitutes the paradigmatic split of doing sustainability (Neumayer 2013; Dedeurwaerdere 2014). According to the weak principle of sustainability, the goal is to maintain the overall value of all types of capital (social, economic and ecological), allowing for substitutions between produced and natural capital, if not in total, then at least at the level of actual use (Bartelmus 2012). In contrast, the strong principle of sustainability assumes that natural capital cannot be easily replaced by any other type of capital due to environmental characteristics that constrain the substitution of natural capital by manufactured capital. An example of such a characteristic is *irreversibility* as it applies to critical components of functions and services of natural capital that uniquely contribute to human wellbeing. These characteristics underlie the development of the category of *critical natural capital*, which assumes that some natural goods and services are irreducibly valuable and important in environmental, social and economic ways and as such cannot be replaced by any other form of either natural or manufactured capital (Chiesura and de Groot 2003). The various degrees of scarcity and threats to the critical natural capital co-determine how to go about the use, preservation and conservation of natural resources (De Groot et al. 2003).

From the perspective of environmental thought, sustainability discourse represents both a shift in thinking and a promising way forward – a way to bring together a host of concerns that have too long been talked about in isolation from one another. Most obviously, sustainability has the potential to overcome a rather persistent dichotomy in environmental thinking – conservation versus preservation[8] – both sides of which aimed to push back against unfettered development (Dereniowska et al. 2015). Conservationism advocates on utilitarian grounds that public ownership and management of forests protects natural resources for long-term use while also preventing a select few from reaping the benefits that should belong to the greater public (Pinchot 1998). By keeping forests (and later grasslands, etc.) under common, public control and management, citizens could more wisely use their natural resources. Preservationism stands sharply against some of the uses admitted by the conservation approach, such as grazing sheep or building dams in public parks or forests. From a preservationist perspective, nature needs to be protected not *for* human use, but *from* human use, or at least from the sort of use that would radically alter a natural place (Muir 1991). These competing approaches have together provided a framework within which several other competing views have been arranged. The intrinsic versus instrumental arguments, for example, could be lined up under preservation and conservation, respectively. Conservationism represents anthropocentric values, whereas the preservationism camp is often couched in ecocentric terms. Although there is an apparent complementarity between conservation and preservation – the former relating to the wise use of the environment; the latter focusing on preserving wild nature from certain kinds of human use – their methods and the results of their application can be often quite different (Dereniowska et al. 2015), alluding to the distinction between weak and strong sustainability.

Although sustainability is frequently taken to be yet another realm of application of standard economic analysis, it includes inherent tensions reflected in the commitment to often conflicting priorities such as economic development and social and environmental justice. From a policy-making perspective, sustainability adds complexity to the issue of the priority of the principles of distributive justice. The classical problem of the trade-offs between principles of *efficiency* and *freedom* is further complicated by introducing *environmental sustainability* as a third incommensurable principle. For example, the irreversibility of decisions pertaining to how much nature should be left, and in what condition, for future generations has been recognized as having such ethical significance that this should not be a matter solely of market interactions, as there is no guarantee that the free market will invest enough in the future (Baumol and Blinder 2011). In contrast, substantive environmental rights can threaten freedom and democracy, for example, by 'being too stringent with environmental and resource controls [that] could compromise future people's effective capacities for productive development' (Hayward 2003, p. 122). The irreducible tensions within the *efficiency-freedom-environmental sustainability* nexus suggest that sustainable development cannot be relentlessly reduced to its axiomatic representation without simultaneous considerations regarding its ethical underpinnings, aspects and implications. This point motivates Söderbaum to search for alternative tools of analysis and approaches to decision-making that comprehensively account for normative components of alternative sustainability and development narratives (Söderbaum 2007, 2012, 2014).

The distinction between weak and strong sustainability brings us to the axiological underpinnings of sustainable development and corresponding conceptions of environmental ethics, often classified as *anthropocentric* versus *non-anthropocentric* ethics (e.g. ecocentric ethics).[9] Anthropocentrism is frequently defined in contrast to the belief that at least some non-human entities also possess intrinsic value. This radical form holds that only human beings have moral standing. Anthropocentrism is a very ambiguous conception, however (Meinard et al. 2016). Two additional value distinctions must be evoked to better illuminate its meaning: (a) that between intrinsic and extrinsic values of nature and (b) that of objectivity versus subjectivity of value. The categories of intrinsic and extrinsic value are useful to articulate different types of environmental threats. For example, an ecosystem can be considered as valuable because a local economy depends on it, but as such its value is expressed in purely instrumental terms. Yet there are numerous important considerations at play in environmental valuing, decision-making and environmental activism, such as rareness, aesthetic or symbolic value, uniqueness, which allude instead to intrinsic worth of nature. The distinction between subjective and objective values has also played a major role in the philosophical literature: if value is generated by human beings, the valuation process is prone to the bias of human chauvinism. It has been frequently argued that an environmental ethics program, to bring about change in normative orientation and human practices, has to be based on objective foundations (Sylvan [Routley] 2003; Rolston III 1989), which the intrinsic value of nature was supposed to provide (see discussion in O'Neill 1993, Chapter 2).

Although a detailed analysis of the issues involved in the anthropocentrism versus non-anthropocentrism debate is intricate and deserves a separate study, here it is sufficient to say that some forms of anthropocentrism are inescapable. Indeed, as human agents, our experience and cognitive structures are bound to be 'anthropocentric' (Piątek 1988), which is to say that our concern with the environment, conservation and related values are inescapably human issues (Williams 1992), and valuation is an expression of human attitude toward the world (Burms 1991). Thus certain kinds of anthropocentrism do not preclude that people ascribe intrinsic value to the environment. Alternatively, then, anthropocentrism can also refer to the issue of *moral signification* and *moral priority* in the sense that although humans might not be the only entities that have intrinsic value and directly matter morally, humans are worth so much more than anything else that they are, in a practical sense, the only things that matter. That is, the value of non-human entities and things is entirely determined by their participation in the satisfaction of human needs and wants (Minteer 2009). Although on this interpretation anthropocentrism does not preclude the ascription of intrinsic value to nature, some advocate that whether non-human nature has intrinsic value (or enough to matter), as opposed to merely making instrumental contributions to human ends, is of critical importance for decision makers. It makes a difference whether environmental protection is seen as a principle or as a resultant policy (Gillroy 2002), as the anthropocentrism versus ecocentrism split co-determines our understanding of the purposes of governance systems and influences the concepts of environmental law (Bosselmann 2008).

In response to the anthropocentric view, philosophers have proposed various versions of non-anthropocentric positions: *sentientism* views all sentient beings as possessing moral worth (or intrinsic value); *biocentrism* expands this to include all living beings and *ecocentrism*, a kind of holism, takes ecosystems to be the locus of value. These ask us to pay attention to a different set of entities and consequently to a different set of goals and ways of achieving those goals. For example, under an ecocentric approach, the value of individual organisms is derivative of their role in an ecosystem; particular individuals might be sacrificed for the well-being of the whole. In contrast, the individualist approach of biocentrism would have the value of an ecosystem be dependent upon how well it benefits the individual entities that depend upon it.

Although holistic versions of non-anthropocentrism, such as ecocentrism, are seemingly in stark theoretical contrast to more individualistic positions, moral intuition, or commonsense morality, raise the possibility that both ecosystems and individual humans and animals count morally. Furthermore, distinguishing between anthropocentrism and non-anthropocentrism in policy debate does not necessarily imply a clash of a magnitude resulting in impasse. It is more constructive to express this debate without taking an absolutist or radical stance; for basing environmental policy, the choice between these positions is 'highly contextual and thus requires a subtle examination of the concrete policy situation' (Katz 1999). Such context-specific analysis should account for conflict of values in environment stakes, respect value pluralism and pay attention to the importance of history and narrative in environmental valuation, as argued by O'Neill et al. (2008). Last, but not least, attempts to bridge the gap between anthropocentrism and non-anthropocentrism accentuate the need for a clear articulation of ethical underpinnings of various perspectives participating in the sustainability debates.

From a pluralistic perspective the sort of argued here, delineating the scope of the moral community – that is to say, which beings and entities are included in moral considerations – does not predetermine the outcome of moral evalua-tions or how to resolve environmental dilemmas. It primarily determines which considerations are to be taken into account in the process of moral reasoning in a decision situation. Once we decide on the set of morally relevant considerations, the next step is the balancing of interests (in other words, weighting and assign-ing priority). A pluralistic perspective would suggest context-sensitive criteria for weighting, ranking and balancing of interests. Conversely, a strongly monistic ver-sion of ecocentrism might claim that, for example, ecosystem integrity (as a policy goal) should have overriding priority over the welfare of individual components of the ecosystem, irrespective of specific conditions and context. A view that accepts a pluralism of relevant moral considerations (e.g. anthropocentric, biocentric and ecocentric concerns) might delineate instead a space for more nuance and judgement, even though it might tell us nothing unambiguously about how to weight the various concerns. These normative positions, as Dereniowska et al. (2015) describes, can be seen to relate to each other analogically to utilitarianism and deontology: most moral agents employ both outcome and duty-based considerations even though these two approaches are inconsistent or at least incommensurable with each other. Although various outcomes can be compared with one another within utilitarianism, rights and duties of a deontological sort cannot so obviously be put on a single scale with utility to be directly considered. Giving up one or the other to achieve consistency or clear-cut guidance for legitimate policy decisions, however, would entail giving up a significant part of what many consider important. Thus, weighting of competing considerations necessitates a way that is not (indiscriminately) rule-bound but makes use instead of reflexive, multisided judgement in a discursive setting (Dereniowska et al. 2015). Such a de-centered model, in line with John Dryzek's insights, can better serve ecologically important democracy projects (1995). Imposing single-minded solutions to wicked situations (especially involving weighing competing claims) where human and ecological values are at play is reductionist and counteractive to democratic decision-making.

In favor of a practical pluralistic approach, one final point of clarification is in order regarding why we should embrace pluralism instead of concluding merely that much disagreement exists. After all, many positions (even in science) turn out to be wrong. Likewise, one might say that things being complex and challenging do not show that things are pluralistic by nature. Dereniowska et al. (2015) suggest instead that pluralism can be embraced as a methodology, or practical response, to the seeming intractability of many disagreements, even if more perfect (but currently unattainable) knowledge would clarify for us which answers to the problems we face are correct and which incorrect. Pluralism as a practical position is a reasonable response to the need to arrive at answers under post-normal circumstances.

Within sustainable development debate, as it has developed over past decades, multiple, but often inconsistent, in the sense that they cannot be made to fit under some unifying normative theory without remainder, views have coexisted. The vagueness of the sustainability concept makes it difficult to translate between concept and practice (Arler 2003) or to achieve progress. For this reason, 'narrowly defined sustainability of economic activity stands a better chance of success than holistic visions of development' (Bartelmus 2012, p. xiv). However, the disagreements are not going to disappear simply by jettisoning the ethical components and alternative normative perspectives on sustainability since they are about things that really matter and are not merely about matters of fact (Barry 2013). Although precision and agreement is desirable, too much narrowing through consensus or other means will inevitably result in leaving out some important values and priorities. This does not imply any sort of depreciation of working toward a core understanding of sustainability. After all, developing a shared understanding of moral and political commitments and looking for points of agreement lies at the heart of a healthy democracy (Dereniowska et al. 2015). Rather, the growing recognition that sustainability inevitably raises issues of values asks us how we can take up the sustainability challenge also in terms of our collective capacity to deliberate on the sustainable vision of the future (Robinson 2004) and to constructively engage with existing differences.

Moral pluralism and democratic (inter)action for sustainability

The assumption behind positional analysis is that sustainable solutions are intrinsically related to the functioning of a reflexive and deliberate democracy and so socially and ecologically relevant economics must be able not only to account for complexity and uncertainty in a pluralistic mode but also to engage and communicate with society and policymakers. Profoundly political and moral issues are involved in both decision-making and science itself, making the principle of democracy a top priority (Söderbaum 2008) for safeguarding legitimacy, trust and cooperation.

Positional analysis, as I see it, reaffirms the idea of participatory democracy, which combines elements of representative and direct democracy in a process of collective decision-making (Aragonès and Sánchez-Pagés 2009); it is related to a Deweyan notion of democracy as a social and ethical ideal – a way of life that goes beyond governance matters (Dewey 1997). In this context, the promise of the sustainability concept can be sought in the inclusion of ecological, social and economic dimensions in addressing intra- and intergenerational equity under one policy framework and in its ability to blend global concerns with the local. The democratic and participatory advantage of acting locally is vested with a global perspective for thinking about moral responsibility and action.

The project of democracy is essentially a project of an ongoing moral transformation (Graeber 2014). Similarly, sustainability transformation is essentially a moral, normative project involving a vision of our sustainable 'common future' and (more or less implicitly) of how to get there. There is considerable concern that an insistence on democratic processes may possibly weaken the efficacy of sustainability orientation insofar as there exists little hope for unanimity regarding the specific outcome or processes to be used. One could argue, in an absolutist vein, that successfully enacting sustainability would require that all citizens value sustainability equally and perhaps even similarly rank specific sustainability values, giving to sustainability goals not only legitimacy but also priority in public policies. Setting aside for now the merits of this point, a more sceptical objection arises: the role of public participation in decision process can potentially hinder rather than improve the realization of progressive solutions due to the possibility of some engaging in power games and pursuing narrow interests disguised within social controversies that lead to a polarization of public debate. The deeper problem, however, lies not in an either/or choice about inclusive politics for sustainability but rather pertains to the contested meaning and scope of democratic procedures and their legitimacy. Furthermore, looking at environmental controversies and expressions of collective concerns provides a breadth of resources for public policy analysis and for analytically recasting the questions of democracy as meta-ideology and democratic legitimacy both in outcome and the processes leading to it.

Descriptively, democratic interactions employ various means and modes of political engagement, varying in their accounts of, for example, rationality of choice, closure mechanisms of the decision-making process, the role and value of controversy and disagreement and emancipatory social action. Citizens' engagement in political processes and collective action may have politically corrective implications in rethinking democratic procedures and outcomes and their legitimacy. Such considerations can enrich an economic and political outlook regarding disagreements over social and environmental goods (see e.g. Bromley and Paavola 2002). Democratic agents express their discontents in various forms ranging from rational and publicly acceptable acts, civil disobedience to more radical activism. Civil disobedience acts or more radical forms of social activism may, on the one hand, and to varying degrees, violate the procedures shaping democratic interactions, but on the other hand, frequently are radical, last-resort expressions of deep dissatisfaction with the politics of exclusion and disempowerment. It remains that without making visible the conflict and what stands behind it, a truly democratic process cannot take place. Since sustainable development is devised precisely to deal with the social-environmental inequalities nexus, it seems importantly relevant to expand policy analysis against structural inequalities resulting in the politics of exclusion. The participatory bend implied in positional analysis is sensitive to the problem of existing political inequalities and the asymmetric distribution of power between different parties and actors, an issue too frequently overlooked even by democratic pluralists (on this point, see e.g. Blokland 2011).

Democracy as an ethical ideal that protects difference and secures some minimal, procedurally fair standards has potential for universalizing sustainability values. It is in the democratic, discursive setting that some shared principles and values can become universalized, such as the value of sustainable society and economy. This is not to say that universalized principles and values would, or should, gain an absolutist status dictating the value hierarchies, nor that they are abstracted from cultural and local conditions of their realization.[10] Rather, this is to suggest that a more nuanced account of pluralistic thinking and action is required in tacking between the universal and the particular, which may also illuminate on democratic interactions that enable fostering sustainability as common good through more cooperation and understanding. Furthermore, the argument for reintroducing ethical debate in policy analysis raises the question of standards by which to evaluate conflicting claims in a world of moral pluralism. To that end, some remarks on the meaning of moral pluralism are in order.

Moral pluralism holds, in Martin Benjamin's words, that several 'good and important ethical values and principles are inherently incompatible. They cannot be combined into a single harmonious scheme of morality for all' (2003, p. 125). Moral pluralism, thus, does not necessarily imply relativism in the sense that moral answers are always relative to something. Rather, it refers to the belief that there exist, as Susan Wolf puts it, 'pockets of indeterminacy' in moral reasoning: 'No principle or decision procedure exists that can guarantee a unique and determinate answer to every moral question involving a choice among different fundamental moral values or principles' (Wolf 1992, p. 785, 788). This indeterminancy is due to *rationally irreducible difference* with respect to moral principles, values, beliefs, theories and the like. It is not always due to our human or theoretical insufficiencies that such conflict remains, but rather, as Isaiah Berlin argues, because 'not all the supreme values pursued by mankind now and in the past were necessarily compatible with one another' (2000, p. 7). In other words, even if a world of objective values exists or our knowledge is complete, these values often clash because of being inconsistent (not mutually realizable) or incommensurable (not reducible to a common denominator).[11]

One of the concerns is whether explicitly seeking to accommodate difference would lead to relativism, giving way to pursuing narrowly constructed interests. There is, however, a difference between *descriptive relativism* and *moral relativism*. The former is not a moral theory but an empirical claim about the world. It holds that there are, in fact, moral disagreements between people and cultures. Moral relativism is saying something more. Not only is there difference, but moral right and wrong are defined by a culture's particular moral views. One can be a descriptive relativist to some degree without embracing moral relativism since from actual disagreement about some moral claims we cannot conclude without added premises that right and wrong are defined by culture. There is also a distinction to make between radical and weak versions of relativism in ethics. *Radical relativism* is the claim that there are no standards by which to make cross-cultural evaluations of moral claims, values, and so on and that because of this each belief can only be judged within its cultural context. *Weak relativism* simply claims that all moral claims, values, and so on are culturally (or historically, geo-politically, etc.) developed, although there are nonetheless some ways to make judgements across cultures, based presumably on our shared humanity and moral imagination. This relativism seems to fit fine with pluralism of the sort argued here.

The specific case of moral pluralism – one that can be found in the characteristics of 'wicked' problems and post-normal contexts – is one that may result in equally legitimate but rationally irreducible opinions and judgements about specific situations. Differences that justify pluralism can be located at various levels of moral thinking – theory, worldviews, and so on – although to be moral pluralism, these must result in differences in evaluations of particular cases. Reasonable but irresolvable difference may also be in terms of the rankings or weightings of principles, values, sets of virtues, and so on. Since they are all interconnected (and are not always conceptually or ontologically distinct – for example, values are expressible as beliefs or judgements), it would be surprising if pluralism existed with respect to one but not others. Importantly, moral pluralism is an attempt to respond to the fact of rationally irresolvable differences of beliefs and values with an emphasis on both tolerance and the ability to rationally evaluate competing claims. Defined in this way, it is not inconsistent with some version of universalism, which can be understood as the observation that moral beliefs and values are shared cross-culturally. On a strong, monistic interpretation, universalism may sometimes be equated with absolutism, meaning that there are singular substantive values, principles and orderings of these in each situation, for everyone, which implies inter-culturally shared standards of moral evaluations without exceptions. On a weak interpretation, however, universalism (that there are *some* shared moral beliefs and values across cultures) can be interpreted to be proximate of a weak version of descriptive relativism (that there are *some* differences). A pluralist would most likely accept this weak version of either theory.

Speaking about pluralism entails the expectation that pluralism about pluralism exists (Lassman 2011). Nevertheless, despite the breadth of positions, some shared pluralist intuitions about moral life and conflict management can be identified. Hinman points to the existence of some principles that embody fundamental intuitions of ethical pluralism (2003, pp. 32-33). The extent to which these principles are put into practice and how they are realized marks the place of moral pluralism in the spectrum between relativism and absolutism. Articulated as an alternative to these two extremes, pluralism can be seen as a strength in moral life, not its weakness (Hinman 2003). In what follows, I build on Hinman's articulation of basic pluralistic intuitions and extend this into a provisional list of some of the principles through which constructive expressions of democracy are channeled in practice:

- *The principle of mutual understanding:* In situations of perpetual disagreement or even in cases in which we dislike some aspects of different opinions or cultures, we can at least try to understand different views in virtue of our moral and spiritual imagination. The principle of understanding does not imply approval of the positions we seek to understand or that we cannot compare or criticize them (Hinman 2003). It is, however, a precondition for further engagement with difference. It is a prerequisite of effective and constructive communication not predicated on consensus (Rescher 1995), involving speaking and listening (Dobson 2014). Notably, social and economic transition can occur if there is a common understanding of what people want to achieve (although this does not automatically claim that people need to univocally agree on what they want), for which the understanding of the manifold cultural context in which any transition process takes place is crucial.
- *The principle of tolerance:* Pluralism suggests a cautious tolerance rather than blind acceptance, allowing other individuals, groups or cultures as much as possible to foster their moral vision (Hinman 2003), without contenting that any view is as good as any other. Absolutist interpretation of the principle of tolerance does not comport with the pluralistic spirit, as it renders meaningless any possibility of rational evaluation of competing claims, making public discourse meaningless, and in some cases, it could give ways to forces diminishing and eradicating diversity – an issue addressed by the next principle.
- *The principle of standing up against evil:* If pluralism ever hooks close to absolutism, this is the point on which, throughout history, pluralistic thought has drawn lines between what is acceptable and what is not. On behalf of tolerance, no pluralist would and should accept exclusionary movements pretending to hegemonic status, as they endanger the cultivation of diversity (Hinman 2003); a pluralist will not condone violence or violations of human rights and dignity.

The principle of preventing harm falls under this category, as suffering should be minimized as much as is possible (Berlin 2000; Connolly 2005). Thus, ethical pluralism stands against flagrant wrongdoing.

- *The principle of fallibility:* Occasionally, when confronted with difference (e.g. cultural differences, incommensurable ideologies), we may recognize that it is our attitude, values or elements of our worldview that need modification or adjustment. In the clash of values or in the midst of conflict, we may become more aware of our own biases and prejudices; it is through the acceptance that our own position is not infallible that we are called to openness, tolerance and respect toward others (Hinman 2003).

- *The principle of respect:* This principle extends the perspective of understanding and tolerance by including the 'democratization ingredient' of the 'cultivation of care' for the perspectives of others and emphasizing relational situatedness of the self (Connolly 1995; Schlosberg 2002). Through recognition and responsiveness, this principle prevents overly quick invalidations of the perspectives of others.

- *Audi alteram partem* (hear the other side) – the *principle of adversary argument:* Borrowed from common law, adversarial reasoning is based on the recognition that the clash between two contradictory claims sheds new light on matters in a way that no single position is capable of. The demand to a fair hearing can be seen as a necessary, universal feature of fair procedure: 'it is reasonable to be a universalist in the cause of reasonableness in the regulation of conflicts (hear the other side), but not a universalist in defense of particular outcomes of particular conflicts of moral opinion' (Hampshire 2001, pp. 52-53). Adversarial reasoning enables us to activate the constructive and synergistic potential included in differences of perspectives, thus facilitating the cultivation of a dialogic ethos.

- *The principle of extended responsibility:* Participation in social and political discourse not only requires recognition and hearing of others but also calls for self-scrutiny and taking responsibility for one's own views, beliefs and actions. Also, from a positional perspective, greater accountability on behalf of decision-making parties is required by acknowledging that dissensus on matters of public policies informed by science can exist and calling for the process of decision-making and policy formation that is more open, inclusive, with power games and interest conflicts clearly articulated. Moral responsibility is inherently bound up with the exercise of autonomy and freedom of moral agents. Not only must those with the power to exercise their freedom be held accountable for their actions (and inactions) but respecting the morally considerable claims of all who will be impacted by their decisions (i.e. moral patients)[12] provides a building block of ethical and democratic legitimacy. In addition to the received notion of individual responsibility, it is relevant here to consider what collective responsibility might mean and require.

The above list is just a provisional outline meant to open up complex and intertwined axiological, motivational and ideological components of pluralistic thinking and acting stretched across the relativism-absolutism spectrum. It provides some pointers for entering and constructively engaging with difference and navigating perpetual conflicts – although certainly there are other important principles and related virtues and values that could facilitate further this objective.

The principles included in this minimal, provisional primer may be differently interpreted depending on specific perspectives and positions and thus given more or less substantive weight in shaping democratic processes and interactions. By implication, in a dynamically changing globalized world that poses adaptive challenges to the exercise of democracy and moral judgement, also legitimizing procedures and their conceptualizations may be subject to scrutiny and adjustments. This idea has been expressed differently by Joshua Cohen with reference to the procedure-substance dichotomy: 'Moral pluralism causes no more trouble for agreement on substance than for agreement on democratic procedure' (1994, p. 618).

These basic intuitions – shared across various pluralistic strands of thought – make it possible to conceptualize democratic practices as stretched between affirming conflict (as an expression of irreducible difference) and seeking for its resolution. They can be construed as providing some minimal both normative and procedural standards for the anti-nihilistic, axiological orientation of ethical pluralism merged with agathological components of standing up against oppression; pluralistic principles call for cultivation of virtues of understanding, care, respect and responsibility. Pluralism that enhances constructive democratic expressions celebrates difference in relational, not atomistic terms, with 'relational sensitivity' (Connolly 2005) as one of the prerequisites.

In this context, the search for democratic legitimization of sustainability values and broader normative orientation is not a completely relativistic endeavor in the sense of 'anything goes', even in situations of rationally insoluble disagreements and communication not necessarily predicated on consensus. This suggests that beyond the search for consensus as the sole common ground for democratic action, an understanding not predicated on consensus in communication can be sought. Such an understanding base requires, borrowing from Armstrong (1988), a *pluralistic literacy*, that is, the ability to interpret and to deal effectively with cultural differences and negotiating with competing claims of multiple ways of interpreting and understandings. Pluralistic literacy can be construed as a practical requirement for what Söderbaum calls 'paradigms co-existence' in the community of inquiry in contrast with encouraging a setting in which one leading paradigm marginalizes other valid options (2008).

An illustration of pluralistic literacy at work can be found in illuminating insights of David Schlosberg (2002) into how diversity of environmental justice movements can be the strength holding great potential for collective change. It takes something more to make this diversity a strength rather than an obstacle. Schlosberg analyses factors that contribute to strengthening movements and to what I call democratic action, such as orientation toward network building, development of discursive, dialogical relationships or communication across difference based on tolerance and respect (2002). In a similar vein, democratic interactions based on normative and procedural principles that enable us to seek dialogic understanding, enact pluralistic literacy and navigate disagreements and conflicts even in the face of dissensus are considered as facilitators in fostering sustainability change. These aspects can be seen both as conditions and constructive expressions of democracy in practices at individual and collective levels.

Concluding remarks

In this chapter, I briefly identified some of the questions that positional analysis raises at the crossroads of sustainability, ethics and democracy. Specifically, I focused on moral complexity endemic to sustainability as a policy issue and competing normative conceptions of sustainability. The chapter provided some conceptual clarifications and the elements of a pluralistic approach that is a middle ground between dogmatic absolutism and subjective relativism; applied to sustainability, this points to the possibility of universalizing thinking and democratic action. Against this ground, I investigated some of the procedural aspects of sustainability transformation in decision-making and policy formation as implied by positional analysis, pointing to constructive ways of dealing with factual and moral complexity.

As sustainability exposes characteristics of 'wicked problems', scientific facts alone cannot provide sufficient ground on which to base sustainability policy, calling for integrating ethical and positive analyses. Sustainability is irreducibly a collective and ethical problem that poses adaptive challenges. The role of ethics cannot be overlooked in activating the potential within the plurality of sustainability disputes, nor can ethics be abstracted from the pressing reality of social and environmental problems that require immediate action. Such a practice-driven outlook demands ethical scrutiny in public and political discourse on sustainability goals. The practical challenge is how to communicate across different perspectives and narratives and how to draw constructive, effective and productive potential out of difference and conflict and how differences can be integrated in a wide spectrum of democratic processes and practices.

Positional analysis calls for a pluralistic practice. The recognition and acknowledgement of pluralism, although important, do not necessarily entail that democratic action, or a normative orientation (be it toward sustainability or any other socially or environmentally just vision), will be fostered in an inclusive, transformative and dialogical way. The constructive potential embedded in difference pertains, rather, to attitudes and strategies employed in dealing with difference and disagreement. This raises the importance of processes and questioning at least minimal standards of pluralistic legitimacy and practices by which to execute these standards, channeling cooperative expressions of democracy. To that end, this chapter provided a minimal primer of pluralistic principles for shaping democratic interactions and differences accommodation in ethical and constructive ways. The capacity to effectively respond to critical future challenges within the sustainability framework depends to a great extent on whether and how the inner tensions are addressed. Performing reflective, dialogical and collaborative actions can enable alterations and a redevelopment of unsustainable trends and patterns.

Notes

1 Fischer notes that policy is not a socially and culturally external phenomenon but rather a social construct: 'as a sociopolitical agreement on a course of action or (inaction) designed to resolve or mitigate a problem, a policy is created discursively' (2009, p. 172).

2 Although 'sustainability' in the interdisciplinary literature is associated with more encompassing, ecologically and socially, normative ideal than 'sustainable development', because of the focus on diverse meanings and interpretations of these terms I use them synonymously here.

3 The ideas of global responsibility, ecological citizenship and a common good reflect these universalizing tendencies in the search for normative standards for a globalized world.

4 For a broader overview of the differences between 'tame problems' and 'wicked problems' see for example Rittel and Webber (1973); Batie (2008).

5 Such a situation has been conceptualized in game theory as the *Prisoner's Dilemma* to explain why rational, disinterested individuals may not cooperate even if, on the collective level, it seems to be in the best interest of each individual. This model has been famously applied to the problem of the environmental commons in Hardin's (1968) *Tragedy of the Commons*. Gardiner (2010b) went further by considering the conflict between present and future generations' interests (the so-called Pure Intergenerational Problem [PIP]). In PIP, there can be no symmetry assumed in calling upon responsibility and thus the standard solutions that usually appeal to received ideas of reciprocity and mutually beneficial interactions do not work.

6 The application of a capability approach to sustainable development is not without its challenges and has been a subject of interdisciplinary debates and modifications – discussion of which falls beyond the scope of this chapter. For an overview, see for example, Lessmann and Rauschmayer (2013), Burger and Christen (2011), and Pelenc et al. (2013).

7 In Sen's words, 'we have to see human beings as agents who can think and act, not just as patients who have needs that require catering' (2013, p. 8).

8 The conservationism versus preservationism debate arose within the North American context, and is linked with the pioneering figures that have influenced environmental protection paradigms all over the globe. Conservationism was largely introduced by Gifford Pinchot (1998), and represented a progressive, science-based approach to the protection of natural resources. The preservationist paradigm was a more spiritually-oriented paradigm as found in the writings of, for example, John Muir (1991), one of the pioneers of the American national parks movement. The significance of this historical distinction pertains to philosophically distinctive paradigms of human interaction with the environment, still echoed in contemporary debates in ecological restoration or conservation biology fields.

9 For a broader overview of environmental ethics positions, see Light and Rolston III (2002) and Wenz (2001).

10 On that matter, both the strong version of universalism (all values and beliefs are shared) and the strong version of descriptive relativism (no shared beliefs and values) are both probably descriptively false. There are some key or central values held across cultures (e.g. minimizing of suffering) but also differences in, for example, rankings of values.

11 I thank Jason Matzke, who studied under Martin Benjamin, for directing me to these sources in working out the challenges of pluralism in ethics.

12 Moral patients are all beings who possess moral standing and are thus objects of moral consideration. Although the class of moral patients includes those who are also moral agents (e.g. a normally functioning adult human being), it also includes those who have standing but do not possess moral autonomy (e.g. very young children or non-human beings). In other words, although not all moral patients can be held responsible for their actions (because they are not also moral agents), their interests, well-being or flourishing must be taken into account by moral agents.

References

Aragonès, Enriqueta, and Santiago Sánchez-Pagés, 2009. A theory of participatory democracy based on the real case of Porto Alegre. *European Economic Review*, Vol. 53, No. 1, pp. 56–72.

Arler, Finn, 2003. Ecological utilization of space: Operationalizing sustainability, pp. 155–185. In Andrew Light and Avner De-Shalit, eds., *Moral and Political Reasoning in Environmental Practice*. The MIT Press, Cambridge, MA.

Armstrong, Paul B., 1988. Pluralistic literacy. *Profession*, Vol. 88, pp. 29–32.

Barry, Brian, 2013. Sustainability and intergenerational justice, pp. 109–121. In Lori Gruen, Dale Jamieson, and Christopher Schlottmann, eds., *Reflecting on Nature. Readings in Environmental Ethics and Philosophy*. Oxford University Press, New York, NY.

Bartelmus, Peter, 2012. *Sustainability Economics: An Introduction*. Routledge, London.

Batie, Sandra S., 2008. Wicked problems and applied economics. *American Journal of Agricultural Economics*, Vol. 90, No. 5, pp. 1179–1191.

Baumol, William J., and Alan S. Blinder, 2011. *Microeconomics: Principles and Policy*. Cengage Learning, Mason, OH.

Benjamin, Martin, 2003. *Philosophy & This Actual World: An Introduction to Practical Philosophical Inquiry*. Rowman & Littlefield Publishers, Lanham, MD.

Berlin, Isaiah, 2000. *The Proper Study of Mankind. An Anthology of Essays*. Farrar, Straus and Giroux, New York, NY.

Blokland, Hans, 2011. *Pluralism, Democracy and Political Knowledge: Robert A. Dahl and His Critics on Modern Politics*. Routledge, Burlington, NJ.

Bosselmann, Klaus, 2008. *The Principle of Sustainability: Transforming Law and Governance*. Ashgate Publishing, Aldershot.

Bromley, Daniel W., and Jouni Paavola, 2002. Economics, ethics, and environmental policy. In Daniel W. Bromley and Jouni Paavola, eds., *Economics, Ethics, and Environmental Policy: Contested Choices*, pp. 261–76. Blackwell, Oxford.

Brown, Douglas, 2002. *Insatiable Is Not Sustainable*. Praeger, Westport, CT.

Burger, Paul, and Marius Christen, 2011. Towards a capability approach of sustainability. *Journal of Cleaner Production*, Vol. 19, No. 8, pp. 787–795.

Burms, Arnold, 1991. Antropocentrisme en ecocentrisme [Anthropocentrism and ecocentrism], pp. 140–144. In A. Liegeois, J. Selling, L. Anckaert, J. De Tavernier, B. Roebben, J. Verstraeten, eds., *Aspecten van een christelijke sociale ethiek*. KULeuven, Bibliotheek van de Faculteit Godgeleerdheid, Leuven.

Cato, Molly Scott, 2013. *The Bioregional Economy: Land, Liberty and the Pursuit of Happiness*. Routledge, New York, NY.

Chiesura, Anna, and Rudolf de Groot, 2003. Critical natural capital: A socio-cultural perspective. *Ecological Economics*, Vol. 44, No. 2-3, pp. 219–231.

Cohen, Joshua, 1994. Pluralism and proceduralism, *Chicago-Kent Law Review*, No. 69, pp. 589–618.

Connolly, William E., 1995. *The Ethos of Pluralisation*. University of Minnesota Press, Minneapolis, MN.

Connolly, William E., 2005. *Pluralism*. Duke University Press, Durham, NC.

Curtin, Deane, 2005. *Environmental Ethics for a Postcolonial World*. Rowman & Littlefield Publishers, Lanham, MD.

De Groot, Rudolf, Johan Van der Perk, Anna Chiesura, and Arnold van Vliet, 2003. Importance and threat as determining factors for criticality of natural capital. *Ecological Economics*, Vol. 44, No. 2-3, pp. 187–204.

Dedeurwaerdere, Tom, 2014. *Sustainability Science for Strong Sustainability*. Edward Elgar, Cheltenham.

Dereniowska, Malgorzata, Jason Matzke, and Peter Söderbaum, 2015. From the contested terrain of sustainability concept toward pluralistic and democratic practice, pp. 22–51. In Krystyna Najder-Stefaniak, ed., *Philosophy and Practice of Sustainable Development*. Zakład Filozofii WNS SGGW, Warsaw.

Dewey, John, 1997 [1888]. The ethics of democracy, pp. 182–204. In *Pragmatism. A Reader*, Louis Menand, Ed., Vintage, New York, NY.

Dobson, Andrew, 2014. *Listening for Democracy: Recognition, Representation, Reconciliation.* Oxford University Press, Oxford.

Dryzek, John, 1995. Political and ecological communication. *Environmental Politics*, Vol. 4, No. 4, pp. 13–30.

Edwards, Andres R., 2008. *The Sustainability Revolution. Portrait of a Paradigm Shift.* New Society Publisher, Gabriola Island.

Ekins, Paul, Sandrine Simon, Lisa Deutsch, Carl Folke, and Rudolf De Groot. 2003. A framework for the practical application of the concepts of critical natural capital and strong sustainability. *Ecological Economics*, Vol. 44, No. 2-3, pp. 165–185.

Fischer, Frank, 2009. *Democracy and Expertise: Reorienting Policy Inquiry.* Oxford University Press, New York, NY.

Funtowicz, Silvio O., and Jerome R. Ravetz, 1993. Science for the post-normal age. *Futures*, Vol. 25. No. 7, pp. 739–755.

Gardiner, Stephen M., 2010a. Ethics and global climate change. In Stephen M. Gardiner, Simon Caney, Dale Jamieson, and Henry Shue, eds., *Climate Ethics: Essential Readings*, pp. 3–35. Oxford University Press, Oxford.

Gardiner, Stephen M., 2010b. A perfect moral storm: Climate change, intergenerational ethics the problem of moral corruption, pp. 87–98. In Stephen M. Gardiner, Simon Caney, Dale Jamieson, and Henry Shue, eds., *Climate Ethics: Essential Readings*. Oxford University Press, Oxford.

Gillroy, John Martin, and Joe Bowersox, 2002. Introduction: The roots of moral austerity in environmental policy discourse, pp. 1-22. In John Martin, and Joe Bowersox, eds., *The Moral Austerity of Environmental Decision Making: Sustainability, Democracy, and Normative Argument in Policy and Law*. Duke University Press, Durham, NC.

Gillroy, John Martin, 2002. A practical concept of nature's intrinsic value, pp. 72–79. In John Martin Gillroy and Joe Bowersox, eds., *The Moral Austerity of Environmental Decision Making: Sustainability, Democracy, and Normative Argument in Policy and Law*. Duke University Press, Durham, NC.

Graeber, David, 2014. *The Democracy Project: A History, a Crisis, a Movement.* Penguin Books, London.

Hampshire, Stuart, 2001. *Justice Is Conflict.* Princeton University Press, Princeton, NJ.

Hardin, Garrett, 1968. The tragedy of the commons. *Science*, Vol. 162, No. 3859, pp. 1243–1248.

Hayward, Tim, 2003. Constitutional environmental rights: A case for political analysis, pp. 109–129. In Andrew Light and Avner De-Shalit, eds., *Moral and Political Reasoning in Environmental Practice*. The MIT Press, Cambridge, MA, and London.

Hinman, Lawrence M., 2003. *Ethics: A Pluralistic Approach to Moral Theory.* Thomson Wadsworth, Belmont, CA.

Jamieson, Dale, 2010. Ethics, public policy, and global warming. In Stephen M. Gardiner, Simon Caney, Dale Jamieson, and Henry Shue, eds., *Climate Ethics: Essential Readings*, pp. 77–86. Oxford University Press, Oxford, NY.

Jaspers, Karl, 1953. *The Origin and the Goal of History*, trans. M. Bullock, Yale University Press, New Haven, CT.

Kane, Robert, 1996. *Through the Moral Maze. Searching for Absolute Values in a Pluralistic World.* North Castle Books, Armonk, NY.

Katz, Erik, 1999. A pragmatic reconsideration of anthropocentrism. *Environmental Ethics*, Vol. 21, No. 4, pp. 377–390.

Kośmicki, Eugeniusz, 2010. *Zrównoważony Rozwój W Warunkach Globalizacji Gospodarki* [Sustainable Development in the Context of Economic Globalization]. Wydawnictwo Ekonomia i Środowisko, Białystok, Poznań.

Kothari, Rajni, 1994. Environment, technology, and ethics, pp. 228–238. In Lori Gruen and Dale Jamieson, eds., *Reflecting on Nature: Readings in Environmental Philosophy*. Oxford University Press, New York, NY.

Lassman, Peter, 2011. *Pluralism.* Polity Press, Cambridge, MA.

Lessmann, Ortrud, and Felix Rauschmayer. 2013. Re-conceptualizing sustainable development on the basis of the capability approach: A model and its difficulties. *Journal of Human Development and Capabilities* Vol. 14, No. 1, pp. 95–114.

Light, Andrew, and Holmes Rolston III, eds., 2002. *Environmental Ethics: An Anthology.* Blackwell, Malden, MA.

Meinard, Yves, Malgorzata Dereniowska and Jean-Sébastien Gharbi, 2016. The ethical stakes in monetary valuation methods for conservation purposes. *Biological Conservation,* Vol. 199, pp. 67–74.

Minteer, Ben A. 2009. Anthropocentrism, pp. 58–62. In Callicott, J.B., Frodeman, R. eds., *Encyclopedia of Environmental Ethics and Philosophy.* Macmillan, Detroit, MI.

Mugerauer, Robert, and Lynne Manzo, 2008. *Environmental Dilemmas: Ethical Decision Making.* Lexington Books, Lanham, MD.

Muir, John, 1991. *Our National Parks.* Sierra Club Books, San Francisco, CA.

Neumayer, Eric, 1998. Preserving natural capital in a world of uncertainty and scarce financial resources. *International Journal of Sustainable Development and World Ecology,* Vol. 5, No. 1, pp. 27–42.

Neumayer, Eric, 2013. *Weak Versus Strong Sustainability: Exploring the Limits of Two Opposing Paradigms.* Edward Elgar, Cheltenham.

Nussbaum, Martha C., 2010. *Not For Profit. Why Democracy Needs The Humanities.* Princeton University Press, Princeton, NJ.

O'Neill, John, 1993. *Ecology, Policy and Politics: Human Well-Being and the Natural World.* Routledge, London.

O'Neill, John, Alan Holland, and Andrew Light, 2008. *Environmental Values.* Routledge, London and New York.

Pelenc, Jérôme, Minkieba Kevin Lompo, Jérôme Ballet, and Jean-Luc Dubois, 2013. Sustainable human development and the capability approach: Integrating environment, responsibility and collective agency. *Journal of Human Development and Capabilities,* Vol. 14, No 1, pp. 77–94.

Pezzey, John, 1992. Sustainability: An interdisciplinary guide. *Environmental Values,* Vol. 1, No. 4, pp. 321–362.

Piątek, Zdzisława. 1988. *Aspekty antropocentryzmu* [Aspects of Anthropocentism]. Jagiellonian University Press, Kraków.

Pinchot, Gifford, 1998, *Breaking New Ground.* Island Press, Washington, DC.

Pryshlakivsky, Jonathan, and Cory Searcy. 2013. Sustainable development as a wicked problem, pp. 109–128. In Samuel F. Kovacic and Andres Sousa-Poza, eds., *Managing and Engineering in Complex Situations.* Topics in Safety, Risk, Reliability and Quality 21. Springer Netherlands, Dordrecht.

Rescher, Nicholas, 1995, *Pluralism: Against the Demand for Consensus.* Clarendon Press, Oxford.

Rittel, Horst W. J., and Melvin M. Webber, 1973. Dilemmas in a general theory of planning. *Policy Sciences,* Vol. 4, No. 2, pp. 155–169.

Rolston III, Holmes, 1989. *Philosophy Gone Wild. Environmental Ethics.* Prometheus Books, Buffalo, NY.

Robinson, John, 2004. Squaring the circle? Some thoughts on the idea of sustainable development. *Ecological Economics,* Vol. 48, No. 4, pp. 369–384.

Schlosberg, David, 2002. *Environmental Justice and the New Pluralism: The Challenge of Difference for Environmentalism.* Oxford University Press, Oxford.

Sen, Amartya, 2013. The ends and means of sustainability. *Journal of Human Development and Capabilities,* Vol. 14, No. 1, pp. 6–20.

Söderbaum, Peter, 2007. Toward sustainability economics: Principles and values. *Journal of Bioeconomics,* Vol. 9, pp. 205–225.

Söderbaum, Peter, 2008. *Understanding Sustainability Economics. Towards Pluralism in Economics.* Earthscan/Routledge, London.

Söderbaum, Peter, 2012. Democracy and sustainable development. Implications for science and economics, *real-world economics review*, No. 60, 20 June 2012, pp. 107–119.

Söderbaum, Peter, 2014. The role of economics and democracy in institutional change for sustainability. *Sustainability*, Vol. 6, No. 5, pp. 2755–2765.

Sylvan (Routley), Richard, 2003. Is there a need for a new, an environmental ethic? pp, 47–52. In Andrew Light and Holmes Rolston III, eds., *Environmental Ethics: An Anthology*. Blackwell, Malden, MA.

Thorseth, May. 2015. Limitations to democratic governance of natural resources, pp. 36–52. In Dieter Birnbacher and May Thorseth, eds., *The Politics of Sustainability. Philosophical Perspectives*. Routledge/Eartscann, London.

Van der Sluijs, J., 2006. Uncertainty, assumptions, and value commitments in the knowledge-base of complex environmental problems, pp. 67–84. In Ângela Guimarães Pereira, Sofia Guedes Vaz and Sylvia Tognetti, eds., *Interfaces between Science and Society*. Green Leaf Publishing, Sheffield.

Waddock, Sandra, 2013. The wicked problems of global sustainability need wicked (good) leaders and wicked (good) collaborative solutions. *Journal of Management for Global Sustainability*, Vol. 1, no. 1, pp. 91–111.

Wenz, Peter S., 2001. *Environmental Ethics Today*. Oxford University Press, New York, NY.

Williams, Bernard, 1992. Must a concern for the environment be centred on human beings? pp. 60–68. In C.C.W. Taylor, ed., *Ethics and the Environment*. Corpus Christi College, Oxford.

Williams, Bruce A., and Albert R. Matheny, 1998. *Democracy, Dialogue, and Environmental Disputes: The Contested Languages of Social Regulation*. Yale University Press, New Haven, CT.

Wolf, Susan, 1992. Two levels of pluralism. *Ethics*, Vol. 102, No. 4, pp. 785–798.

Woods, Kerri, 2015. Climate justice, motivation and harm, pp. 92–108. In Dieter Birnbacher and May Thorseth, eds., *The Politics of Sustainability. Philosophical Perspectives*. Routledge/Eartscann, London.

World Commission on Environment and Development (WCED), 1987. *Our Common Future*. United Nations, Oxford.

8 Positional analysis and practical ethics

Małgorzata Dereniowska

Introductory remarks

Positional analysis (PA) is an approach that emphasizes an adaptive rationality and encourages expressions of democracy via a dialogical, open and inclusive process of searching for multifaceted illumination of a situation. The positional aspect implies thinking *about, across* and *with* difference – an aspect frequently overlooked, being treated as an inhibitor of knowledge integration and progress on policy matters. Yet through the focus and deliberation on differences between opinions and ideological orientations of different actors, a wealth of learning opportunities may occur. This raises a question about tools, modes of reasoning and competences enabling fruitful (even if not based on consensus) communication and the learning process. In this way, PA, with its emphasis on the importance of an ethically open process in arriving at sustainable outcomes, motivates the inquiry into what specific practical tools of ethical reasoning and procedures can be employed in democratic public dialogue for adjudicating among conflicting claims. In a PA framework, participatory research and decision-making on environmental and sustainability policy are encouraged. In both contexts, coupling factual and ethical analysis are required (Becker 2012; Tuana 2012; Tuana et al. 2012). The ethical components of scientific practices, public discourse and decision-making regarding sustainability are too often left unspoken and unanalyzed. Identifying ethical issues in public debate and connecting ethical reasoning with social action are essential to both navigating the challenges and inducing systemic, radical change (Brown 2012). This motivates me to focus specifically on ethical analysis as an inherent component of the PA framework and the challenges that ethics needs to address in participatory research and policy making.

The positions of individual and collective actors in public debates and policy making are frequently infused with values, ideologies, specific interests and power games that constitute the (often hidden) backdrop of many conflicts. Thus, it is no surprise that along with the uncertainty about facts, there is deep disagreement and lack of consensus about what is really at stake in decision-making regarding sustainability (or any social, economic or environmental policy, for that matter). Sustainability problems often involve multiplicity of ethically significant considerations. Part of the challenge is how to perform in a situation of dilemma and conflict, with a necessity to make urgent decisions and act in the face of *uncertainty* (most likely we do not know all of the relevant pieces of information, contextual aspects of the particular case to make the most informed decision; moreover, we have limited information about the consequences of our decisions), *indeterminacy* (it is not possible to determine one single most reasonable and rational answer to the problem in question) and *risk*.

This chapter considers the mechanisms of deliberation closure and making decisions in situations in which participants do not share a common ideological and value orientation and where there is no possibility of reaching full agreement about the outcome. This specific context has been to some degree neglected within the domain of moral philosophy insofar as moral dilemmas and conflicts are considered to result either from inconsistencies in our principles or from mistakenly having a plurality of principles without a covering theory or principle. Classical solutions focused on finding ways to prioritize principles, developing a covering theory or arriving at careful exception clauses (Marcus 1980).[1] A contrasting casuist method – a case-based reasoning approach sometimes used in applied and experimental ethics and jurisprudence – goes so far as to question the need and usefulness of more systematized ethical reasoning and theory building. Such an approach dissolves the possibility of universalized ethical thinking into discrete particularisms, which does little to enhance social cohesion and coordination of democratic action in the transition toward sustainability.

Of the various strategies for dealing with moral disagreement and value inconsistency, that developed by American philosopher Martin Benjamin is of special interest for a PA framework; it provides procedural tools for dealing with adaptive, dilemmatic, post-normal situations that are at the center of our current inquiry.[2] Such situations are characterized by circumstances that impede consensus and call for other modes of conflict accommodation, such as compromise. Benjamin differentiates five circumstances of what he calls *integrity-preserving compromise* (Benjamin 1990a, 2001, 2003):

- *Factual and metaphysical uncertainty.* In decision situations that require us to take a position, we rarely have fixed answers to our grand questions, such as whether nature possesses intrinsic value, whether an embryo is a moral person possessing full human rights, or how much nature do we need for future generations? These and similar questions about the ontological status of entities, endemic to scientific practices, constitute inherent difficulties in making decisions on the basis of observable facts. Making moral judgements in situations where reason, evidence and argument cannot provide for decisive and immutable responses suggests the intractability of ethical questions, or rather – under further constraints – calls for ethical compromise based on disciplined ethical reasoning.
- *Moral complexity.* Frequently the complex moral tapestry of the real world lends support to opposing morally relevant views, in light of which little hope exists for a quick elimination of differences by means of advanced singular ethical theory.

- *Continuing cooperative relationship.* Occasionally, individuals are engaged in collective projects (e.g. in the work place, academic projects, political action, etc.), being embedded in a web of relationships with others. Analogically, organizations do not operate within a social and economic vacuum, and occasionally cooperation and network building require taking consideration of the position of other organizations or collective actors.
- *Impending nondeferrable decision.* On policy matters that require urgent decisions, relevant parties usually do not enjoy the luxury of interminable debate. Typically, a practical choice without philosophical or factual certainty must be made, making compromise an alternative to consensus. Even if no flawless solutions can be advanced, their limitations are not sufficient to discard them if a position must be taken on the matter and when the available alternatives may be shown to have limits or flaws as well.
- *Limited resources.* Even in situations not constrained by factual or metaphysical uncertainty, there are at least two classes of circumstances that may call for compromise: (a) disputes over the distribution of scarce goods and services, such as access to land or goods like transplantable organs or access to health care services and (b) cases where time limits the possibilities for increasing knowledge or achieving adequate deliberation for consensual agreement. For instance, climate change negotiations can be considered to fall under this constraint. Moreover, sometimes even in situations in which a decision is not urgent, postponing of a decision may drastically increase the financial, social or ecological costs of inaction.

These circumstances of compromise are those conditions that provide both the motivation and the justification for political compromise. Sustainability controversies frequently are characterized by these conditions, motivating the inquiry into how we can consistently envision compromise as a procedural model of political conflict resolution and whether it could undermine both dealing with multiple moral frameworks and the need for a continuous ethical debate and ethical scrutiny. Last, but not least, isn't compromise a morally dubious rule for public deliberation?

The goal of this chapter is to inquire into procedural foundations for moral reasoning in decision-making. Building on Benjamin's practical ethics model, my objective is to discuss tools of practical ethical analysis and practical reasoning for dealing with radical dissensus in the specific case of a decision situation characterized by the conditions of compromise. PA and Benjamin's philosophy of conflict share some important procedural points linked to moral pluralism and its implications for public debate and decision-making processes with no necessary stopping point, where outcomes are always subject to revision. PA allows conflicts to be made visible and perspectives and ideologies to be discussed through employment of various participatory methods. This poses questions about how such an open approach to decision-making can provide good solutions without succumbing to anything goes relativism and how to engage competing ethical frameworks, ideologies and values in the face of insoluble conflicts.

The first part of the chapter outlines and examines the six-component model of practical ethics developed by Benjamin, preparing the ground for fleshing out the relationship between Benjamin's philosophy of conflict and PA as a decision-making approach. It is argued that his model of practical ethics is well suited to addressing the ethical dimensions of scientific practices, decision-making and public debate for sustainability. In the second part, elements of Benjamin's practical ethics model will be related to some of the theoretical and practical challenges of PA and sustainability decision-making. Benjamin's model provides a tool for thinking about the process that occurs both when PA is carried out and afterwards for deciding on alternatives. That pertains to how conditional input can be used, through what kind of decision-making procedure, in post-normal situations, and what rule to use for arriving at a decision using multidimensional information.

Martin Benjamin's practical ethics model

The emphasis on the issue of moral pluralism and an ethical dimension in PA for sustainable development raises questions of how the role of ethics is to be understood. This is the case in accounting for the normative aspects of sustainable development and in the question of how to reintroduce ethical reasoning in policy context and put ethical requirements into practice. The contextuality and situatedness of moral claims suggest moral pluralism as an inevitable element of moral life, and that any workable model of practical ethics needs to deal with the question of how to address dilemmas, cognitive and moral dissonance and conflict, especially in areas where legitimate differences cannot be rationally settled. Acceptance of various forms and levels of pluralism is important for building democratic capacity for change. However, accepting pluralism is not sufficient for ensuring that the constructive potential of this diversity will be used to build a dialogic space for collective action due to the fact that diverse attitudes toward difference exist (Najder-Stefaniak 2014). A model of ethical decision-making that is not necessarily predicated on consensus, but which at the same time constructively addresses rationally irreducible differences and power-laden conflicts can be facilitated with Benjamin's practical ethics model, of which he distinguishes the following points (2001):

1   Interdisciplinary considerations
2   A pragmatic conception of moral reasoning
3   Moral pluralism
4   Democratic temperament
5   Conflict accommodation and compromise
6   A correspondingly complex conception of ethical theory

These elements, which I briefly present and discuss below, provide concrete ethical tools for making multiperspectival judgements and procedures for resolving conflicts. They are particularly appealing and suitable for dealing with sustainability issues by addressing the need for interdisciplinary considerations and providing procedures for situations characterized by indeterminacy, uncertainty and multileveled risk. Indeed, the dual realization that the external world does not operate deterministically as a closed system but is rather an open system characterized by increasing complexity not fully grasped by even the most refined scientific models, and that science works with and is characterized by significant uncertainty (for a comprehensive overview of uncertainty and how science deals with it, see Van der Sluijs 2006) reminds us of the importance of addressing the limits of our knowledge and ethical scrutiny.

Inter- and transdisciplinary considerations

Practical ethics,[3] in addressing complex problems such as organ transplants, climate policies and the like, necessarily draws from factual knowledge. For this reason, as Benjamin argues, in practice, 'there can be no compartmentalized division of labor between theoretical and practical ethics and factual understanding' (2001, p. 25). The empirical claims that are important to our ethical thinking are not so easy for philosophers to ascertain on their own, and, as it is often noted, no clear line exists between facts and norms. Thus, philosophers need to collaborate with one or more specialists or take great pains to learn another discipline's work on their own. Analogically, 'hard' science analysts need philosophers to adequately account for the ambiguity of the interface between science and values.

Applied sciences, by default, are normative: prescriptive judgements are formed as part of standard applied research practice and used for informing policy choices. The interdisciplinary debate about the economic valuation of nature illustrates how both ethical convictions of researchers as well as the ethical underpinnings of specific economic concepts interact in shaping scientists' attitudes (e.g. conservation biologists concerned primarily with the intrinsic value of nature versus the anthropocentrism of standard economic valuation methods) and the take on the subject of study (O'Neill et al. 2008; Meinard et al. 2016). Practically and methodologically it matters whether the prescriptive judgements are elaborated in a discursive and cooperative way (Nowak 2013). Especially in the context of sustainable development, applied sciences that contribute to its understanding and solutions have to face this issue. The multidisciplinary and transdisciplinary nature of work in sustainability have been widely acknowledged, raising calls for various versions of pluralism as a way of approaching the breadth of sources from which they draw and for integrating factual and ethical analyses (Popa et al. 2015; Spangenberg 2011; Becker 2012).

Crossing of disciplinary boundaries has a two-fold advantage. As Benjamin puts it, 'no hard and fast line between facts and values, science and ethics' is provided; 'values are revisited in the light of facts, and facts are revisited in the light of values' (2003, p. 121). In other words, conducting ethical analysis as part of practical reasoning involves not only ethical theory (principles, values, etc.) and empirical facts: the interaction between these two realms may also lead to changes in our conceptions of each (Benjamin 2001). The genesis and development of environmental ethics as a discipline illustrate this point well: the scientific knowledge base of human-induced ecological crises motivated rethinking the mainstream anthropocentric moral thought, arguing for a necessary extension of our moral considerations to the non-human world. Also ethical debates within the public sphere about the social and environmental consequences of scientific practices may lead to questioning how we arrive at facts and how different methodological routes can lead to different factual images. Noteworthy here are the transdisciplinary collaborations between environmental justice activists and concerned scientists searching for new ways to produce knowledge more relevant to local needs and social action via community-based participatory research methods, leading in some cases to significant transformation of science and engineering (Ottinger and Cohen 2011).

The importance of considering ethically and politically laden sustainability questions from an interdisciplinary perspective arises also due to the fact that environmental problems are so thoroughly integrated with other issues (most notably, economic and social matters) that solving them in isolation may only raise or exacerbate problems elsewhere (Dereniowska and Matzke 2014). For example, setting aside tillable land to provide protected habitat for threatened ground birds might raise the cost of food, a situation felt most sharply by those already economically marginalized. Or similarly, turning to hydroelectric power to curb carbon emissions can permanently destroy both aquatic systems and the means by which local people make a living. Whatever the answers, the various issues cannot be separated. Drawing on a wide array of disciplines and ways of knowing facilitates a better understanding of real-world issues, and grounds it in multiple cultural, historical and social conditionings present both in societal belief systems and scientific inquiry. A better awareness of these conditions is crucial for developing more meaningful and efficacious understandings and policies (Dereniowska and Matzke 2014).

Moral pluralism

A common thread in diverse accounts of moral pluralism is the belief that more than one set of competing values, principles, theories or judgements of particular cases can be morally legitimate but nevertheless rationally evaluated (see Chapter 7). According to Benjamin, the position of moral pluralism is best understood as a middle ground between subjective relativism and objective absolutism (Benjamin 2003). Objective absolutism correctly holds out for objectivity but wrongly links it with something absolute or outside of human experience and thought (Benjamin 2003, p. 119). By 'objective' Benjamin meant, following Hilary Putnam, 'objective from the point of view of our best and most reflective practice', in other words, 'objectivity humanly speaking' (Putnam 1994, 177n). Subjective relativism emphasizes a certain kind of legitimate relativism: judgements, principles, theories are relative to the best available background beliefs and non-moral theories at our disposal. However, it hardly follows that they are 'merely' subjective, little more than matters of taste or naked preference (Benjamin 2003, p. 120). Accepting pluralism does not presuppose any particular position with regard to validation and the legitimization of claims. Conversely to descriptive relativism, which assumes that any particular opinion or claim is relative to something (be it culture, agent, etc.), pluralism does not imply that opinion and so on, is relative to anything. In the first place, pluralism recognizes the existence of diversity, but this diversity can have different sources, can occur at many levels and also can result from all sorts of biases. Thus, Benjamin distinguishes, following Cohen (1993) and Rawls (1993), between *pluralism as such* and *reasonable pluralism*. The former pertains to plural and conflicting values resulting from selfishness, prejudice, ignorance, bad reasoning, and so on, together with plural and conflicting values that remain even when these things are overcome. The latter falls under *reasonable* pluralism (Benjamin 2003, p. 125).[4] Moral pluralism is a fact about the world, and an applied ethical theory and its practical requirements must take account of it:

> To embrace only a single dominant value from which others may possibly be derived is to invite a different kind of madness, a monomaniacal narrowness that borders on fanaticism and repudiates the richness and complexity of human life. A more plausible (and mediating) possibility is to embrace a useful, relatively rich and coherent, but occasionally conflicting, subset of good values and principles while acknowledging the reasonableness of certain alternative subsets.
>
> (Benjamin 2003, pp. 128–129)

From a moral and philosophical point of view, the most interesting is that form of pluralism, in which different reasonable interpretations lead to rationally irreducible difference at the level of judgement about a particular case. This is the kind of pluralism that interests Benjamin the most, and which seems to be particularly relevant from the perspective of sustainability and moral decision-making, motivating the pluralistic orientation. The requirement of adaptiveness for sustainability policies points to the increased role of deliberation between various political actors. These different players represent, however, different and sometimes divergent values and ideologies. The objection is that moral pluralism may be potentially incompatible with ideas of collective change in beliefs, moral outlook and ideology and make public discourse meaningless. The pragmatic conception of moral reasoning and justification will provide some insights into how to prevent such relativism and eclecticism.

Pragmatic conception of moral reasoning and justification

What it is to do practical ethics is an important concern. For Benjamin, this involves the description (and prescription) of a process that involves moving among various levels of cognition (such as theory and judgements about particular cases), ways of thought (such as imagination and reason) and kinds of beliefs (such as those regarding how the world works and value commitments). His account, which is general enough to accommodate a wide range of views regarding the metaphysics of morals, is based on pluralistic moral epistemology that involves a simplified representation of a working moral framework as a *ship of morality* (Benjamin 2003). Benjamin uses Otto Neurath's metaphor of the 'ship of knowledge'[5] to articulate and clarify the operation of moral practices. Moral practice, on this account, cannot be based entirely on abstract, impersonal reason removed from the affective motives; nor does it assume the possibility of resolving every moral conflict without reminder.

According to this moral epistemology, moral beliefs arise from a combination of biology (kin selection, altruism and survival instincts) and society (constructed norms that are tied in some way to our biological inheritance). At some point, we are of an age to participate more in the critical evaluation of our beliefs and values. We do so like fixing and rebuilding a ship while sailing in the ocean, with no chance to take to dry dock and inspect. Importantly, no aspect of a moral framework is, in principle, immune to correction or improvement. Yet we do, on reflection, note that some of our beliefs are more firmly held than are others. Once we identify particular moral judgements in which we have great confidence, we then look for rules and principles that organize or support them. These rules and principles unify and reveal the underlying rationales for our judgements of particular cases (Benjamin 2003, p. 122). However, even though we each experience only a small part of the world, shared human experience and problems create the need for, according to Benjamin (2003), *reflective equilibrium* and *inter-subjective discourse* that shape our inherited moral views.

Reflective equilibrium originated in the philosophy of science. Nelson Goodman developed it as a way of assessing the justification of rules of inference in inductive and deductive logic (1995), and it was subsequently adapted for social-political theory, most notably by Rawls (1971),[6] and eventually ethics (Daniels 1996; Benjamin 1990a,b, 2003; Vokey 2001) as a way to deal with diversity of views and the incommensurability of values. In this latter use, it seeks a middle ground between unjustified optimism that we can find single correct answers to moral questions and postmodern relativism that says truth is a matter merely of cultural or personal perspective.

The term 'equilibrium' is taken in economics as having specific connotations to market equilibrium and thereby carries the associated baggage of underlying philosophical assumptions such as that it is possible to attain a perfect, lasting equilibrium state. Although both economic equilibrium and equilibrium in moral and political philosophy can be considered subsets or cases of mathematical equilibrium, their content and the way they are used differ tremendously. Reflective equilibrium in moral and political thought is larger in the sense that it includes the processes that lead to an outcome. It is sometimes entirely a procedural concept (Rawls 1971), while economists take account of process only insofar as it may change the outcome. In moral and political philosophy, equilibrium pertains to the thought processes balancing at least two of the various levels of thinking: (a) judgements regarding particular cases, (b) principles or theories or (c) background beliefs and worldviews. Thus, reflective equilibrium is a procedural concept referring to the process of achieving equilibrium, however, dynamic and modified through time.

Reflective equilibrium as presented by Benjamin (1990a, 2003, 2005) is a process (not a finished and final end state) of seeking as much consistency among our various beliefs, theories, models, metaphors, paradigms and any other element of our mental and emotive lives. The 'glue' among these elements consists of *connectedness, interdependency* and *mutual support* among these various levels of our thinking and feeling. It privileges no single belief but recognizes differences between beliefs based on how well they fit with other beliefs. When inconsistencies are discovered, possible responses include rejecting that belief, modifying it to fit with other beliefs or modifying or rejecting other beliefs to make room for the new belief. Wide reflective equilibrium, on Benjamin's account, has primarily practical value, being a procedural tool for dealing with partial and different perspectives,[7] both within and between individuals.

To clarify further, in this context, 'reflective' does not mean purely rational, but something more like reasonable. It refers to an ongoing process that is at least thoughtful and critical; this ongoing process admits that achieving 'equilibrium' is only temporary, demanding continuous reflection and adjustments in the face of the complexity of human life, complete with ethical conflicts and disagreements. Second, 'equilibrium' describes the goal of attaining as much coherence as possible within personal and interpersonal spheres, even when complete unity of beliefs and values is out of reach. Personal coherence simply means the matching process in decision situations that satisfies the conditions of wide reflective equilibrium better than other alternatives. Interpersonal coherence implies that individual answers considered along with the answers of others strive toward as much congruence between each other as possible, without implying the necessity of complete unanimity for the sake of making joint decisions (Benjamin 2003, p. 122).

Third, although reflective equilibrium is a process one can undertake within a specific area of human thought (such as ethics), it becomes 'wide' reflective equilibrium when its scope is expanded to include a more comprehensive variety of beliefs (also based on science, religion, etc.). The reason to include also our general beliefs in the process of moral evaluation is to provide a background against which we can eliminate the illegitimate arguments (e.g. those based on oppression, domination or hatred) in the deliberative process. Conversely to the Rawlsian thought experiment in which original position implies impartiality, Benjamin claims that in practice we are entering the decision situation while already carrying the luggage of existing views, beliefs and so on, each of which impact our perceptions, judgements and choices (2005).

Understood in this way, and with an emphasis on *an ongoing process* with no final end state, the method of wide reflective equilibrium is quite commonsense, as this is the process in which every subject engages with (more or less consciously) from the first moment of self-realization (Wenz 2007). Through articulation and a more conscious engagement in gauging among various aspects of our moral frameworks, we become better democratically tempered to tackle the collective, complex challenges of public policies on sustainability (and other matters).

Democratic temperament

One of the underlying intuitions of moral pluralism is the scepticism about the feasibility of a Platonic quest for final harmony. Benjamin challenges the modern over-reliance on rationalization as the means for achieving that harmony (1990a). Rather, given the indisputable fact of moral pluralism, our best alternative in the realm of ethics is to treat it as an ongoing process of deliberative reflection that strives toward greater consistency and depends to a great extent on competences for making reasonable judgements. However, if through sustained deliberation consensus is impossible to reach, the matter may be left undecided or put to a vote. Wanting to move beyond the deadlock without using one's power or privilege to force an answer requires one to exhibit certain personal capacities (Benjamin 2001, p. 28). Benjamin builds here on Miller's (1997) term, 'democratic temperament',[8] to denote a capacity to combine 'support for particular positions on moral and political issues with respect for opposing yet reasonable positions on the same issues' (Benjamin 2001, p. 28).

In cases of reasonable disagreement, democratic temperament disposes one to 'share the power to shape and make decisions with those affected by them' (Benjamin 2001, p. 29). It implies that socially embedded individuals are simultaneously both agents and spectators (although in various proportions and to different degrees): 'As agents, we are inclined to act on our particular values and principles. As spectators, we are inclined to respect those, who act on opposing but nonetheless reasonable, values and principles' (Benjamin 2003, p. 124). This is the arena where moral pluralism raises equivocality in our human inclinations, and bringing together the aspects of agent and spectator requires a certain capacity. The democratic temperament outstretches the spectrum through which the moral subject is moving from an objective, impersonal spectator embracing universal ideals, to an embodied subject fully immersed in her experience (Benjamin 2003). This idea is implicit in Söderbaum's account of the individual's functioning in the society: 'a healthy individual has a strong ego but is able to at the same time more or less internalize the interests of others' (2008, p. 59). The notion of democratic temperament explains the possibility of the varying degrees to which a person can accommodate other-regarding concerns, while the interplay between the agent and the spectator makes clearer the intertwining affective and cognitive elements and how they play out in interactive public deliberation.

Approximating an impersonal position need not mean or assume cold rational deduction and disregard for affective aspects of moral behavior. Rather it can be seen as an exercise of mutual respect despite stark differences and an imaginative trying out of another person's shoes, so to speak. As Benjamin notes, 'Your democratic temperament leads you to believe both in the superiority of your particular position and in the value of arriving at some sort of agreement on the policy question that reflects the complexity of the question and pays equal respect to those holding the opposing reasonable position on what seems, at least for now, to be rationally irreconcilable conflict' (2003, p. 141). Moral and political agents can be viewed as beings who employ both passions and reason in decision-making and who are both self and others oriented. This idea relates to Söderbaum's (2000, 2008) notion of political economic person (PEP). PEP is viewed as a person in a community, where the logic of 'I' is embedded in a web of relational logic of 'We' (i.e. other-regarding and acting reciprocally in balancing the interests of individuals in their diverse roles and society). The logic of 'We' leads to conceiving reciprocal rationality and an emphasis on norms of cooperating and thinking in the horizon of responsibility that facilitates modifying the attitudes of PEPs (Söderbaum 2000, 2008). It is related to the choice of paradigm for acting within society, which suggests two different underlying epistemologies: of isolation and of participation. Democratic temperament put into practice can explain the possibility of making different judgements about similar cases in diverging circumstances and be a vehicle for the adaptation of individuals to changing contexts. Also the prospect of universalizing some normative aspirations (such as including future generations in our moral community and granting them rights) relies on democratic temperament as the ability to proficiently move between particularisms (e.g. self-interest) and non-particularisms (e.g. collective responsibility) while continuously revising the moral outlook. The notion of democratic temperament aligns with the growing acknowledgement of the important role of skills and adaptive learning in sustainability problem solving.

Conflict accommodation and compromise

The question of how to deal with and to act in the face of moral disagreement is an inescapable component of any ethical program. David Wong emphasized the need for more attention to conflict accommodation in situations in which agreement cannot be reached; these may include arbitration, synthesis, reconciliation and compromise (1992). The problem of conflict accommodation was for quite some time somewhat ignored by moral philosophers, partly due to a more fundamental question about the conceptual possibility of the existence of moral dilemmas.[9] One way to deny the existence of moral dilemmas was to suggest that exception clauses can be added to principles or that principles can be rank ordered to resolve any apparent dilemmas. In either case, the underlying assumption is a monistic quest for a 'complete set of rules, priorities, or qualifications which would, in every possible case, unequivocally mandate a single course of action' (Marcus 1980, p. 124). It is not surprising, then, that the focus on developing a complete, holistic ethical theory results in leaving unattended the practical need of dealing in specific situations with rationally irreconcilable difference.

Speaking about compromise as a way for conflict accommodation evokes the commonly held view of compromise as a betrayal of moral ideals and values: compromising on moral principles is seen to disvalue one's own integrity and credibility as moral agent. Against this view, Benjamin asks whether compromise can be, at least in some cases, *integrity preserving* (1990a). Acceptable compromise is not necessarily agreeing with the other side that a third, middle ground is the correct moral position. Rather, it is acknowledging that, *all things considered*, a third position is the best position. There is a grand difference, then, between *compromising one's moral position* and *compromise as it is necessary for the well functioning of a democracy*. On the latter's account, a compromise position need not be seen as the correct moral position, narrowly defined. Rather, it is about the necessity of taking a position when one considers several additional items, such as the import of non-coercive, peaceful agreement, the length of admissible rationally irreducible differences (Benjamin 2003, p. 141), and the various roles in which the antagonists find themselves (e.g. as citizens, managers, activists and the like). Sometimes, when we take all of this into account, compromise becomes not just acceptable, but required: one is 'committed to resolving the policy question on terms that pay equal respect to the contending reasonable positions and that stand a chance of public acceptability' (Benjamin 2003, p. 141). All the while, each party can continue to try to persuade the other side of the rightness of its position (p. 136).

Compromise is advisable as a method of conflict accommodation in specific situations characterized by the aforementioned five circumstances of compromise. They include factual and metaphysical uncertainty, moral complexity, continuing cooperative relationship, impending nondeferrable decision and limited resources. The more these conditions are obtained, the stronger the initial case for pursuing the compromise although there is no clear-cut formula for determining how many of these conditions need to be meet before going for compromise (Benjamin 1990a, p. 32).

Legitimate compromise, as presented by Benjamin, necessarily consists of both the *process* and the *outcome*. Paying attention only to compromise as an outcome can wrongly give support to agreements arising from unequal distributions of power and coercion. This cannot be fair compromise (Benjamin 1990a, pp. 4–8). Similarly, fair procedure of compromise can potentially lead to an uneven 'splitting the difference', to borrow Benjamin's book title (1990a), between opposing positions. The standard sense of compromise is, therefore, *a settlement of differences by mutual concessions* for mutual gain, through reciprocally regardful 'give-and-take discussion' on a singular course of action for the sake of agreement (Benjamin 2003, p. 136).[10] It is, thus, a discursive method of conflict accommodation engaging adversarial reasoning, but it differs from negotiations insofar as emphasis is put on rational persuasion on mutual concessions. Strictly speaking, the standard case of compromise is not a conflict resolution, as it has a built-in component that does not allow closing down ethical debate. As Benjamin reminds us, 'there is no closure. Although the question of public policy may, for the time being, be settled, the ethical question remains open, and you are free, as an individual, to continue to make the case for the truth as you see it' (Benjamin 2003, pp. 141–142).

Although the standard cases of compromise encompass both process and outcome based on mutual concessions, there are special cases that allow us to devise more substantive policy outcomes. Many decision situations about sustainable projects or environmental goods display such characteristics. For example, under conditions of disagreement over a good that is not sharable or divisible, there is no possibility to substantively split the difference. In such cases, the only possibility may be, as Benjamin (1990a) argues, *a purely procedural compromise* that yields *an intermediate outcome.* The parties partaking in a conflict over a more-or-less indivisible good may come together to 'a mutually satisfactory decision to abide by the outcome of a subsequent process' (1990a, p. 6). In other words, the special case of compromise allows all involved parties to jointly decide on the procedure that will subsequently produce a disproportionate outcome. The agreement on the procedure that pays equal consideration and respect to all participants is, in this specific case, the only plausible participatory way forward that allows all affected parties to engage in the decision.

In moral and democratic practice, compromise is not only necessary, but it may be also a condition of an integrated life within the social, collective context. Compromise need not always amount to moral capitulation but can advance, and in fact often is necessary for, the preservation of integrity. Key to this argument is, first, the distinction and interrelation between political and moral compromise (e.g. moral commitments can include democratic ideals and an awareness of irreducible difference). Second, seeing oneself as a part of a larger community in which decisions must be made – as opposed to a tempting but overly idealistic image of one's own perfection against a degraded society – is essential to a full appreciation and effective use of compromise.

Correspondingly complex conception of moral theory

The challenge against which Benjamin formulates the demand for a complex conception of moral theory is well illustrated by Hilary Putnam: 'when a philosopher "solves" an ethical problem for one, one feels as if one had asked for a subway token and been given a passenger ticket valid for the first interplanetary passenger-carrying spaceship instead' (1990, p. 179). The conceptions of theory in 'spaceship ethics' are too detached from practical contexts, whereas 'subway ethics' boils down to mere casuistry or radical particularism. The common underlying assumption between these two extremes, Benjamin argues, is of the comprehensiveness and singularity of the ethical theory. The disputants on each side just formulate and approach it in different ways:

> Casuists and particularists emphasize the inadequacies of such theories for real-life decision-making and conclude that efforts to systematize and find general theoretical justification for our moral choices and judgments are misconceived. Kantians and utilitarians [representative of the 'spaceship ethics'] try to develop such a theory, but invariably fall short when confronted with the kinds of cases and contexts emphasized by casuists and particularians.
>
> (Benjamin 2001, p. 30)

Many moral and political theorists have challenged the idea that it is a reasonable expectation that ethical theory must be singular and comprehensive (Berlin 2000; Benjamin 2001; Nagel 2000). A more modest and complex conception of ethical theory would aim, as Benjamin suggests, not so much for one umbrella theory but for 'a *family* of non-comprehensive ethical theories achieving as much systematic generalization and justification as the various contexts and subject matters will allow' (Benjamin 2001, p. 30). This proposal addresses the concerns about the potentially undemocratic character of strong versions of the monistic non-anthropocentric ethics for policy formation, on the one hand (Minteer 2012), and the requirement of communicatively engaging multiple normative perspectives in decision-making good practices, on the other hand (Dryzek 1995; Thorseth 2015).

The demand for a correspondingly complex moral theory is linked with a practical question about how to do problem-driven ethics. Ethical consideration must not rely only on the question of what ethics requires in the abstract; after all, different ethical theories may lead to different, or even conflicting, positions on particular matters. From the perspective of environmental ethics, the question of the adequacy of philosophical theories and concepts when applied to urgent global problems like climate change is not solely a question of theoretical reorientation but also a question of how to use them in practice, which entails the ability to make reasonable judgements. In a practical context, given the uncertainty we face at every level, we are forced to draw from experience and understanding to make judgements. It seems plausible to assume that there is no overarching, all-covering model or theory by which to do this with exactitude at all situations at all times. A theory or approach should facilitate instead of replace good judgement (Wenz 1988, p. 314). Nevertheless, theory building remains an important task as it plays a role, for example, in the articulation and evaluation of social values and beliefs (Dereniowska and Matzke 2014).

Furthermore, one could point to limited hope in the feasibility of the project of arrival at the monistic theory that will provide easy and unambiguous guidance for policy (at least any time soon). In such contexts, pluralism does not suggest eclecticism or embracing views that are diametrically opposed to one's own beliefs, but it does suggest that compromise may be integrity preserving under circumstances of reasonable disagreement. How, then, could the role of ethics in a policy context be defined? Ewa Nowak sums up as follows:

> Ethics does not provide ready answers. Neither does it take over citizens' right to rationally co-decide which solutions are the best for the whole, diversified and pluralistic, society. Rather, it is the source of normative tools and argumentative procedures that allows agents to reach their independent conclusions. At least this is what it should look like in a democratic society.
>
> (2013, p. 54)

PA and ethical decision-making

In this part, I consider in more detail some of the components of Benjamin's practical ethics that raise challenges as a complementary procedural tool for PA application in policy making. They include some of the questions that the pragmatic conception of moral reasoning and compromise raise from the positional perspective.

Pragmatic conception of moral reasoning and justification – grounded by Benjamin in wide reflective equilibrium – raises questions about the possibility of inter- and intra-personal application. From the perspective of the PA framework, one of the objections for the use of wide reflective equilibrium on the collective level pertains to the question of how this tool accommodates differences. Reflective equilibrium as a tool can be used in various ways and takes into account in various ways difference and pluralism.[11] With reference to moral practice, for a monist, the goal would be to eventually find the single right moral theory or set of principles that we could then apply in all similar cases. Unlike the monists' use of reflective equilibrium, an appreciation of rationally irreducible difference is, for pluralists, an assumption one brings to the process. Reflective equilibrium can be taken as a balancing of arguments understood by one person or between more people and can be applied to situations where people do not necessarily share an ideological orientation. Wide reflective equilibrium is not constructed to deny differences in opinions and ideologies but rather to help in searching for points of *convergence, mutual support* and *interconnectedness* (even among incommensurable elements) of our thinking about the world, even if incomplete and dynamically changing.

Wide reflective equilibrium is related to PA and Söderbaum's account of decision situations (see Chapter 1, Figure 1.1), in which making a decision is understood as a process of matching an ideological orientation of an individual and the impact of each alternative of choice (see Figure. 8.1).

Translating into reflective equilibrium language, an ideological orientation pertains to the beliefs of an individual (or a mission of an organization) and specific values and principles held. The projected impact of alternatives is a judgement about a particular case. To put it in other words, the decision-making process understood as a matching of ideological positions and expected outcomes can be construed as a specific case of reflective equilibrium. The suggestion here is to widen the perspective to include the third component – that is, background beliefs – to make explicit room in PA for the widely held ideals (such as the importance of

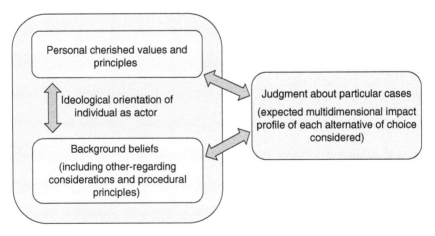

Figure 8.1 Positional decision-making as a process of wide reflective equilibrium.

democracy, freedom, dignity and the like) and to ensure the attunement of each party involved in decision-making to the voices of others (both as a widely held procedural principle to respect and to listen to others, and – during the process of matching, or balancing – as an intersubjective, collectively shaped arena of constantly reformulating these ideals, values, knowledge, etc.). It is not to say that in PA the process of taking decisions involves only narrow balancing, possibly too relative to specific ideologies; indeed, it emphasizes the importance of public scrutiny and deliberation to avoid such biases, and the reference to wide reflective equilibrium is meant to articulate further these points.

An example of collective reflective equilibrium comes from practices within the scientific community of inquiry. Within science, a more narrow reflective equilibrium is undertaken when observations are found to be inconsistent with the dominant view. As Kuhn (1962) notes, in normal science (as opposed to the rare moments of paradigm shift), the challenging observation is sometimes set aside for further research under the assumption that it will be made eventually to fit with the dominant theory. However, other times the new observation might be made to cohere with the reigning theory by making adjustments somewhere in the theory. For example, predator/prey models that held that predator and prey populations follow each other's increases and decreases with some mathematical precision were challenged by field data that suggested otherwise. In this case, the options available to researchers included, among others, that the specific species studied are simply related in more complex ways, that the study noticed a mere anomaly that left the theory untouched or that the theory itself needed modification.

The process of wide reflective equilibrium can be illustrated by two historical examples. The first draws from Kuhn's favorite example of paradigm shifts in science: the gradual rejection of Ptolemaic astronomy in favor of the Copernican model. As Kuhn (1962) points out, the latter was not necessarily better at making accurate predictions but was favored by some because its elimination of the need for epicycles to plot planetary movements was more elegant. New paradigms are accepted not simply for the reason they more accurately describe a phenomenon but for reasons ranging from ontological simplicity to generality in application. To see wide reflective equilibrium at work in this example, it is instructive to notice the reaction of the Catholic Church, which rejected the new model because it did not cohere with certain religiously held beliefs. If the earth is not the center of the universe (or solar system), perhaps human beings are not the center of God's attention. One way in which consistency of belief could be maintained was through the rejection of the heliocentric model. However, others responded differently by altering certain beliefs they already held to make room for what they saw was an otherwise attractive model; this group concluded that the physical arrangement of the universe has nothing to do with the non-physical centeredness of humanity in a religious system. The second example is similar. Darwinism was rejected by many precisely because it challenged their views of Biblical interpretation, beliefs in creation and special status of human beings. Others made room in their belief system for evolutionary explanations by coming to see evolution as one of the ways the divine acts in the cause-effect material world; it is how God creates. Still others chose to reject belief in the divine all together, seeing no need for divine intervention when a purely physical explanation was at hand. The point in both of these familiar examples is that wide reflective equilibrium involves the continued search for consistency among a wide range of views as we are confronted with new ideas and experiences.

A point of clarification is in order: as I consider this method at the science, policy and society interface, it would be a misdescription of our situation to think that we start with new empirical models from science and beliefs/values from elsewhere and try to construct from the ground up a consistent set of beliefs that would then inform our policy directions. Rather, we already have – both within each of us and communally – deeply held beliefs of all sorts. As we come together to better understand new issues, we are putting together ideas (new and old) in novel ways. Inevitably we notice conflicts both within science and ethics (and other ways of understanding) and between them. We move to resolve inconsistencies, acknowledging complexity, incommensurability and disagreement. Some ideas will congeal more thoroughly with others although it is plausible to assume that we will not find complete harmony, at least anytime soon.

Wide reflective equilibrium helps to better articulate the requirement for scrutiny and transparency. It makes pluralistic approaches (e.g. methodological or to decision-making) fairly immune to the objection that they offer merely an eclecticism or a coin-flipping. The standard objection to a pluralistic model is that it may allow anyone (researchers, special interest groups or decision makers) to use any of the potentially incommensurable arguments to construct support for their narrow interests. An actor resistant to climate policy that limited their continued use of fossil fuels to generate electricity, for example, could pick and choose climate models strategically. However, it is wide reflective equilibrium's constant push for consistency that may prevent this objection from materializing. In fact, both the elements of reflectiveness and equilibrium put boundaries on acceptable positions in taking decision. Some ideas (e.g. race as a scientific classification system) are not going to fit genuine and wide reflective equilibrium given the number, strength and connection of other empirical views as well as ethical and political convictions.

PA is an ethically open approach, and it is at the same time a learning process. Each actor is responsible for her own arguments and may change them (and modify her ideological orientation) when confronted with the arguments of other decision makers or concerned actors. However, on the collective level, this raises questions about representation and whose ideas about reflective equilibrium or compromise count, and how they come together.[12] A potential problem exists in relation to the criteria of *interdependency, connectedness* and *mutual support* as they bring together the content under the process of reflective equilibrium – given its role in crafting compromise. Wide reflective equilibrium, following Benjamin, is about the process of reasoning that does not predetermine the outcome or the content of a reached equilibrium. It does not naively presume the necessary trade-offs between moral efficiency, on the one hand, and concrete efficiency that allows narrow interests to materialize, on the other hand. Nonetheless, it may raise the problem of disparity in representation and misrecognition, with the criteria of interdependency, connectedness and mutual support between the positions admitted to the debate and decision-making. The question is whether it can prevent the possibility that only those voices that are most numerous or well articulated will be granted significance in producing the outcome, increasing the disempowerment of those in minority positions.

To respond to this problem, a few points can be made. As a purely procedural tool, narrow reflective equilibrium can be used in a technocratic way, to rationalize power interests in the name of coherence with the majority-shared ideology. However, the widening of perspective against the possibility of rationalizing bias or prejudice necessitates the inclusion in our considerations of both substantive claims of interests and procedural commitments. The latter encompass, for example, the right to be heard or that minority voices are granted an equal consideration against the disparity of representation. This is to ensure that both the process and resulting output do not perpetuate the existing structural, systemic inequalities that disempower or oppress different or minority voices (a problem that motivated Rawls to envision an ideal situation). Wide reflective equilibrium, thus, offers considerable potential if used in give-and-take discussions based on mutual respect, providing grounds for fair outcomes even if consensus is out of reach. A compromise in such contexts requires not only *an equal consideration* of asserted reasonable claims of underrepresented positions, even if these are radically different from the majority view, but also *equal priority* in crafting solution. In other words, equal consideration is paid to all involved parties through the process and in the outcome resulting not just from a search for mutual connection, interdependence and mutual support between substantive claims articulated by the parties to the dispute but also between procedural commitments that secure the process from misrecognition, exclusion and deprivation.

The motivation behind bringing together the procedural and substantive commitments on one spectrum in situations that call for a compromise (and in democratic interactions more generally) is twofold. First, new or radical ideas that diverge from mainstream beliefs are not often easily assimilated regardless of how reasonable they might be. Numerous factors stand behind the resistance to change. For example, Söderbaum points to inertia or path dependence of various kinds (including cognitive habits, social commitments and promises to act in certain ways or vested interests) (2008, p. 59). Furthermore, behind the layers of advocacy for substantive claims that radically challenge dominant positions often lies the search for new means of participation and for broader institutional change processes to counteract existing injustice. This is well illustrated by even a cursory analysis of environmental justice activism fighting an unequal distribution of environmental risks, burdens and benefits. The environmental justice movements are characterized by wide heterogeneity of substantive claims and notable differences in functioning of its organizations across continents and countries. Nonetheless, they all share some essential elements that pertain to the procedural dimension of justice, advocating for a more integrative and inclusive approach to public health and environmental decision-making. Schlosberg demonstrates that the common distributive approach, aimed to satisfy broad demands by fairly distributing risks and resources, does not say anything about the process and procedural requirements, assuming that '(re) distributional equity can occur within existing social, economic, and institutional conditions' (2009, p. 74). Schlosberg makes the case for equal and due attention to interrelated issues of recognition, participation and capabilities within a pluralistic justice framework precisely because 'distributional equity simply *cannot* come about otherwise' (2009, emphasis in original). Participation and recognition of those who have been outside of decision-making processes play essential roles in environmental justice movements due to power asymmetries that cannot be addressed alone within a purely outcome-oriented framework and by looking only at substantive merits, without due attention to procedural aspects in calling out justice in existing conditions.

The goal of compromising is not to end or completely resolve conflict but to enable navigation of disagreement on jointly held stakes, while allowing for continued ethical debate (Benjamin 1990a, p. 7). In fact, the notion of compromise is best understood as a positional concept that requires positional thinking. Compromise in each case refers to a specific point in time and to specific situations in which parties, with their own perception of the problem, try to make the best of what would otherwise be an impasse. Using compromise as a mechanism for closure in deliberation over matters of disagreement does not dissolve differences and does not require changing one's position (although it may encourage such revision), values or principles; nor does it prevent each side from advocating and making appeals to others. In this way, as long as we decide to work together and the moral dispute goes on, compromise in politics does not obscure democratic processes or democratic ideals. Whether compromise will give a more lasting or stable solution is a matter that can be determined only ex post. Also, whether a successive commitment will emerge out of it also cannot be predetermined; however, sharing power to make decisions through an inclusive process provides some basis to consider integrity-preserving compromise a promising way toward that.

Concluding remarks

The idea of an ethically open-ended conception of economics developed by Söderbaum within a meta-ideological framework of democracy is a response to complexity. It suggests isolating monetary and non-monetary impacts through the analysis of impacts and groups affected in the present and in the future. The outcome of the analysis is not predefined by substantive normative constraints: 'Instead of assuming that the scientist knows what the "correct societal values" are, it is suggested that he or she should reason in conditional terms, referring, for instance, to the kind of alternative development views' (Söderbaum 1990, p. 28). PA is an approach that explicitly tackles ethical and political components in policy relevant information, emphasizing the need to incorporate moral reasoning into more participatory decision-making. The conditional output of PA in the form of various alternative pathways to decide upon, necessitates the craft of making judgement and thinking in the horizon of responsibility, which raises questions about how to implement moral deliberation and what forms it can take.

This chapter examined the questions of how to take up decision-making and make joint progress in situations that are irremediable imperfections, requiring making decisions in situations under constraints of risk, uncertainty and indeterminacy. Drawing on Martin Benjamin's model of practical ethics, it considered what kind of ethical tools of analysis and reasoning best aid shaping procedures and decision-making for sustainability policy in situations of rationally irreducible difference of perspectives and alternatives. It illuminated how various ideologies can come into play in participatory forms of democracy without blocking decision-making – even in cases when consensus is out of reach and/or when communication cannot be grounded on consensus.

On Söderbaum's account, the rationality of choice in complex and conflict-laden situations is not something that can be pre-calculated, but rather it is an outcome of deliberative, pluralistic discourse (Söderbaum 2000). Neither the outcome nor the communication during the process of arriving at outcome is necessarily predicated on consensus. In the face of pluralism, power struggles and incommensurability of values, objectives and interests, urgent decisions may require conflict accommodation or compromise. Although deliberation is an element of the process, there is no a priori requirement that deliberation must result in consensual or univocal agreement instead of just a mere agreement; the shift from consensus demand toward more inclusive solution called integrity-preserving compromise illuminates on the relationship between personal ethical convictions and pluralistic politics. The spirit of democratic temperament assumes the interplay between the impartiality of involved actors as spectators in the non-ideal world and their affective subjectivity. The engagement in democratic practices of all those affected by decisions made in deliberative processes occasionally requires political compromise, while remaining open to listening to alternative views, learning and modifying one's views in light of other people's concerns and values in a way that strives to achieve as much consistency as possible in balancing the inevitable tensions between the individual and collective, universal and particular. Ethical practice in positional terms entails, in other words, mediating way of thinking and acting.

Notes

1 This rather common position views moral decision making as unidirectional application of principles and other elements of ethical theory into specific cases. Ethics, in other words, is considered in its application (but not necessarily in discovery) as a top-down approach in which moral practice upon an appropriate calibration can be axiomatically represented and codified. Ruth Barcan Marcus refers to John Lemmon's account of inconsistency in moral dilemma, which illustrates this position: 'It may be argued that our being faced with this moral situation [of conflicting duties] merely reflects an implicit inconsistency in our existing moral code; we are forced, if we are to remain both moral and logical, by the situation to restore consistency to our code by adding exception clauses to our present principles or by giving priority to one principle over another, or by some such device. The situation is as it is in mathematics: there, if an inconsistency is revealed by derivation, we are compelled to modify our axioms; here, if an inconsistency is revealed in application, we are forced to revise our principles' (Lemmon 1965; adapted from Marcus 1980, p. 580).

2 From now on, when referring to decision situation, I mean the situations of rationally irresolvable conflict in a context characterized by indeterminacy, risk and uncertainty, as expressed in Benjamin's circumstances of compromise.

3 *Practical ethics* can be contrasted with *theoretical ethics* that is concerned with development and justification of ethical theories, and *applied ethics* that is a matter of applying theory to descriptions of situations. Practical ethics has different methods, and takes account of both ethical theories and folk morality, and it is concerned with providing tools for making moral decisions and navigating ethical and cognitive dissonance in a non-ideal world.

4 One may note, as Judy Brown pointed to me, that the line drawn between pluralism *as such* and *reasonable* pluralism is hardly unconditional/non-arbitrary. This issue itself can be a subject to procedural constraints, such as who is to evaluate, and how this is to be done, the various reasons given for competing claims and values. The lack of attention to the dynamically shaped and subtle lines between the requirement of legitimacy, validation, and discrimination of the "unreasonable" can provide a way to close down more critical or radical views (i.e. as being 'unreasonable' or 'extreme').

5 Otto Neurath's famous metaphor of the *ship of knowledge* expressed the idea of the fallibility and uncertainty of knowledge in science: 'There is no way to establish fully secured, neat protocol statements as starting points of the sciences. There is no tabula rasa. We are like sailors who have to rebuild their ship on the open sea, without ever being able to dismantle it in dry-dock and reconstruct it from its best components. Only metaphysics can disappear without a trace. Imprecise "verbal clusters" [Ballungen] are somehow always part of the ship. If imprecision is diminished at one place, it may well re-appear at another place to a stronger degree' (Neurath 1983, p. 91).

6 It is to Rawls's famous veil of ignorance that reflective equilibrium is strongly associated with the attitude of impartial observer and equilibrium as an end-state. Rawls in his *Theory of Justice* was concerned with granting the *real freedom* a status of principle. Consequently, a theory of justice that imposes in a paternalistic way the rules of the society would be inconsistent with his main concern. Thus, in order to justify the principles of his theory of justice, Rawls invented the fiction of the veil of ignorance. Under the veil of ignorance, individuals do not know their place in society, their class position, their social status, their fortune in the distribution of natural assets, abilities, and so on (1971, p. 12). As choosing principles of justice is different from determining one's interest and in order to avoid that interest conflicts with the objective of choosing impartial principles of justice (what is required by the definition of justice), the function of the veil of ignorance is to secure the choice of principles of justice from bias. It does not refer to a real historical situation, but to an experiment of thought that each of us can do at any time; some facts are kept distant, while agents are assumed to be impartial players. The main thesis of Rawls through his work is that under the veil of ignorance, people would choose the theory of justice that he advocates. The methodological tool he employs is reflective equilibrium, and the fictional veil of ignorance allows ranking the main traditional conceptions of justice. For Rawls, reflective equilibrium plays the role of construction and justification of an impartial theory of social justice.

7 Benjamin's account of wide reflective equilibrium differs both from that of John Rawls and Norman Daniels. While Rawls focuses on the justification of theories of justice and Daniels on theory of acceptance, Benjamin is concerned with moral reasoning in its most general form (Benjamin 2005).

8 Miller's *Democratic Temperament: The Legacy of William James* (1997) was a tribute to the philosophical contribution of William James's mediating way of thinking.

9 Moral dilemmas refer to situations in which doing one of the two or more mutually inconsistent actions called by duty leaves remaining option(s) wrongly unfulfilled.

10 The classic compromise, according to which all parties both gain and sacrifice something valuable, has been also discussed by philosophers Amy Gutmann and Dennis Thompson (2010). Similarly to Benjamin, they are skeptical about the common ground agreements, and see compromise as essential for the well-functioning of democracy: 'Classic compromises serve the common good not only by improving on the status quo from the agreeing

parties' particular perspectives, but also by contributing to a robust democratic process … Governing a democracy without compromise is impossible. To restrict political agreements to common ground or common goods, especially in a polarized partisan environment, is to privilege the status quo, even when all parties agree that reform is needed' (pp. 186–188).

11 For a detailed illustration of multiple possibilities and ways for achieving reflective equilibrium in one situation, see (Wenz 2007, pp. 17–20).

12 I want to thank Peter Söderbaum for his comments that led me to emphasize the procedural characteristic of WRE, which is aimed at organizing thought processes for deriving reasonable outcomes, but does not in itself predefine the outcome or its reasonability.

References

Becker, Christian U., 2012. *Sustainability Ethics and Sustainability Research*, Springer Netherlands, Dordrecht.

Benjamin, Martin, 1990a. *Splitting the Difference. Compromise and Integrity in Ethics and Politics*, University Press of Kansas, Lawrence.

Benjamin, Martin, 1990b. Ethical reasoning and analysis: The elements. *Center for the Study of Ethics in Society Papers*, Vol. 3, No. 3, pp. 1–25.

Benjamin, Martin, 2001. Between subway and spaceship: Practical ethics at the outset of the twenty-first century. *Hastings Center Reports*, Vol. 31, No. 4, pp. 24–31.

Benjamin, Martin, 2003. *Philosophy & This Actual World: An Introduction to Practical Philosophical Inquiry*, Rowman & Littlefield Publishers, Lanham.

Benjamin, Martin, 2005. Moral reasoning, moral pluralism, and the classroom, pp. 23–36. In Kenneth R. Howe, ed., *Philosophy of Education*, Philosophy of Education Society, Urbana, IL.

Berlin, Isaiah, 2000. *The Proper Study of Mankind. An Anthology of Essays*, Farrar, Straus and Giroux, New York, NY.

Brown, Donald A., 2012. *Climate Change Ethics: Navigating the Perfect Moral Storm*. Earthscan/ Routledge, New York, NY.

Cohen, Joshua, 1993. Moral pluralism and political consensus, pp. 270–292. In David Copp, Jean Hampton, and John Roemer, eds., *The Idea of Democracy*. Cambridge University Press, Cambridge.

Daniels, Norman, 1996. *Justice and Justification: Reflective Equilibrium in Theory and Practice*, Cambridge University Press, Cambridge.

Dereniowska, Malgorzata, and Jason Matzke, 2014. Interdisciplinary foundations for environmental and sustainability ethics: An introduction. *Ethics in Progress*, Vol. 5, No. 1, pp. 7–32.

Dryzek, John, 1995. Political and ecological communication, *Environmental Politics*, Vol. 4, No 4, pp. 13–30.

Goodman, Nelson, 1995. *Fact, Fiction, and Forecast*. Harvard University Press, Cambridge, MA.

Gutmann, Amy, and Dennis F. Thompson. 2010. The mindsets of political compromise, *Perspectives on Politics*, Vol. 8, No.4, pp. 1125–1143.

Kuhn, Thomas S., 1962. *The Structure of Scientific Revolutions*. The University of Chicago Press, Chicago.

Lemmon, Edward J., 1965. Deontic logic and the logic of imperatives, *Logique Et Analyse*, Vol. 8, No 29, pp. 39–61.

Marcus, Ruth Barcan, 1980. Moral dilemmas and consistency, *Journal of Philosophy*, Vol. 77, No. 3, pp. 121–136.

Miller, Joshua. 1997. *Democratic Temperament: The Legacy of William James*. University Press of Kansas, Lawrence.

Meinard, Yves, Malgorzata Dereniowska and Jean-Sébastien Gharbi, 2016. The ethical stakes in monetary valuation methods for conservation purposes, *Biological Conservation* Vol. 199, pp. 67–74.

Minteer, Ben A., 2012. *Refounding Environmental Ethics: Pragmatism, Principle, and Practice*. Temple University Press, Philadelphia, PA.

Nagel, Thomas, 2000. *Mortal Questions*. Cambridge University Press, Cambridge.

Najder-Stefaniak, Krystyna. 2014. Value of an encounter from an ethical perspective, *Ethics in Progress*, Vol. 5, No. 1, pp. 113–122.

Neurath, Otto, 1983. *Philosophical Papers*. Reidel, Dordrecht.

Nowak, Ewa, 2013. *Experimental Ethics. A Multidisciplinary Approach*. LIT Verlag, Berlin.

O'Neill, John, Alan Holland and Andrew Light, 2008. *Environmental Values*. Routledge, London.

Ottinger, Gwen, and Benjamin Cohen, eds., 2011. *Technoscience and Environmental Justice. Expert Cultures in a Grassroots Movement*. The MIT Press, Cambridge, MA, and London.

Popa, Florin, Mathieu Guillermin, and Tom Dedeurwaerdere, 2015. A pragmatist approach to transdisciplinarity in sustainability research: From complex systems theory to reflexive science, *Futures, Advances in Transdisciplinarity 2004–2014*, Vol. 65, pp. 45–56.

Putnam, Hilary, 1990. How not to solve ethical problems, pp. 179–192. In James Conant, ed., *Realism with a Human Face*, Harvard University Press, Cambridge, MA.

Putnam, Hilary, 1994. Pragmatism and moral objectivity, pp. 151–181. In James Conant, ed., *Words and Life*, Harvard University Press, Cambridge, MA.

Rawls, John, 1971. *Theory of Justice*. Harvard University Press, Cambridge, MA.

Rawls, John, 1993. *Political Liberalism*. Columbia University Press, New York, NY.

Söderbaum, Peter, 1990. *Economics in Relation to Environment, Agriculture and Rural Development. A Non-Traditinoal Approach to Project Evaluation*. Report 31. Swedish University of Agricultural Sciences, Department of Economics, Uppsala.

Söderbaum, Peter, 2000. *Ecological Economics. A Political Economics Approach to Environment and Development*. Eartscan/Routledge, London.

Söderbaum, Peter, 2008. *Understanding Sustainability Economics. Towards Pluralism in Economics*, Eartscann, London & Sterling, VA.

Schlosberg, David, 2009. *Defining Environmental Justice: Theories, Movements, and Nature*. Oxford University Press, Oxford.

Spangenberg, Joachim H., 2011. Sustainability science: A review, an analysis and some empirical lessons, *Environmental Conservation*, Vol. 38, No. 3, pp. 275–287.

Thorseth, May, 2015. Limitations to democratic governance of natural resources, pp. 36–52. In Dieter Birnbacher and May Thorseth, eds., *The Politics of Sustainability. Philosophical Perspectives*. Routledge/Eartscan, London and New York.

Tuana, Nancy, 2012. Embedding philosophers in the practices of science: Bringing humanities to the sciences, *Synthese*, Vol. 190, No. 11, pp. 1955–1973.

Tuana, Nancy, Ryan L. Sriver, Toby Svoboda, Roman Olson, Peter J. Irvine, Jacob Haqq-Misra, and Klaus Keller, 2012. Towards integrated ethical and scientific analysis of geoengineering: a research agenda, *Ethics, Policy & Environment*, Vol. 15, No. 2, pp. 136–157.

Van der Sluijs, J., 2006. Uncertainty, assumptions, and value commitments in the knowledge-base of complex environmental problems, pp. 67–84. In Ângela Guimarães Pereira, Sofia Guedes Vaz and Sylvia Tognetti, eds., *Interfaces Between Science and Society*, Green Leaf Publishing, Sheffield.

Vokey, Daniel, 2001. *Moral Discourse in a Pluralistic World*, University of Notre Dame Press, Notre Dame, IN.

Wenz, Peter S., 2007. *Political Philosophies in Moral Conflict*, McGraw Hill, Boston, MA.

Wenz, Peter S., 1988. *Environmental Justice*, SUNY Press, Albany, NY.

Wong, David B., 1992. Coping with moral conflict and ambiguity, *Ethics*, Vol. 102, No. 4, pp. 763–784.

9 Democracy, sustainability and positional analysis

An interview with Peter Söderbaum (with introduction by Judy Brown)

I initially came across Peter Söderbaum's work on positional analysis in the early 1990s while working on my PhD on accounting and labour relations. I was looking for ways to think about accounting in more pluralistic ways and his advocacy of pluralism in economics really resonated with me (not the least because it helped explain why I had felt so frustrated by the monologic accounting and economics education I received as a student!!). I have maintained a strong interest in his writing over the years and drawn on it heavily in my own research endeavours – which combine an interest in pluralism and strong dissatisfaction with mainstream accounting theory and practice. Mainstream accounting is heavily influenced by neoclassical economics – ontologically, methodologically and politically – and this is recognized as a major problem by social, environmental and critical accounting academics. A particular appeal for me in positional analysis is its surfacing of the inherently *political* character of economics – raising questions about which politics and whose values should be taken into account in a democratic society.[1]

To set the context, I would like to preface this interview with Peter with some comments about the issues his work raises from an accounting perspective.[2] Accounting has traditionally been a narrow discipline, with strong capitalist assumptions and a focus on corporations, financial markets and shareholder wealth maximization. All this is inherently linked with its roots in neoclassical economics, and, relatedly, the role neoclassical economics has played in legitimizing neoliberalism. Such a limited focus is unacceptable for a profession that claims to serve the public interest, particularly given the far-reaching economic, social and environmental impacts of corporate activity. Even when corporations and accountants report on sustainability-related issues, they do so by applying business framings and concepts. For example, their decision-making models and information systems record costs and benefits from managerial viewpoints so the focus is on whether there is a 'business case' – rather than citizen case – for social and environmental accounting (SEA). Since the 1980s accounting technologies have also played a key role in neoliberal governance regimes in the public sector and structural adjustment programmes in developing countries, with increasing use of market-like mechanisms and metrics.

As accounting has become entangled in politically contentious areas such as sustainability, the need for new pluralistic approaches has become increasingly evident. Environmentalists, trade unions, indigenous peoples, ethical investors and new social movements all have concerns – about corporate accountability, environmental degradation, poverty, inequality, human rights and globalization – that are currently ignored or glossed over in accounting. When these issues are addressed, as noted above, a 'business case' lens is applied – which focuses on the implications for finance capital and shareholder wealth maximization. SEA is thus absorbed into mainstream accounting in a way that poses little, if any, challenge to neoliberal capitalism. For example, sustainability reporting becomes more about 'stakeholder management' rather than accountability or democratic participation. Indeed, accounting has played a pivotal role in neoliberal agendas that promote the externalization of capitalism's harmful impacts, considering them other people's problems and shifting costs onto others. As such, accounting is arguably deeply complicit in many of the crises and unsustainable trends confronting the planet.

In attempting to address the democratic deficiencies of traditional accounting, SEA academics have sought to develop and support more socially responsible approaches. However, in spite of continued calls for change and ongoing efforts to work with business leaders, professional accounting bodies and policymakers, progress has been very limited. As in other disciplinary areas, these largely top-down approaches have done little to provide constituencies beyond finance capital with an effective accounting voice. The social and critical accounting communities have become increasingly aware that SEA's aspirations to 'democratize' accounting have been under-theorized, and that this has significantly hindered the development of accounting and accountability systems oriented to citizen and societal interests.

What would it mean to democratize accounting? In an effort to answer this question, I have drawn on Peter Söderbaum's research and worked with colleagues as part of a multidisciplinary *Spaces of Democracy* network arguing for the value of pluralism and conflict in a healthy democracy, outlining a conceptual framework for dialogic accounting that seeks to take ideological differences seriously. This framework raises questions about *what* is accounted for in conventional accounting systems, *how* and on *whose* terms. The aim of dialogic accounting is to enable actors with divergent perspectives to account for things that traditional accounting disregards and in a way that accords with their own philosophical and political standpoints. Fair trade investors, for example, might seek disclosures about human rights, workplace conditions and supply chains not demanded by traditional investors. Dialogic accounts could be used for decision-making and social accountability purposes and to stimulate democratic debate. This framework is based on an agonistic understanding of democracy which cautions against overly consensual or universalistic understandings often apparent in more deliberative conceptions of democracy. As discussed in Chapter 5 of this book, it also specifically rejects minimalist, market-like understandings of democracy.

Key concerns remain in realizing the potential of dialogic accounting. SEA academics and others have run into major obstacles when challenging mainstream accounting. For example, traditional accountants are taught to view accounting as an impartial, value-free discipline and, perhaps unsurprisingly, find it difficult to see why it needs to change or, indeed, how it could operate differently. When stakeholders have sought new accountings (e.g. in the labour or environmental context), the profession and corporations have engaged them very superficially, translating their concerns into business language (e.g. the 'business case' for employee reporting or sustainability). Existing accounting systems thus often do not capture information required for serious democratic debate. New theorizations of the role of accountants, civil society engagement and information systems are needed to help SEA academics and others challenge traditional practices and develop more ideologically open forms of accounting. There is considerable scope here for the development of new styles of accounting (e.g. Peter Söderbaum's positional analysis, counter accountings), academic-civil society alliances, the use of new social media technologies, and the like. Drawing on heterodox streams of economic thought – as a challenge to neoliberal and neoclassical economic orthodoxy – will be a crucial part of efforts to democratize accounting. In this sense, it is important to see proposals for dialogic approaches to accounting as just one part of a far broader rethinking of, *inter alia*, capitalism, economics, governance, politics, public policy, law, science and educational processes in ways that might help deepen democracy. Of particular interest here is how heterodox understandings of economics – that offer alternatives and challenges to neoclassical economics and technocratic approaches such as cost–benefit analysis – might help to support significant changes in accounting (and vice versa).

In the following interview with Peter, I focus specifically on his work on positional analysis that I think has the potential to make a very important contribution to efforts to rethink accounting. Adapting his definition of economics discussed in Chapter 3 of this book, for example, we might conceive of dialogic accounting as 'multidimensional accounting of (limited) resources in a democratic society' for decision-making and accountability purposes. Ideological differences of opinion could then be made visible through political economic approaches such as positional analysis.

Judy Brown: What do you see as the main challenges in implementing positional analysis and getting it accepted into policymaking arenas? How might we best address these issues?

Peter Söderbaum: Behind positional analysis is an idea to accept a degree of complexity and to strengthen democracy. However, many politicians and decision makers expect clear-cut recommendations from experts. They have become accustomed to cost–benefit analysis (CBA) and other similar technocratic approaches where reference is made to one optimal solution. Hiding behind experts can be an attractive option for some politicians.

I think that the kind of alternative economics advocated in the early chapters of this book together with PA as a method can play a role in strengthening and legitimizing other modes of thinking and arguments than traditional thinking as in CBA. PA may then play a role without being implemented in the sense of a written document where alternatives are systematically being assessed. However, of course, the existence of written PA studies is essential for success of this way of thinking.

Those who teach or write textbooks about the use of CBA are, of course, happy with a continued dominance for CBA and neoclassical economics more generally. They tend to avoid open debate about alternative approaches and have, so to say, 'internalized' the conceptual framework and values of CBA. CBA is close to economic growth in gross domestic product (GDP) terms as an ideological orientation and as we all know the present growth and market centred ideology while being challenged is not easily changed.

Sustainable development in its modernization or radical interpretations will not easily be taken seriously among actors in business for example. However, public debate will go on with university scholars among the participants and there may be – after all – some reasons for optimism.

So, there is an ideological challenge where the combined dominance of neoclassical economics and neoliberalism is part of the problems faced. As I see it, pluralism in economics plays a key role but at issue is how that pluralism may come about. Students have a role just as their professors in economics and even politicians may act when they realize that economics is not just science in a narrow sense but at the same time ideology. Even citizens and social movements can, of course, contribute to make university departments of economics more compatible with democracy.

Judy Brown: Given the problems with neoclassical economics and accounting, perhaps it would be better for citizens to avoid them altogether?

Peter Söderbaum: I think that the close to monopoly position of neoclassical theory is one of the problems we have to deal with. Economics is at the heart when actors think about development. In Chapter 4, reference was made to different kinds of inertia, for example, cognitive and emotional inertia. Economists as well as other actors are locked into specific ways of perceiving the world. They see prices, money and markets everywhere and believe that rationality should be dealt with in terms of monetary and financial calculation. Each year millions of students learn about management of resources and accounting in what can be described as one globally standardized way. These cognitive habits and connected standardization – even at a global level – are attractive because it means that economists essentially use the same language. However, if this language is inappropriate in relation to sustainability or other issues, then we have a problem. The problem is not so much with neoclassical theory as with the monopoly position and the protectionism of the advocates of this theory. Pluralism and 'competition' seem to be helpful, an argument that neoclassical economists should understand.

Should we forget about neoclassical theory and accounting systems (closely connected with neoclassical theory) altogether? This would not be realistic, but I like the idea of a thought experiment, that is, thinking about a society where neoclassical theory did not exist or was less dominant. What kind of economics and accounting systems would then emerge?

I am certainly a biased person – actually we are all biased with our ideological orientations – but I would imagine or guess that non-monetary variables and accounting systems would then play a more important role. When a person is employed in a business company his or her salary becomes a financial outlay and monetary cost as part of the ambition to increase profits. When a person on the other hand loses his or her employment, this may increase profits. However, the fact that a person is employed is seen as a positive thing by many and not only by the employed person. Unemployment is, as we all know, a significant problem in many parts of Europe these days. While the financial aspect matters, social, health and environmental considerations should not be reduced to their monetary aspect. We clearly need some kind of separate SEA systems (as discussed in Chapters 5 and 6 of this book).

Neoclassical theory is, however, one of the theories to be considered as part of a pluralist strategy. In the present book and elsewhere, I have repeatedly used neoclassical theory for comparative purposes. When arguing that some kind of ecological or institutional economics is preferable for some purposes, a systematic comparison and assessment is needed. What are the differences and how can some non-neoclassical school of economics contribute?

Judy Brown: As noted in my introduction, I felt quite frustrated when I was an accounting student about the lack of pluralism within the accounting and economics curricula. I have been intrigued – and heartened – by the efforts of economics students who have actively petitioned their professors and university administrations demanding more pluralism in their courses. I am thinking here, for example, of the activities of the Heterodox Economics Students Association and ideas about 'Occupy Economics'. Do you think progress is being made in the educational context?

Peter Söderbaum: I am afraid that progress is slow, but one observation is that students from different universities increasingly work together. I am thinking of the 'International Student Initiative for Pluralism in Economics' signed by economics student associations in more than 30 countries. There are, of course, also some university professors who in journals and books support this call for pluralism. *The International Journal of Pluralism and Economics Education* focuses, as the name suggests, on the need for competition between perspectives. Moreover, there are books, for example, *The Handbook of Pluralist Economics Education* (Reardon 2009) and *The Economics Curriculum: Towards a Radical Reformulation* (Madi and Reardon 2014).

Paradigm issues in economics are discussed at many places suggesting that some professors respond to the initiatives by students and colleagues. The World Economics Association (WEA) exists since 2011 with its book series and journals (*Economic Thought, Real-World Economics Review, World Economic Review*). However, many university departments of economics still appear to be closed for this kind of new thinking. Students and professors of economics certainly have important roles, but I believe that more would be happening if other actors in society understood that the monopoly of neoclassical theory is a danger for society. Journalists, politicians, members of civil society organizations have important roles. In her book *The Blockage. Rethinking Organizational Principles for the 21st Century* (2007), Kras points specifically to the importance of listening to 'visionaries', that is, persons who are ready to challenge dominant thinking patterns in terms of theoretical and ideological perspectives.

Judy Brown: In terms of positional analysis, what do you see as the major theoretical and practical issues that still require further work?

How important do you see cross-disciplinary initiatives and/or citizen-academic collaborations in dealing with these issues?

Peter Söderbaum: Many societies claim to observe the imperatives of democracy. However, 'democracy' is interpreted differently by different actors. Some refer to a minimalist interpretation where democracy is connected with the right to vote and majority rules. Some argue or believe that even CBA is an approach useful in a democratic society. However, CBA is, as we have shown, an extremely technocratic approach where economists and the analyst in particular claim to know about correct values in terms of prices as part of an aggregation of impacts to a so-called present value.

For others the idea of democracy is, fortunately, much broader. The idea of consensus about values or ideological orientation is abandoned in favour of acceptance of tensions between different ideological orientations. Criticism is acknowledged as part of a constructive dialogue. This suggests that tolerance versus those who hold a different view (as long as that ideological orientation does not go against democracy itself) becomes a virtue. My conclusion here is that democracy as a contested concept needs to be discussed further even in countries like Sweden. When democracy is taken seriously, CBA will be abandoned and approaches like PA will become the natural choice.

Impact studies and evaluation are not limited to economics. Actors within other social sciences, humanities and even natural sciences dispose of knowledge that become relevant and indeed needed as soon as we take non-monetary impacts seriously. Cross-disciplinary cooperation will improve learning processes for all actors involved. Similarly, citizen-academic collaboration can be beneficial, for example, in making economists understand that individuals and organizations are not just stakeholders with specific interests. In addition to such limited interests, they can be expected to have ideas about what is good for society at large. This is what we have referred to as ideological orientation.

Judy Brown: Do you see positional analysis as useful in both developing and developed country contexts? What specific contextual issues might need addressing in developing country contexts?

Peter Söderbaum: I understand the question, but the challenge of sustainable development should perhaps make us reconsider our understanding of 'progress' and 'development'. Is a nation with extremely high levels of emissions of CO_2 equivalents per capita a 'developed country'? Can a country that increases its amounts of radioactive waste each year or systematically pollutes the air or its waters be regarded as developed?

My position when it comes to the usefulness of PA in different contexts is that thinking in terms of PA and making PA studies is (not unexpectedly) a good idea at many places. PA was first presented as a PhD thesis in management science at Uppsala University, suggesting that this was an approach for business organizations. However, also examples of applied studies at the societal level were presented, and in a gradual manner, PA became mainly regarded as an alternative to CBA.

PA is probably even more needed in so-called developing countries where a lot happens in terms of building infrastructure, mining projects and the like. Neoclassical ideas about social profitability in terms of CBA are perhaps even more dangerous in such countries. Fortunately, there are sometimes counteracting institutions in terms of laws about environmental impact statement (EIS) as well as guidelines about corporate social responsibility (CSR). Such manuals can at least be thought provoking and have the potential of representing moves in the right direction. At the global level, naïve neoclassical ideas about trade as being beneficial for all parties involved can be challenged by reference to methodological elements from PA. We need to know about negative changes in positional terms in each of the trading countries, and we should try to understand possible conflicts of interest in each of the trading countries. And again, ideological orientation is an issue. Any conclusions will then become conditional and related to each ideological orientation articulated and considered in analysis. Why should all of us agree about the ideological orientation built into international trade theory of the neoclassical kind?

Finally, one test of a specific method is if it can be used meaningfully at the level of the individual when she or he faces decision situations. I think the multidimensional and ideologically open approach of PA is by far more appropriate than CBA. However, like CBA advocates, I am a person with vested interests in a specific method and related ideology. This preference for PA does not worry me much since this method is designed to strengthen rather than weaken democracy. Besides we should all realize that we are guided by something that can be called 'ideological orientation'.

Judy Brown:　Is there something that you want to add?

Peter Söderbaum:　Perhaps not add, but I want to return to where we started – the issue of complexity. All methods involve some simplifications. However, it is possible to go too far in eliminating complexity and simplifying analysis. Some people argue that only that which can be quantified counts. This is built on an idea of how politicians and other decision makers think. Such ideas then represent an entrance point for simplistic mathematics. Some economists move one step further arguing that only that which can be expressed in monetary terms counts. CBA is built on such heroic assumptions.

Some analysts or other actors also start with an assumption that there is one single solution to each societal problem faced. One-dimensional analysis aiming at optimal solutions then becomes the usual approach. However, in the case of problems at the level of society, this does not go well with democracy as understood here. In a decision situation, there are normally actors and stakeholders with different interests and ideological orientations, suggesting that perception of 'problems' and 'solutions' will differ. The ranking of alternatives will then be conditional in relation to each ideological orientation considered as explained in the early chapters of this book.

Finally, other insights from 'post-normal science' dealing with uncertainty, ignorance and so on will make us more modest but at the same time more relevant in our efforts to get closer to a sustainable society.

Judy Brown:　Thank you Peter.

Notes

1　As we have discussed elsewhere, until around 1870, economics was referred to as 'political economics', and it was arguably a mistake to ever abandon this terminology (Söderbaum and Brown 2011). Rather than try to overcome or apologize for the heterogeneity of different schools of economic thought – feminist, institutionalist, Marxian, neoclassical, Keynsian and the like – a multiplicity of viewpoints should be seen as a *strength* in a democratic society.

2　For further discussion of some of these issues, see Söderbaum and Brown (2010).

References

International Journal of Pluralism and Economics Education. Inderscience. www .inderscience.com

International Student Initiative for Pluralism in Economics. Available at www.isipe.net (Accessed 2016-11-06)

Kras, Eva, 2007. *The Blockage. Rethinking Organizational Principles for the 21st Century.* American Literary Press, Baltimore, Maryland.

Madi, Maria Alejandra and Jack Reardon, 2014. *The Economics Curriculum: Towards a Radical Reformulation.* World Economics Association Book Series. Available at: https://www .worldeconomicsassociation.org/books

Reardon, Jack, ed., 2009. *The Handbook of Pluralist Economics Education.* Routledge, London.

Söderbaum, Peter and Judy Brown, 2010. Democratizing economics: pluralism as a path toward sustainability, *Annals of the New York Academy of Sciences*, Vol. 1185, *Ecological Economics Reviews*, pp. 179–195, New York Academy of Sciences, New York.

Söderbaum, Peter and Judy Brown, 2011. Pluralism and democracy in economics, *International Journal of Pluralism and Economics Education*, Vol. 2, No. 3, pp. 240–243.

10 Philosophy, ethics and positional analysis

An interview with Peter Söderbaum (with introduction by Małgorzata Dereniowska)

I encountered Peter Söderbaum in 2010. At that time, I was a PhD student in philosophy, working on ethical dimensions of sustainable development. I was particularly interested in how the ethical stakes in economics for sustainability are articulated and appraised by economists and whether and how such articulations differ from discussions within philosophy.

With Peter's emphasis on the need for philosophical and ethical insights and contributions, we explored numerous bridging points between respective disciplines; the discussion that began back then has continued through to today. As a result of our discourse, my own views and pluralistic orientation have developed further in depth and complexity. It is not only his ideas that have influenced me tremendously but also his dialogical style, his inexhaustible curiosity and his persistent pursuit of numerous philosophical questions at the intersection of our respective research programs, which has led me to fully appreciate the value of interdisciplinary exchange. Through these exchanges, I soon began to notice various patterns within the disciplines of economics and philosophy that related to pluralism. In the interview shared here, I focused particularly on the pluralism debate, as it is tied to other relevant themes, such as sustainability economics and democratization. The stakes in the monism/pluralism debate have practical import and constitute broader attitudes about how to do science. In this context, I addressed also some more general questions that Peter Söderbaum's work raises from a philosophical perspective.

Peter is a scientist concerned with the pursuit of relevant knowledge, critical of reductionism in scientific analysis and public deliberation. He is a concerned scholar devoted to critical scrutiny and the search for ethical imperatives to guide economics in the service of society and a sustainable future. A clear ideological orientation inevitably raises the issue of scientific subjectivity, which Peter is not afraid to confront. In his work, he spells out, when necessary, his own subjective position and ideology; such methodological clarity and reflectiveness on so-called extrascientific elements of knowledge production are a commendable element of sound sustainability research.

Pluralism often invokes postmodernism, which results in the mistaken association of pluralism with the impossibility of making comparisons and choices and with a lack of critical standards. However, the philosophical tradition contains a much more constructive account of pluralism than what could be found by tracing it through the moral and epistemological relativism of postmodernism. This more solid footing can aid in the integration of a more refined account of pluralism into economic methodology.

A Polish philosopher Mieczysław A. Krąpiec claims that the richness of philosophical questions and insights, however diverse, always boils down, one way or another, to issues pertaining to the monism and pluralism debate – which is as old as philosophy itself (1991). In many ways, the monism/pluralism dichotomy is no different in economics than in other disciplines although there are shifts in discussion from issues such as the acceptance of pluralism and its consequences to more subtle questions of, for example, what pluralism implies. In philosophy, one would hardly object anymore to the fact of value and cultural pluralism or pluralism in science. Nevertheless, there remain debates about how to approach pluralism, such as whether it implies an anything-goes relativism of values and goods or methodological eclecticism.

The notion of pluralism, when taken seriously, is open to multiple interpretations and conceptualizations. The mere fact of diversity of models, however, does not imply an equal appraisal of any and all positions, nor does it eliminate the ability to make critical judgments. In fact, meaningful pluralism requires the ability to make comparisons, which asks further inevitable questions about criteria of evaluation. At this point, specifically, pluralism poses many challenges regarding the legitimacy of claims and the validity of models, theories and so on. One of the worries is that it invites unwanted relativism and eclecticism, leaving us without hope to better understand the world and to make progress toward greater integration of our body of knowledge.

A part of recasting and operationalizing pluralism is the development of an understanding of the normative aspects of economics. The ambiguity of the science and values interface involves the questions of an appraisal of uncertainty, risk and diversity of perspectives and how to accommodate such a quest in the process of knowledge production. Looking at the normative layer of sustainability economics, as a science for a sustainable society, touches upon various facets of the above philosophical questions.

A slightly different but related question pertains to challenges of disaggregated analysis vis-à-vis public decision-making, especially with an emphasis on international, global and intergenerational dimensions. These dimensions are involved in climate change and sustainability policies, raising questions of cross-country comparisons, decision-making procedures and the compatibility of economic analyses with democracy. All those profound issues generate growing attention in various fields of research, from the humanities to the social sciences. In this light, the question about the status and role of economic tools at the interface among science, society and policy takes on a different shape. Indeed, thinking of the linkages between democracy and economics implies a paradigmatic shift toward more process-oriented, holistic thinking, where not only the outcome matters. The process that leads to the sustainable outcome is of equal importance.

The importance of the insights offered by Peter for philosophy is timely: for a long time, the discipline of philosophy – once thought to be the queen of the sciences – has been considered in non-philosophical circles to be overly abstract and detached from the real world; the image frequently held is that of the philosopher enclosed in her ivory tower of pure ideas. And in fairness, there has often been a tendency in philosophy to search for absolute, ultimate solutions to our queries, which resemble the monistic tendencies of mainstream economics. Some of the criticisms of mainstream moral philosophy from the perspectives of multiculturalism and value pluralism are not unfamiliar: ethicists themselves tried to establish a formulaic calculus to be able to derive one single unambiguous answer to each moral decision situation. Nevertheless, once we accept some diversity of perspectives and distance ourselves from the claim to absolute truths, engaging humbly in dialogue and a joint search for (however partial) perspectives on truth and solutions to real-world problems, we can learn from each other for the benefit of sustainability problem solving.

Małgorzata Dereniowska: You tend to refer repeatedly to 'pluralism'. Pluralism is a contested concept in the sense that it is used differently by different persons. Can you clarify how you use 'pluralism' in your text?

Peter Söderbaum: As I see it, pluralism is very much connected with democracy and recognition that there are competing conceptual and ideological perspectives in any society. As previously argued, economics is political economics, and there is more than one kind of political economics, each with its specific theoretical and ideological features. A social science 'paradigm' then is characterized by its theoretical (conceptual) and ideological features. This fact that ideology is involved makes it undemocratic to present one single paradigm as the only possibility.

A scholar as a political economic person normally believes more in one theoretical or ideological paradigm than another. Our scholar may know about other paradigms and respect them (as long as they do not contradict democracy itself) but perhaps keep them at a distance. However, each scholar needs to learn about more paradigms than one. Understanding one particular paradigm (such as the institutional version of ecological economics advocated in this book) is largely based on comparison with other existing paradigms (such as the dominant neoclassical theory and ideology). As I see it, comparing one theoretical or ideological paradigm with another is at the heart of pluralism. Each paradigm is largely understood in relation to other perspectives. It can be added that comparing one paradigm with another is also a way of respecting democracy compared with exclusive attention to one paradigm (as in neoclassical textbooks for example).

I also believe that systematically comparing one paradigm with another can be a constructive way of doing research. The neoclassical approach, for example, is a possible reference point (known by many) for articulating different paradigms (conceptual frameworks with connected ideology). From this emphasis on pluralism, it follows that the history of economic ideas is an essential part of economics education, and that examples of today's heterodox schools of economics have to be included in the curriculum.

It should finally be made clear that pluralism does not by itself solve all problems but is an essential – and as I see it – necessary first step when attempting to deal with present sustainability issues. The present tendency to limit attention to only one paradigm in textbooks for students has to come to an end.

Małgorzata Dereniowska: Your definition of pluralism implies both theoretical and methodological pluralism. Yet many mainstream economists in their research practices diverge from the neoclassical assumptions, representing a wide range of heterogeneity in both theoretical and methodological layers – even if the question of pluralism per se is not addressed or dashed aside. What constitutes, according to you, the main factors that prevent pluralism from being a legitimate topic of concern in mainstream circles? What factors constitute the anti-pluralism tendencies in economics? Why is the discussion about pluralism largely absent from mainstream practices and teaching?

Peter Söderbaum: If we focus on neoclassical introductory textbooks in economics, there is not much heterogeneity as I see it. Where economics research is concerned, there can be more heterogeneity, but the interesting thing is that respected economists such as Amartya Sen and Joseph Stiglitz seldom, if ever, relate their research to heterodox schools of thought. I think a kind of opportunism is behind the anti-pluralist tendencies that you mention.

Another factor that may be important is the 'physics envy' aspect of neoclassical economists and neoclassical economics. There is a belief in value neutrality and in the paradigm-shift idea of Thomas Kuhn. This is a bit strange because there is some pluralism even in natural sciences.

Małgorzata Dereniowska: If some pluralism does exist, both on the level of theory and methodology, in mainstream economics, then there must be something about pluralism that makes this subject either non-existent or controversial. How much pluralism do we actually need? What is according to you, at the heart of the split between pluralist and mainstream economists (usually considered as not pluralist enough in the non-mainstream literature)? What is really at stake with this distinction?

Peter Söderbaum: I can, of course, only speculate, but I think that there is a lot of opportunism and rent seeking behind the present tendency to protect neoclassical theory. Actually, public choice theory can be questioned as I have done at a conference with International Economic Association (IEA) (Söderbaum 1991), but if this particular theory can explain rent-seeking behavior of specific professional categories, then I would suggest the category of neoclassical economists. It is a relatively homogeneous group while, for example, farmers can be divided into different groups depending on ideological orientation. Some are 'eco-farmers', others defend conventional agriculture.

However, what is at stake as you say? I suggest that mainstream economics and mainstream market ideology [in terms of gross domestic product (GDP)-growth, etc.] are closely connected, and that this mainstream makes our present political economic system legitimate. This means that not only the economics paradigm is at stake but also mainstream ideology (neoliberalism) and our political economic system. It is judged to be controversial if someone raises such issues. Sometimes I feel that only retired persons like myself can point to radical alternatives at the levels of perspectives and institutional arrangements.

Małgorzata Dereniowska: Being a pluralist, you accept the need to be open and critical toward different schools of thought and methodologies, and at the same time, you recognize that in conducting economic analysis, we need to make specific methodological choices. This issue raises the inherent tension of pluralism: between eclecticism on the one hand, and more structured pluralism that allows us to give some meaning and to make necessary choices that limit available options. How would you define the criteria of choosing between different alternatives? What, according to you, can help a pluralist to assess the legitimacy of various options at hand and how?

Peter Söderbaum: Those who believe strongly in one theory with connected ideology may get frustrated when hearing about alternative perspectives. Questions are then raised about an 'anything goes' attitude suggesting that the person embracing pluralism thinks of an infinite number of alternative perspectives.

However, heterodox economists, while often being more open than orthodox economists, have their own preferences with respect to theoretical perspectives. And such preferences have a lot to do with ideology. An economist who takes sustainable development seriously may prefer a version of ecological economics to the mainstream alternative(s). The important thing for the mainstream economist is to understand and accept that there are alternative perspectives also outside the mainstream.

Małgorzata Dereniowska: When discussing sustainability economics – with an explicit normative orientation – what are the standards and the criteria for relevant ideological orientations?

Peter Söderbaum: Sustainability and sustainable development with its explicit ideological orientation need to be discussed and clarified as you suggest. In a FAO publication, I proposed at an early stage (1982) four ethical principles for public policy. They are about 'non-degradation of the natural resource base' and included a 'philosophy of cautiousness'.

National environmental policy in Sweden these days is formulated with an overall generational goal and 16 sets of sub-goals. This is in line with the spirit of positional analysis where multidimensional impact studies are prepared, and issues of negative irreversible impacts are observed as carefully as possible.

When you ask for 'standards and criteria for relevant ideological orientations', my main response is that since ideology is involved, criteria based on democracy are relevant. Official goals where governments articulate some idea of sustainable development should be respected but also interpretations of ideological orientations of different groups in society. For analysis to be tractable, only a limited number of ideological orientations can be articulated, but the set of ideological orientations considered have to be 'many sided' reflecting the tensions between ideological orientations in a particular society. Even the personal political ideas of the scholar may be articulated and made the subject of debate and dialogue. There are no final responses. All ideological orientations can be challenged, and new studies may be made to add to the knowledge and information available.

Małgorzata Dereniowska: One of the main challenges for sustainability economics pertain to climate change, for which it is difficult to describe spatial patterns of impact or to isolate impacts on different interested stakeholders (or even delineate who counts as stakeholder). Do you think that positional analysis can incorporate the challenges of intergenerational justice in climate decision-making? How can positional analysis aid in dealing with such challenges? What are the advantages and limits of a disaggregated approach to decision-making in discussing matters of international, global importance?

Peter Söderbaum: Positional analysis is about 'illuminating' an issue rather than pointing to a specific solution. Solutions will be conditional in relation to each ideological orientation considered in the analysis. And some ideological orientations emphasize climate change issues more than others. I agree that a method in itself cannot solve these complex issues. However, conceptual frameworks and methods can make a difference. We are back to the fact that the concept of ideology is made visible as well as tensions between ideological orientations.

I think that disaggregated approaches are becoming more and more accepted in public policy. Consider Sweden's 16 environmental goals. Positional thinking in relation to these objectives means that you also focus on possible lock-in effects and irreversible impacts when choosing among options. A single monetary indicator, such as GDP, will never tell the whole story. However, this is common sense. Neither will PA tell a whole story but rather a number of fragmented stories. Again this is a matter of accepting complexity rather than assuming it away. Positional analysis opens the door for separate ideological orientations, including global issues, while, for example, cost–benefit analysis (CBA) essentially relies on one ideological orientation and closes the door for other options.

Małgorzata Dereniowska: In your definition of economics as 'multidimensional management of (limited) resources in a democratic society', you emphasize democracy, which is a strong normative requirement. If you were to give just one main reason for why according to you it is necessary to address democracy in economic analysis, what would it be? Also, do you think that democratization of political regimes is a necessary step for a globalized world in search of a sustainable future or rather should we aim for democratic openness, debate and scrutiny in the public sphere? In other words, democracy as a political concept or a normative ideal? Or, would you recommend something else in thinking about democracy, economics and the globalized world?

Peter Söderbaum: As argued in earlier chapters of the book, there is a tension in economics between technocracy and democracy, and that neoclassical theory and method, for example, CBA, is extremely technocratic. Essential steps toward democracy need to be taken. Democracy means that we should listen to citizens as part of a problem-solving process. Not only science but also the ideological orientations of various actors should be with us, especially in a situation where development paths need to be reconsidered.

I think countries such as China and Russia have problems these days. When it is dangerous to criticize the national government or actors in power, then this will be a barrier to necessary environmental policy interventions. It may be added that also in countries that function a bit better in terms of democracy, it is often the case that whistle-blowers in relation to chemical pollution, for example, may be in trouble. 'Joining the mainstream' in economics and elsewhere is easier, it seems.

Personally, I believe that democracy as meta-ideology is superior to dictatorship in our search for a better world. Today, dictatorships with little internal debate have to rely on the critical dialogue that takes place in democracies. However, again there are limits to democracy also in our countries. It would make a difference, for example, if democracy was taken seriously in introductory textbooks in economics.

Małgorzata Dereniowska: An increasing number of economists argues that economic valuation can play some role and may be useful in the decision process, but it cannot be a substitute for the decision process itself. How would you respond to the idea that CBA cannot be a base for a political decision, or a substitute for it, but it can play some role in decision-making processes? In other words, the problem with CBA is, according to you, inherent in the very tool, or is it the problem of how it is used, and of the political and social consequences of communicating the results of CBA by economists?

Peter Söderbaum: The problem with CBA is that it is not compatible with democracy. The CBA advocate or analyst dictates how various impacts should be valued in relation to each other and therefore excludes all ideological orientations but one. Ezra Mishan, himself a textbook writer on CBA (1971), later argued that CBA is built on an idea of consensus in society about the CBA rules of valuation (1980). In relation to environmental issues, it is not realistic to expect a consensus, he argued.

In a society, it is theoretically possible for politicians by majority rule to decide that CBA should be used for certain kinds of investments, but those politicians would, as I see it, be very unwise persons and not understand the essentials of democracy.

It is, of course, also possible to abandon the neoclassical idea of correct values in favor of some sensitivity analysis where there are alternative monetary prices for specific impacts and thereby alternative recommended solutions. This response to the criticism of CBA appears a bit desperate and is of little interest as I see it. This is still a case of aggregation and 'monetary reductionism'.

When asked if I can see any positive feature of CBA, my response is that alternatives of choice are on an equal footing when the analysis begins. This is the case also with PA while environmental impact statement (EIS), for example, enters the scene when some actor group has proposed a specific alternative. This tends to lead to modification of the alternative at best.

Małgorzata Dereniowska: Amartya Sen also has been writing about the importance of positional analysis although in a slightly different way: Sen emphasizes the role of 'positionality' both in the process of scientific knowledge production and in the consolidation of beliefs and the need for a 'trans-positional' assessment, in defining the positional view of objectivity as a more plausible alternative to a positivist, value-neutral ideal of objectivity as independent of the subject. How do you see possible convergences and divergences between the positional component in your and Sen's thought?

Peter Söderbaum: Thank you for informing me about Amartya Sen's article 'Positional Objectivity' (1993), which I have now read. Sen's article is of interest, and it is clear that he uses positional thinking somewhat differently. Let us first point to the fact that there are different versions of positional thinking in the literature, for example, 'positioning' as part of business strategy and marketing of products (Ries and Trout 2001).

My use of positional thinking and analysis is more like 'positional decision-making in chess', where each move conditions future moves. The idea is to consider irreversible impacts, lock-in effects and other aspects of inertia that influence future options in a positive or negative manner according to some ideological orientation.

When I chose to refer to the 'position' rather than 'state' or 'stock' of various objects of description, I felt that it was easier to refer to 'positions' of individuals than to the 'state' of individuals as in the cases of social position, professional position and health position. Some impacts in a decision situation refer to individuals; other impacts may be of an environmental kind, for example, land-use changes or pollution of various kinds.

In any decision situation, history and present position are of interest. Amartya Sen is concerned about the 'positionality' of the social scientist and subjective as well as objective ways of perceiving various phenomena. In PA, the focus is on actors in relation to an issue or decision situation, and we are interested in the 'situatedness' of various actors and the stories told by them. The individual is a political economic person guided by an 'ideological orientation' and so forth.

In relation to present unsustainable development, we have to bring in concepts such as 'ideological orientation' and discuss orientations that are clearly unsustainable and those that represent steps in the right direction. So, my advice to Amartya Sen is to consider this kind of concept in his analysis of positionality. Gunnar Myrdal's dictum that 'values are always with us' must be taken seriously. Myrdal continues, 'There can be no view except from a viewpoint. In the questions raised and the viewpoint chosen, valuations are implied' (Myrdal 1978, p. 778). Also the economist as analyst is guided by an ideological orientation. However, his or her analysis should be 'many sided' and not limited to his or her own ideological orientation. Analysis should be compatible with democracy including social control by various actors to limit manipulation.

Małgorzata Dereniowska: If you were to confine your main message and academic mission to one idea or concept, what would it be? Or, if it is not possible to easily choose, what particularly would you like to convey to our readers?

Peter Söderbaum: Many present development trends are unsustainable. We can no longer avoid a debate about perspectives in economics and ideological orientations. Marginal changes in institutional arrangements do not appear to be enough.

Małgorzata Dereniowska: Thank you Peter.

References

Krąpiec, Mieczysław Albert, 1991. *O Rozumienie Filozofii.* (Understanding philosophy) in series *Dzieła* (Works), Vol. 16, Lublin: RW KUL.

Mishan, Ezra J. 1971. *Cost–Benefit Analysis.* Allen & Unwin, London.

Mishan, Ezra J. 1980. How valid are economic valuations of allocative changes? *Journal of Economic Issues,* Vol. 14, No. 1, pp. 143–171.

Myrdal, Gunnar, 1978. Institutional economics, *Journal of Economic Issues,* Vol. 12, No. 4, pp. 771–783.

Ries, Al and Jack Trout, 2001. *Positioning. How to Be Seen and Heard in the Overcrowded Marketplace.* McGraw-Hill, New York.

Sen, Amartya, 1993. Positional objectivity. *Philosophy & Public Affairs,* Vol. 22, No. 2, pp. 126–145.

Söderbaum, Peter, 1982. Ecological imperatives for public policy. *Ceres. The FAO Review on Agriculture and Development,* Vol. 15, No. 2, pp. 28–32. Rome.

Söderbaum, Peter, 1991. Environmental and agricultural issues: what is the alternative to public choice theory?, pp. 24–42 in Partha Dasgupta, ed., *Issues in Contemporary Economics, Volume 3. Policy and Development.* Macmillan (in Association with the International Economic Association), London.

Appendix
The early history of positional analysis

Peter Söderbaum

Introduction

In 1973, I presented my PhD thesis in Swedish. An English version of the title is as follows: 'Positional analysis for decision-making and planning. An interdisciplinary approach to economic analysis'.[1] This publication was the result not only of various social movements in the scientific community, such as an increased interest in interdisciplinary perspectives (or perhaps transdisciplinary perspectives in present language) but also of specific events and experiences in my own career. I will start by choosing this latter personal perspective, but everything that happens to a person is normally related to a context or rather various contexts.

Positional analysis (PA) was given a specific meaning in the mentioned thesis. Already at this stage, I want to emphasize that things have been added so that my present understanding of PA differs a bit from the first publication. Essentially, PA has become part of a larger perspective where paradigm issues are involved. This is the result of applied studies with PA undertaken by others and myself and also of the ongoing dialogue with advocates of neoclassical cost–benefit analysis (CBA) or other methods that may share some features with PA. I am thinking of multi-criteria approaches, for example.

The main reason for the attempt to bring together early writings on PA here is that a large part of it was written in Swedish and that some of these writings in Swedish (reports from university departments and books) are not easily available today. In some sense, one can regret that not everything was written in English from the very beginning, but I believe that there are also advantages of writing in two languages and of moving between them. English language is certainly rich but as with all single languages, there is a risk of being locked into it. Also other languages, such as Swedish, can contribute constructively to an understanding of essential issues in our societies.

It should be made clear that these 'early writings' cover a period from 1967 (my licentiate thesis) to 1990. Since then, a majority of publications have been written in English. Some work from 1990 to the present will still be mentioned below to indicate how things developed and to prepare the way for a discussion of the limited success of PA so far and the potential for this approach and similar efforts in the future.

First, a few words about my personal background: at Uppsala University (UU), I began by studying political science and continued with statistics, economics and business management. I became a student advisor at the Department of Economics, UU, and later a teacher in international economics at the same department for two or three years. Already at this stage in the early 1960s, I made the judgement that economics developed more in the direction of a single paradigm with few openings while business management developed in a more interdisciplinary direction. I went to l'Université Catholique de Lovain in Belgium one year for studies of various forms of European economic cooperation. Upon my return, I became a teacher at the Department of Business Management, UU, more precisely responsible for various courses in marketing and (later) consumer behavior. In economics, the tendency is to stick to the neoclassical paradigm and try to modify it a little bit, whereas studies of organizations and marketing as part of business management education tend to be more interdisciplinary in kind. If psychology and sociology have something to offer in understanding consumer behavior, then why should one not interact with and learn from actors connected with such disciplines.

Economics of information and knowledge

About 1962 while still at the Department of Economics, UU, I wrote a paper 'Economics and Information' questioning the assumption of perfect (or complete) information generally made in neoclassical theory. This paper was met with skepticism by some colleagues at the department that was one reason for me to move to the Department of Business Management.[2] The professor of this department, Sune Carlson, offered me a part time position at the Royal Academy of Engineering Sciences and thereby a chance to continue elaboration of my ideas about the search for information and knowledge. I assisted a section of the academy focusing on 'economics and organization', and my task became to study the economics of research and development (R&D). Sune Carlson also facilitated contact with a group of large Swedish corporations at the time (Fagersta, Volvo, Pharmacia) who were very active in R&D activities. This was the background for my licentiate thesis in 1967 with the title 'Profitability of Investments and Changes in Stock of Technical Knowledge' (Söderbaum 1967).

In the mentioned companies, large sums of money and considerable human resources were used for R&D. At issue is then the rationality when choosing among R&D projects. A focus directly and only on monetary performance was judged not to be very meaningful. I do, of course, not claim to solve these problems in any final sense, but I made the judgement that keeping the monetary and knowledge dimensions separate from each other and reasoning in multiple steps in positional terms concerning the knowledge dimension might be a good idea. 'Stock of knowledge' became the first positional concept and the potential of reasoning in terms of decision trees in positional terms emerged. Later (in the mentioned PhD thesis), positional thinking was generalized to non-monetary dimensions other than knowledge.[3]

The choice of one alternative rather than another in a decision situation involves a commitment that both opens and closes possibilities for the future. Inertia is involved.[4] Reference can also be made to 'lock-in effects' or irreversibility, and the future opportunities resulting from the choice of one specific alternative at one point in time can be judged positively or negatively by a specific actor. An analogy to a game of chess was present already in this study of R&D. Each step or move in positional terms by one chess player opens and closes possibilities for the future. Reversing one move in positional terms when it has taken place is not possible. The analogy between R&D and chess playing, however, has some limitations in the sense that a game of chess is finished at a point, whereas in the case of R&D, the result of each move is only a new starting point for further moves in a potentially never-ending process.

Each R&D project influences somehow the stock of technical knowledge available at future points in time. Success of a project may lead directly to profitable investments in production facilities and will also influence the future search costs in terms of time, energy and money for specific additional pieces of knowledge and thereby monetary performance. It was argued that keeping monetary and knowledge dimensions separate in strategy consideration and formulation could be a way of dealing with the problem faced by business corporations.

A study of consumer behavior

As a responsible teacher in marketing and consumer behavior I wanted to contribute to dialogue in the latter field as well. I wrote a report with the title 'System, functions, activities. A cognitive model of purchasing behavior' (Söderbaum 1970). A lot of literature not only on marketing existed at the time but also on the role and perspectives of consumers and purchasers deserved some interest. Two early models of consumer behavior built on social psychology with learning theory as a component had been presented by Howard (1963) and Engel et al. (1968). I thought that something was missing in these models or rather that something could be added to their socio-psychological frame of reference.

A commodity, such as a piece of furniture, has to be adapted to other (perhaps already existing) furniture and elements in an apartment. Thinking in terms of systems was suggested. A potential additional piece of furniture or painting has to be adapted to other elements in the total system. 'System adaptation' was the terminology used. A functional and multidimensional perspective was furthermore added. In relation to a specific user of the system, it may be relevant to distinguish between different functions such as

- Physical–technical function
- Social function
- Aesthetic function
- Biological function
- Function in monetary terms

- Time-saving function
- Psychic or psychological function
- Communication function
- Transportation function and so on. (1970, p. 39).

References to activities and patterns of activities of the users (of the system), such as life style, represented an attempt to deal with the time aspect. Also positional change aspects were considered and referred to as 'system flexibility'. A piece of furniture or other commodity may be well adapted not only to the present system but also to alternative configurations of components that may be considered in the future. The duration or sustainability of a well-functioning commodity or the system as a whole is of course also a relevant consideration. When rereading what I wrote in 1970, I also realize that other elements of what was later presented as PA was part of the systems model. Interested parties (stakeholders) can be identified in relation to a system and impacts from the point of view of one interested party can be considered as costs and benefits where monetary and non-monetary impacts are separated rather than aggregated.

The PhD thesis

As already mentioned, the PhD thesis was written in Swedish. There is, however, an English summary (1973, pp. 324–329) that is subdivided into different chapters. The titles of the different chapters are not given in the mentioned English summary but are translated here:

Chapter 1: Introduction
Chapter 2: Points of departure
Chapter 3: Interested parties and their objectives
Chapter 4: A general explanatory model for adaptations of economic subjects
Chapter 5: Inertia and its different forms of manifestation
Chapter 6: Evaluation of impacts from the point of view of different interested parties/stakeholders I
Chapter 7: Evaluation of impacts from the point of view of different interested parties II
Chapter 8: Describing the development of decision processes over time
Chapter 9: Adaptation under uncertainty
Chapter 10: The strategic aspect of decision-making over time
Chapter 11: How positional analysis can be used for planning purposes
Chapter 12: Forming a basis for decision-making. Principles and examples
Chapter 13: A holistic view of decision-making and planning at the level of economic subjects
Chapter 14: Application of positional analysis I. Three case studies
Chapter 15: Application of positional analysis II. The case of Brofjorden
Chapter 16: Ecology and economics Summary in English

Today, I can only regret that the thesis was written in Swedish. This should, however, not be seen as a sign of my inability to write in English at the time (since my licentiate thesis was written in English). It was rather a matter of tactics from my point of view as a PhD student. I understood that my thesis project could be considered strange in relation to a Department of Business Economics compared, for example, with other PhD studies, and I wanted to increase the probability that my supervisors would understand my message. I succeeded in this respect and became a 'docent' that can be seen as a quality indicator of the thesis and the way it was defended.

The purpose of the study was to work along three mutually supporting lines: description of decision processes, explanation of decision processes and preparation of a base of knowledge and information for purposes of decision-making. Describing a decision process is of interest in itself and may reveal the role and power positions of different actors, but it may also improve explanation and understanding of decision processes and also contribute to the formation of a relevant base of information for decision-making.

My ideas about PA and economics more generally in the thesis can be described as follows:

- A *behavioral and socio-psychological point of departure* (references to Herbert Simon 1947; Cyert and March 1963, among others).
- *Interdisciplinary openings* – References to systems theory (Buckley 1968) and cybernetics (Ashby 1956).
- A *holistic and multidimensional idea of economics* (in the sense that all kinds of impacts are considered 'economic'. Things do not become 'more economic' by assessing them in monetary terms).
- Reference to *all kinds of scales for measurement* (including distinctions of a qualitative nature) rather than focusing exclusively on quantification.
- *Recognizing* that *different stakeholders* in relation to a particular issue refer to different interests (references to Rhenman 1964) – they are different interested parties – and that it is not very meaningful to add the values connected with different interests as part of a societal analysis.

A main theme of the thesis was, however, the attempt to *make inertia in its different forms visible* as part of decision-making and impact studies. Focus was here on different forms of inertia, such as commitments of various kinds, lock-in effects and irreversibility in various dimensions. Existing or future positions may be valued positively or negatively depending on an individual's situation and perspective. Life, and also decision-making at a collective and political level, can be seen as a matter of avoiding negative series of positions and acting in a way that leads to positive series of positions over time. Land for agriculture and forestry may be lost for urbanization purposes or road building. Some actors will value such changes positively and others negatively.

Ecological economists have emphasized the existence of inertia in energy terms and even regarded Georgescu-Roegen (1971) as the founder of ecological economics. Reasoning and analysis in energy and emergy terms have been seen by some as that which separates ecological economics from neoclassical environmental economics. I agree that energy analysis is a relevant issue of inertia, but I like to warn against any tendency to replace monetary reductionism with a reductionism in terms of energy. Economic analysis has to be holistic and multidimensional. Measurement in energy terms is not the only physical aspect of inertia, and it was argued that a number of other dimensions less connected with physical impacts were also relevant. In the thesis, the following list of dimensions was presented and exemplified with respect to positional thinking and issues of inertia:

- Psychological dimensions
- Dimensions related to information and knowledge
- Social dimensions
- Ethical dimensions
- Legal or juridical dimensions
- Aesthetic dimensions
- Physiological dimensions
- Biological dimensions
- Chemical dimensions
- Ecological dimensions
- Physical–technical dimensions
- Spatial dimensions
- Historical dimensions
- Monetary dimensions
- and so on. (1973, p. 65).

The list can, of course, be extended or presented in a different way, but it represented my understanding of multidimensionality at the time. Positional thinking can also be applied to the decision process itself. Inspired by Holbaek-Hansen's (1958) reference to 'commitments', I suggested that a decision process can be understood in terms of successive commitments that again refer to different dimensions:

- Exclusively cognitive commitments
- Cognitive commitments, plus social commitments
- Cognitive commitments, plus social, plus legal commitments
- Cognitive plus social, plus legal, plus physical–technical commitments

This was referred to as a 'principle of successive commitments' when the openings for, and number of, alternatives are reduced in a step-by-step fashion. Understanding decision processes in this way may refer to decisions made by single individuals as well as to town planning or transportation issues at a collective level.

As mentioned already, 'path dependence' has emerged later in the literature as a concept of inertia. North (1990) has used this term and concept mainly in relation to institutional change, but I suggest that it should be seen as part of inertia in a much broader (and multidimensional) sense.

PA claims to be useful at all levels from the individual through the organization and to the societal level. When PA in its early versions was developed, I expected the approach, for example, to be applied in business circles and at the university Departments of Business Management. There was certainly some interest among colleagues at such departments and even single applied studies, but it soon became clear to me that PA was mainly regarded as an alternative to CBA at the societal level.

Positional thinking can be regarded as the main idea in the thesis. There are about 30 diagrams with a time axis. Reversibility and irreversibility are illustrated for various scales, and attempts are made to deal with uncertainty in terms of subjective probabilities to attain specific objectives. A recommendation is that issues of inertia are taken seriously before making a decision. It should at the same time be made clear that positional thinking is not the only essential element of PA. A somewhat simplified version of the scheme of analysis presented in the thesis (pp. 214–216) looks as follows:

1   Describe the planning task and the preconditions concerning decision maker(s) and environment.
2   Identify all interested parties or stakeholders.
3   Identify systems that will be affected differently depending on alternative chosen among those considered.
4   Use a checklist for possibly relevant dimensions for impact studies in positional and other terms.
5   Describe initial position for relevant systems and dimensions.
6   Identify relevant explanatory models concerning relations between alternatives and their impacts in case of implementation.
7   Choice of future points in time for estimates of impacts.
8   Choice of alternatives to be considered in analysis.
9   Prognosis of impacts for each alternative considered.
10 A study of inertia of different kinds (commitments, irreversible impacts, etc.).
11 A study of uncertainty concerning relevant objectives, alternatives and impacts.
12 A study of similarities and differences between the interests of different stakeholders and possible cooperative or competitive relationships between them.
13 Put together the total information basis for decision-making. Use diagrams, matrices and so on for clearness and transparency.
14 Consider the possibilities to reduce the number of alternatives for further study.
15 Study the possibilities for control and goal achievement from the point of view of each stakeholder category.

PA may appear as a quite complex approach from the above list. Those who made the first studies also considered simplified versions of the approach. It will also become clear later on that a scheme of analysis as used today differs in some ways from the above list. However, it is still of interest, I believe, to have a look at the original version of PA.

Examples of early applied studies

Where did 'positional thinking' come from? I think that thinking in positions or states is close to our everyday experiences. While writing these lines, I am sitting on a chair and in a specific position that may continue for some minutes and then be changed to a new position or a series of positions. I may go for a walk and so on. It is not difficult to imagine such examples of positional changes in various dimensions. In my case, I thought that such everyday experiences were missing from neoclassical economic theory and textbooks. Positional thinking can thus be compared with the predilection for thinking in equilibrium terms in neoclassical theory. Markets, for example, can be looked upon in other ways than the (anonymous) forces of supply and demand (which tend to move toward equilibrium). This reliance exclusively on equilibrium analysis means that issues of ethics, responsibility and accountability tend to be downplayed or disappear. When things go wrong in some respect, it is the market that fails not any specific market actor. Markets can, however, be made visible as well as the positions of market actors in terms of power at different points in time.

Some of the first applied studies with PA were carried out by students. Most of these studies concerned land use, landscape or natural resources. At the Norwegian University of Agricultural Sciences, a group of students focused on location and design of a new international airport for Oslo, others upon design of ski resorts. At the Department of Business Management in Uppsala, there were studies of the positions of individuals in organizations (e.g. how specific educational activities led to desired professional positions for some persons but not for others) and of the development of the state or positions of product lines of specific corporations.

In some cases, applied studies were published as reports. I will here list some examples with the title in Swedish but with an English translation:

Söderbaum Peter (1976). Tillämpning av positionsanalys vid transportplanering. Exemplet Kungsängsleden i Uppsala (Application of positional analysis for transportation planning. The case of Kungsängsleden in Uppsala). Lantbrukshögskolan, Institutionen för ekonomi och statistik, Rapport 86. Uppsala (A purpose of this road through a ridge and with a bridge across the Fyris river was to connect different parts of the urban area.)

Söderbaum, Peter (1977). Positionsanalys som metod vid utredningsarbete. Översiktlig studie av E18-frågan i Västerås (Positional analysis as a way of preparing decisions. A comprehensive study of the E18 issue in Västerås). Lantbrukshögskolan, Institutionen för ekonomi och statistik, Rapport 103. Uppsala. (This study is about a big motorway through central parts of Västerås, or as an alternative outside the city area.)

Söderbaum, Peter and Elisabeth Rosell (1978). Tillämpning av positionsanalys vid översiktlig planering och detaljplanering i Uppsala kommun. En studie av markanvändningskonflikter, speciellt konflikter mellan tätortsutbyggnad och jord-och skogsbruk (Positional Analysis as an Approach to Land-use and Urban Planning in the City of Uppsala). Swedish University of Agricultural Sciences, Department of Economics and Statistics, Report 137. Uppsala.

Kumm, Karl-Ivar and Peter Söderbaum (1979). Positionsanalys vid vägplanering. Tillämpningsexempel på E4 i Västernorrlands län (Positional Analysis in Road Planning – Case study of Highway E4 in the Province of Västernorrland). Swedish University of Agricultural Sciences, Department of Economics and Statistics, Report 154.

156   *The early history of positional analysis*

Uppsala (This study is among other things about conflicts between recreational interests and transportation interests in relation to the estuary of the river Indalsälven.)

Andersson, Mari (1991). Konsekvensanalys av övervägd bergtäkt I Uppsala län – en tillämpning av positionsanalys (Impacts of bedrock-quarrying in Uppsala municipality – an application of positional analysis). Swedish University of Agricultural Sciences, Department of Economics, Report 35, Uppsala.

Mattsson, Jan-Erik (1991). Val av energisystem för fjärrvärmeverk i Hedemora – försök till allsidig belysing (Selection of system for district heating plant in Hedemora – a many-sided illumination). Swedish University of Agricultural Sciences, Department of Operational Efficiency, Report 190, Garpenberg.

Forsberg, Göran (1993). Finns ekologiskt hållbara energisystem? En uppföljning och konsekvensbeskrivning för Kils kommun (Energy systems and ecological sustainability. The municipality of Kil as a case). Swedish University of Agricultural Sciences, Department of Economics, Report 63, Uppsala.

Brorsson, Kjell-Åke (1995). Metodutveckling av positionsanalysen genom tillämpning på Assjö kvarn. Hållbar utveckling i relation till miljö och sårbarhet (Improving positional analysis as method through applied study of Assjö mill. Sustainable development in relation to environment and security). Swedish University for Agricultural Sciences, Department of Economics, Dissertations 14, Uppsala.

Some attempts in Swedish were made at an early stage to improve the conceptual and theoretical aspects of PA:

Söderbaum, Peter (1975). Utformning av beslutsunderlag vid samhällsplanering. Positionanalys som alternativ till traditionell cost-benefitanalys (A conceptual frame of reference for decision-making at the societal level). Lantbrukshögskolan, Institutionen för ekonomi och statistik, Rapport 63, Uppsala. In an appendix to this report (pp. 46–57) citations in English from writers (Hoos 1972; Kapp 1970; Tribe 1972, Heilbroner 1971) that I considered essential to the debate about CBA and its alternatives were reproduced.

Söderbaum, Peter (1978). Samhällsplanering, ekonomi, miljö (Public planning, economics, environment). Miljöförlaget, Uppsala.

Söderbaum, Peter (1986). Beslutsunderlag. Ensidiga eller allsidiga utredningar? (Approach to decision-making. Reductionist or many-sided studies?). Doxa Ekonomi, Lund.

Söderbaum, Peter (1993). Ekologisk ekonomi. Miljö och utveckling i ny belysning (Ecological Economics. Environment and development in new perspective). Studentlitteratur, Lund.

More interesting for present purposes of informing about PA for actors outside Sweden are publications written in English:

Söderbaum, Peter (1980). Towards a reconciliation of economics and ecology, *European Review of Agricultural Economics*, Vol. 7, No. 1, pp. 55–77. The Hague.

Söderbaum, Peter (1982). Positional analysis for decision-making and planning, *Journal of Economic Issues*, Vol. 16, No. 2, pp. 391–400.

Söderbaum, Peter (1987). Environmental management. A non-traditional approach, *Journal of Economic Issues*, Vol. 21, No. 1, pp. 139–165.

Söderbaum, Peter (1983). Positional analysis in relation to business decision-making. Swedish University of Agricultural Sciences, Department of Economics and Statistics, Report 217. Uppsala.

Söderbaum, Peter (1990). Economics in relation to environment, agriculture and rural development. A non-traditional approach to project evaluation, Swedish University of Agricultural Sciences, Department of Economics, Report 31. Uppsala. (This is a study that was commissioned by FAO in Rome)

Edlund, Jonas och Rodolfo Quintero (1995). Do Wabura – farewell to the river. Application of Positional Analysis to the Urrá I Hydro Power Plant in Columbia. Swedish University of Agricultural Sciences, Department of Economics, Report 94. Uppsala.

An attempt to review my writings up to year 1999 can be found in a 1-year master thesis by Anja Kiviluoto, Helsinki University:

Kiviluoto, Anja (1999). Institutional Economists in Relation to Environmental Issues. A study of the works by Peter Söderbaum. Mälardalen University, Department of Business Studies and Informatics, Report No. 1. Västerås.

PhD studies written in Swedish where PA has been a main theme (by Kjell-Åke Brorsson and Göran Forsberg) have already been mentioned. When I was employed at the Swedish University for Agricultural Sciences also Karl-Ivar Kumm, Gun Lidestav and Bengt Hillring had components of PA in their theses. In Finland, Anti Leskinen wrote his PhD thesis in English:

Leskinen, Antti (1994). Environmental Planning as Learning. The Principles of Negotiation, the Disaggregative Decision-making Method and Parallel Organization in Developing the Road Administration. University of Helsinki, Department of Economics and Management, Section on Land-use Economics, No. 5, Helsinki.

More recent developments

A number of articles and some books have been written since the early 1990s and to get an idea about these developments a selection of publications are listed:

Söderbaum, Peter, 1999. Values, ideology and politics in ecological economics (Tenth Anniversary invited paper), *Ecological Economics*, Vol. 28, pp. 161–170.
Söderbaum, Peter, 2000. *Ecological Economics. A political economics approach to environment and development.* Earthscan, London.
Söderbaum, Peter, 2004. Decision processes and decision-making in relation to sustainable development and democracy – where do we stand? *Journal of Interdisciplinary Economics*, Vol. 14, pp. 41–60.
Söderbaum, Peter, 2006. Democracy and Sustainable Development. What is the alternative to cost-benefit analysis? *Integrated Environmental Assessment and Management*, Vol. 2, No. 2 (April), pp. 182–190. In the same issue of the journal there are contributions from the same symposium at Roskilde University also by Nick Hanley (as advocate of CBA) and Robert Costanza (as representative of what he called a 'pragmatic' attitude)
Söderbaum, Peter, 2007. Issues of paradigm and ideology in sustainability assessment. *Ecological Economics*, Vol. 60, No. 3 (January), pp. 613–626.
Söderbaum, Peter, 2007. Science, ideology and development: is there a 'Sustainability Economics'? *Post-Autistic Economics Review*, No. 43, pp. 24–41.
Söderbaum, Peter, 2008. *Understanding Sustainability Economics. Towards pluralism in economics.* Earthscan, London.
Söderbaum, Peter, 2008. 10th Anniversary Focus: From mainstream 'environmental economics' to 'sustainability economics'. On the need for new thinking. *Journal of Environmental Monitoring*, Vol. 10, pp. 1467–1475.
Söderbaum, Peter, 2011. *Bortom BNP. Nationalekonomi och företagsekonomi för hållbar utveckling* (Behind GDP. Economics and business management for sustainable development). Studentlitteratur, Lund.

Söderbaum, Peter, 2012. Democracy and sustainable development: Implications for science and economics, *Real-world Economics Review*, No. 60, pp. 107–119.

Söderbaum, Peter and Judy Brown, 2010. Democratizing economics: Pluralism as a path toward sustainability. *Annals of the New York Academy of Sciences*, Vol. 1185, *Ecological Economics Reviews*, pp. 179–195. New York Academy of Sciences, New York.

Söderbaum, Peter and Judy Brown, 2011. Pluralism and democracy in economics, *International Journal of Pluralism and Economics Education*, Vol. 2, No. 3, pp. 240–243.

PA today

Large parts of the original version of PA from 1973 remain today. A scheme of analysis in its present form can be found in my two Earthscan books mentioned above. In the 'Ecological Economics' book, chapter 6 (2000, pp. 85–105) about 'Environmental Management and Decision-making', the scheme of analysis is presented on pages 103–104. The title of Chapter 7 in the 'Sustainability Economics' book of 2008 is 'Approaches to Decision-making and Sustainability Assessment' with a scheme of analysis on pages 114–115.

I will not here try to identify in any detail changes in my view of PA, but the purpose of the method is now more closely connected with democracy. The idea is to illuminate an issue in a many-sided (rather than manipulated) way with respect to ideological orientations, alternatives of choice and estimated impacts. Specific focus is placed on inertia, uncertainty and so on.

It is also fair to say that paradigm issues have entered the scene more than before. Individuals are regarded as political economic persons, PEPs, guided by their ideological orientation in decision-making and action. Organizations are PEOs that similarly are guided by their mission. Decision-making is regarded as a matter of 'matching' processes, 'pattern recognition' or 'appropriateness', suggesting that the search for 'optimal' solutions in quantitative terms is downplayed a bit.

Conflicts of interest were originally considered in terms of interested parties or stakeholders. Later such interests have been identified through analysis of activities for individuals and/or organizations that are differently affected depending on which one of the alternatives considered that is chosen. This somewhat technocratic view of interests and values is still relevant, but the main idea of conflicts is now connected with broader differences in terms of ideological orientation. In addition to identifying alternatives, the analyst should identify and articulate relevant ideological orientations among decision-makers and other actors who participate in public dialogue or that appear relevant for other reasons. 'Sustainable development' interpreted in a specific way is one such possible ideological orientation that can be used for purposes of ranking alternatives and conditional conclusions. Similarly, a specific version of a market ideology can point in a different direction with connected ranking of alternatives.

The historical background of a decision situation is also something that needs to be considered if one wants to understand the present position and how different actors have dealt with the issue in the past. Protocols are needed to make individuals and actors visible and accountable in the ongoing decision process. The analyst has therefore a role in describing a decision process and to reproduce the views expressed by different actors. However, also newspapers, radio and television channels and other media are involved in this part of democracy. Listening to many voices is often a good idea.

The PA story continued

How do we measure progress in science? Although problems of measuring progress also exist in natural sciences and engineering sciences, the problems are accentuated in social sciences. Is PA a better method than CBA? Should PA therefore replace CBA as the main approach to decision-making at the societal level?

CBA has been criticized by many. Even Mishan, himself a textbook writer on CBA (1971), argues that CBA can only be used in a society if there is a consensus about the specific rules of valuation (in market terms) that go into CBA. However, in present society, no such consensus can be expected considering environmental issues where there are many opinions about what is good for society (Mishan 1980). This lack of consensus concerning principles of evaluation is enough to argue that CBA cannot be accepted as the one and only approach to decision-making at the societal level.

In a democratic society, citizens, politicians and actors in other roles differ with respect to values and ideological orientation, and it can therefore be argued that such differences have to be respected in the methods used for decision-making. However, who will listen to such arguments or other criticisms of CBA?

I have participated in a national and also international dialogue about PA versus CBA for some 40 years. We may have taken small steps forward in the case of environmental impact assessment (EIA), multiple-criteria approaches and perhaps also some kinds of systems analysis (Clayton and Radcliffe 1996). However, in our societies, CBA has become institutionalized to such an extent that there are many establishment actors that defend this particular approach more or less independently of the arguments that have been put forward. As was previously mentioned, one can with Robert Costanza refer to 'pragmatism'.

Expressed in the language of positional thinking, we are faced with many kinds of inertia:

- Ideas or cognitive habits about science and the role of experts as analysts are quite established in many circles.
- The neoclassical economics paradigm (with CBA as one of its specific branches) is close to a monopoly position at university departments of economics nationally and today even at a global level.
- A market ideology has been and is still dominant in many countries and globally, so-called neo-liberalism.

Technocracy with emphasis on CBA, which is evaluation in specific market terms, follows naturally from the above kinds of dominance. If one wants to open the door for alternative approaches, it is not enough to discuss one method versus another in a narrow sense. The debate has to be broadened to include theory of science, paradigms in economics and ideological orientation.

Actually, this is what has happened with my writings. We need to discuss how values and ideology enters into science; we need to discuss alternative schools of thought in economics, such as institutional theory, and we need to discuss how market fundamentalism as ideological orientation compares with alternative ideological orientations. Is it possible to express the present challenge of sustainable development in market terms? As I see it, the answer is 'no'. Some new thinking is needed.

Our ideas of analysts or experts are very much colored by thinking in terms of technocracy. The expert should be able to point out the best or 'optimal' alternative. As in the case of CBA, the analyst becomes an expert on correct values in addition to her or his abilities to estimate impacts or consequences. While this view is quite established and appreciated by many consultants and other professionals, it has to be reconsidered in the light of democracy.

In the cultural and professional context indicated, it is not so easy to 'sell' a method built on arguments that complexity in all its forms should be respected and as far as possible made visible to decision-makers and those concerned. Appeals for multidimensional thinking, attempts to systematically deal with uncertainty, inertia and so on do not necessarily make you a popular person. Distinctions between ideological orientations and the conditional conclusions that follow will perhaps only make things worse.

I still believe that the time has come when technocracy has to give way to democracy. As already mentioned, I have discussed this issue in articles with Judy Brown (Söderbaum and Brown 2010, 2011). I will, however, here point to an early PhD thesis by Jakubowski *Demokratische Umweltpolitik. Eine institutionenökonomische Analyse umweltpolitischer Zielfindung* (1999). Later, he wrote an article Political Economic Person contra Homo Oeconomicus – Mit PEP zu mehr Nachhaltigkeit (2000) in *LIST FORUM für Wirtschafts- und Finanzpolitik*. Democracy has to become the cornerstone of any method of evaluation at the societal level and increasingly at other levels. We need new ideas about human beings as actors in different roles. (Actually this is what is missing from multicriteria approaches and environmental impact assessments where the ideas about democracy to the extent that they exist tend to be superficial.)

As mentioned earlier, Antti Leskinen wrote his thesis on PA applied to planning procedures in the Finnish road administration. We have had sporadic contacts since then, and I have understood that he is (or was) employed in the City of Tampere as a professional with the role of strengthening democracy in the city administration. How can participation of citizens be improved for example? Even this example points in the direction of some optimism.

A strategy to strengthen PA and other efforts of improving democracy

The tendency among establishment actors and people in general in Sweden and similar countries is to believe that democracy is something that we already have and that it is functioning well. These days we learn about developments in some countries and are congratulating them for getting closer to something that we already have achieved.

My point here is that a lot remains to be done in our own countries. Many kinds of technocratic tendencies have to be counteracted. The dominance of thinking patterns closely connected with the conceptual framework and ideological orientation of neoclassical economic theory (with emphasis on monetary indicators such as gross domestic product (GDP) growth, profits in business, CBA and on self-interest and market relationships of individuals, etc.) is such that one may well speak of a specific market fundamentalism or ideology comparable with dictatorship. I like here to cite the title of another book: *Is Globalization Overpowering Democracy? The Challenge for Ecology, Economy and Culture* edited by Lapka et al. (2007). This book was edited in Prague by persons who expected something better than Soviet imperialism, but who are not sure about their feelings in relation to the political economic system that has emerged as alternative.

So far the present system and the global community with its leading actors have not been very successful in dealing with challenges such as pollution, climate change, loss of biological diversity and so on. Globalization of the present kind does not necessarily lead to a strengthened democracy. Dictatorship in China, for example, appears to be compatible with globalization of markets. Today, students of economics read the same economics textbooks in China as in Western countries and democracy is a term that is absent from the index of such textbooks.

I will end this discussion by once more emphasizing the need to 'democratize economics'. Considering the ideological nature of economics, this discipline has to become pluralistic. There has to be an end to the present monopoly position of neoclassical theory. As a second (and related) step, alternative conceptual and theoretical perspectives in economics have to be strengthened in relation to the sustainability challenge, for example. Remembering that we are all political economic persons with specific responsibilities in relation to other actors, we should participate in public debate and build alliances with actors who share our concerns for the future. And we should always remember that responsibility is a matter of broader societal concerns and not limited to neoclassical self-interest.

Notes

1 The title in Swedish is 'Positionsanalys vid beslutsfattande och planering. Ekonomisk analys på tvärvetenskaplig grund' (Söderbaum 1973).
2 This was a relatively new department at Uppsala University and sometimes named in other ways, for example, Department of Business Administration or Department of Business Studies.

3   The fact that also monetary and financial analysis can be carried out in positional terms was considered common knowledge.
4   While I referred to 'inertia' as the broad category, more recently the concept and term 'path-dependence' has been used in a similar sense (e.g. North 1990).

References

Ashby, W. Ross, 1956. *An Introduction to Cybernetics*. Chapman & Hall, London.

Buckley, Walter, ed. 1968. *Modern Systems Research for the Behavioral Scientist*. Aldine, Chicago.

Clayton, Anthony M. H. and Nicholas J. Radcliffe, 1996. *Sustainability. A systems approach*. Earthscan, London.

Cyert, Richard M. and James G. March, 1963. *A Behavioral Theory of the Firm*. Prentice-Hall, Englewood Cliffs.

Engel, James E., David T. Kollat and Roger D. Blackwell, 1968. *Consumer Behavior*. Holt, Rinehart and Winston, New York.

Georgescu-Roegan, Nicholas, 1971. *The Entropy Law and the Economic Process*. Harvard University Press, Cambridge, MA.

Heilbroner, Robert L. 1971. Introduction in Heilbroner and Ford eds., *Is Economics Relevant?* Goodyear, Pacific Palisades.

Holbaek-Hanssen, Leif, 1958. *Markedsforskning. Ett hjelpemiddel til bedre beslutninger i bedriftene*. Grundt Tanum, Oslo.

Hoos, Ida R. 1972. *Systems Analysis in Public Policy. A Critique*, University of California Press, Berkeley.

Howard, John A. 1963. *Marketing Management. Analysis and Planning*. Richard D. Irwin, Homewood, IL.

Jakubowski, Peter, 1999. *Demokratische Umweltpolitik. Eine institutionenökonomische Analyse umweltpolitischer Zielfindung*. Peter Lang, Frankfurt am Main.

Jakubowski, Peter, 2000. Political Economic Person contra Homo oeconomicus – Mit PEP zu mehr Nachhaltigkeit, *LIST FORUM für Wirtschafts- und Finanzpolitik*, Band 26 (2000), Heft 4, pp. 299–310.

Kapp, K. William, 1970. Environmental disruption: general issues and methodological problems, *Social Science Information* (International Social Science Council), Vol. 9, pp. 15–32.

Lapka, Miroslav J., Sanford Rikoon and Eva Cudlínová, eds. 2007. *Is Globalization Overpowering Democracy? The Challenge for Ecology, Economy and Culture*. Dokoran Publisher, Prague.

Mishan, Ezra J. 1971. *Cost-Benefit Analysis*. Allen & Unwin, London.

Mishan, Ezra J. 1980. How valid are economic valuations of allocative changes? *Journal of Economic Issues*, Vol. 14, No. 1, pp. 143–161.

North, Douglass, 1990. *Institutions, Institutional Change and Economic Performance*. Cambridge University Press, Cambridge.

Rhenman, Eric, 1964. *Företagsdemokrati och företagsorganisation*. (Business Democracy and Organization). Norstedt, Stockholm.

Simon, Herbert A., 1947. *Administrative Behavior*. Macmillan, New York.

Söderbaum, Peter, 1967. Profitability of Investments and Changes in Stock of Technical Knowledge. Department of Business Studies, Report No. 1. Uppsala University, Uppsala.

Söderbaum, Peter, 1970. *System, funktion, aktiviteter – En kognitiv köparmodell* (System, Functions, Activities. A Cognitive Model of Purchasing Behaviour). Department of Business Studies, Report No. 3. Uppsala University, Uppsala.

Söderbaum, Peter, 1973. *Positionsanalys vid beslutsfattande och planering. Ekonomisk analys på tvärvetenskaplig grund* (Positional Analysis for Decision Making and Planning. Economic Analysis on an Interdisciplinary Basis). Scandinavian University Books/Esselte Studium, Stockholm.

Söderbaum, Peter and Judy Brown, 2010. Democratizing economics. Pluralism as path toward sustainability, *New York Academy of Sciences* Volume 1185, Ecological Economics Reviews, pp. 179–195. New York Academy of Sciences, New York.

Söderbaum, Peter and Judy Brown, 2011. Pluralism and democracy in economics, *Int Journal of Pluralism and Economics Education*, Vol 2. No 3, pp. 240–243.

Tribe, Lawrence, 1972. Policy science: analysis or ideology, *Philosophy and Public Affairs*, Vol. 2, No. 1, pp. 66–110.

Index

For Product Safety Concerns and Information please contact our EU
representative GPSR@taylorandfrancis.com
Taylor & Francis Verlag GmbH, Kaufingerstraße 24, 80331 München, Germany